AF719050

Critical Race Theory and Copyright in American Dance

PREVIOUS PUBLICATIONS

Speaking of Monsters: A Teratological Anthology
Edited by Caroline Joan S. Picart and John Edgar Browning

Frames of Evil: Holocaust as Horror in American Film
Caroline Joan S. Picart and David Frank

From Ballroom to DanceSport: Aesthetics, Athletics, and Body Culture
Caroline Joan S. Picart

Critical Race Theory and Copyright in American Dance

Whiteness as Status Property

Caroline Joan S. Picart

palgrave
macmillan

CRITICAL RACE THEORY AND COPYRIGHT IN AMERICAN DANCE
Copyright © Caroline Joan S. Picart, 2013.

All rights reserved.

First published in 2013 by
PALGRAVE MACMILLAN®
in the United States—a division of St. Martin's Press LLC,
175 Fifth Avenue, New York, NY 10010.

Where this book is distributed in the UK, Europe and the rest of the world, this is by Palgrave Macmillan, a division of Macmillan Publishers Limited, registered in England, company number 785998, of Houndmills, Basingstoke, Hampshire RG21 6XS.

Palgrave Macmillan is the global academic imprint of the above companies and has companies and representatives throughout the world.

Palgrave® and Macmillan® are registered trademarks in the United States, the United Kingdom, Europe and other countries.

ISBN: 978–1–137–32196–1

Library of Congress Cataloging-in-Publication Data is available from the Library of Congress.

A catalogue record of the book is available from the British Library.

Design by Newgen Knowledge Works (P) Ltd., Chennai, India.

First edition: November 2013

To my loving and supportive husband, Jerry Rivera

Contents

List of Figures ix

Acknowledgments xi

1 Introduction: Preliminary Remarks 1

2 Comparing Aesthetics of Whiteness and Nonwhiteness in Relation to American Dance 21

3 Loíe Fuller, "Goddess of Light" and Josephine Baker, "Black Venus": Non-narrative Choreography as Mere "Spectacle" 45

4 George Balanchine, "Genius of American Dance": Whiteness, Choreography, Copyrightability in American Dance 67

5 Martha Graham, "Picasso of American Dance," and Katherine Dunham, "Matriarch of Black Dance": Exoticism and Nonwhiteness in American Dance 87

6 Moving into New Directions: Cunningham and Ailey 117

7 Conclusions: Quo Vadis? 161

Notes 175

Bibliography 215

Author's Biography 229

Index 231

Figures

3.1	Public Domain Image of Loíe Fuller's Serpentine Dance	46
3.2	Public Domain Image of Josephine Baker	55
4.1	Public Domain Image of George Balanchine and Suzanne Farrell	68
5.1	Public Domain Image of Martha Graham and Bertram Ross	88
5.2	Public Domain Image of Katherine Dunham	96
6.1	Public Domain Image of Alvin Ailey	139

Acknowledgments

I dedicate this book to both my beloved husband, Jerry Rivera, and my two families: the Picart family in the Philippines and the Terrell family in Tallahassee, Florida. Part of this book was submitted as a thesis for the requirements for a joint MA in Women's Studies and Juris Doctor in Law from the University of Florida (Spring 2013); the thesis was originally titled *Critical Race Theory, Gender, American Modern Dance and Copyright: A Critical Review of Choreography as Intellectual Property*. I thank Berta Hernandez-Truyol, Patricia Hilliard-Nunn, and Anita Anantharam for their comments on earlier drafts, and Judith Page, Anita Anantharam, and Donna Tuckey for their help with administrative details. I am also indebted to the *Cardozo Journal of Law and Gender*, for granting copyright permission to reprint one of my articles, *A Tango between Copyright and Critical Race Theory: Whiteness as Status Property in Balanchine's Ballets, Fuller's Serpentine Dance and Graham's Modern Dances*, which originally appeared in 18 *Cardozo Journal of Law and Gender* 685 (April 2012); the article was a less developed precursor to this book and the germinal idea of the project initially developed under the mentorship of Danaya Wright, Kenneth Nunn, and Jeffrey Lloyd. Finally, a small section of the concluding chapter was adapted from Caroline Joan S. Picart and Marlowe Fox, "Beyond Unbridled Optimism and Fear: Indigenous Peoples, Intellectual Property, Human Rights and the Globalization of Traditional Knowledge and Expressions of Folklore (Part I)," *International Community Law Review* 15, no. 3 (2013), 319–339. I thank the *International Community Law Review* for allowing me to adapt and excerpt the material appropriately. I also thank Berta Hernandez-Truyol and Stephen Powell for their feedback on an earlier version of the article. Nevertheless, as I thank all who have helped me shape the content of this project, I acknowledge that any errors in this book are mine. Finally, I owe a debt of gratitude to Margaret Petty and Leslie Owen, for their painstaking and thorough assistance with preliminary formatting and editing this book into its final form, and to

Margaret Petty, Robert Molt, Nicole Santos, and Nicole Goff for their conscientious help with the index. To close, heartfelt thanks to the staff of Palgrave Macmillan and Newgen Knowledge Works Pvt. Ltd., and enduring thanks to mentor-exemplars John Stuhr, Richard Behling, Raymond Fleming, Judge Richard Posner, and Danaya Wright.

Chapter 1

Introduction: Preliminary Remarks*

Let me start with identifying the ground (however undulating) from which I speak, as I embark on this study. Western philosophy, as influenced by both modernist and scientific traditions, privileges *logos* (factual content) over *ethos* (character) and *pathos* (emotional appeal). Yet having been mentored, very effectively, by Nietzsche, to nurture an appreciation for both rhetoric and philosophy, I believe it is important to pay attention to all three: who speaks, how she or he speaks (and for whom), and what she or he says (and why).

The position from which I spring and to which I eventually return, in my concluding chapter, as outlined in an earlier book, *Inside Notes from the Outside*, moves among, attempting to translate across, multiple hybrid realms of being and becoming—of being perpetually both inside and outside, negotiating differences, and trying, in collaboration with others, to translate, even if "imperfectly," between or among apparent incommensurabilities, knowing that translation, ultimately, can never be absolute or exact.

I begin autoethnographically, drawing from both Donna J. Haraway's theories on "cyborgs"[1] (hybrid beings) as well as my own experiences.

> By the late twentieth century, our time, a mythic time, we are all chimeras, theorized and fabricated hybrids... in short, we are cyborgs.
>
> —Donna Haraway, *Simians, Cyborgs, and Women*

We were visiting with good friends, Roy and Leslie Engle, during the Christmas of 1998 at Stow, Ohio. As we sat across from each other, enjoying the meal, the warmth, and each other's company, I became aware of their three-year-old son's wide-eyed gaze.

"Are you black, or are you white?" Benjamin's adorably dark brown eyes were unblinking. He looked earnestly confused.

I was told by friends that the eminent Slavoj Žižek had asked similar questions as I stood at the podium, introducing him for Florida State University's Colloquium Series in October 2000. "Who is she? You must tell me, where is she from?" he reportedly inquired, with an imperative tone, as I continued with my introduction. When he learned I was from the Philippines, he remarked, "Oh—you mean, like Imelda Marcos?"

It is instances such as these two anecdotes that have spurred me to reflect on bodies, power, and identities. The two instances apparently resolved the question concerning my identity—that is, that I am "brown," neither black nor white, and that I hail from the same place as Asia's glamorous and extravagant "Iron Butterfly"—but seem inadequate as labels. Somehow, there is something about these neat categories that, in Eliot's terms, "slip, slide, and perish . . . [and]will not stay in place."

The politics of race, gender, and class has sparked much interest and even controversy in contemporary academic and wider public circles. The questions with which I attempt to wrestle are not particularly uncommon ones. They are issues that have loomed over anyone who has had to come to terms with concrete, pragmatic questions regarding identity and courses of action within the interacting spheres of race, gender, class, and power. The specific cast I give these questions and my attempts at seeking answers to them are formed by my own experiences as a woman of ambiguous ancestry raised in the Philippines; who was educated in the Philippines, England, and the United States as a biologist and philosopher; and who has traveled in Europe, Asia, and the United States as an academic, artist, US Open DanceSport[2] champion; and most recently, a joint *Juris* Doctor of law and MA Teaching Fellow in women's studies, specializing in Intellectual Property Law and International Law.

Given my lens, it is not uncommon to hear stories of how law school education seems designed to be insulated from the kinds of questions at the heart of women's studies and gender research. Critical Race Theory, LatCrit, and Feminist Legal Theory scholars have done much to show how particularly Criminal Law and Property Law, for example, remain rooted within the historical conditions that produce categories of distinction between those who are privileged and those who are not. However, Intellectual Property, and especially Copyright in relation to dance choreography in particular, for the most part, remain insulated from questions concerning power in relation to race, gender, class, and sexuality.

I remember taking a class on Copyright (which was well organized, engaging, and informational at many levels), but hearing, to my astonishment, the declaration that copyright decisions are absolutely devoid of any aesthetic judgment and are simply based on a purely "objective" code-based evaluation, whose criteria's historical genesis and underlying assumptions, in that particular class, remained largely unscrutinized. Perhaps it is too much to ask of an introductory class on copyright to be critical about the historical and sociopolitical moorings of something as abstract and fluid as copyright. After all, in fairness, a general law school education is geared predominantly to produce practitioners—virtual gladiators—who do not have the time or the luxury to worry about the "whys" behind the rules. All they are tested on, after three years of study, is knowledge of the rules and the ability to apply these rules—to win as many rhetorical battles as possible in the guardianship and application of these rules but not to analyze their foundations or historical genesis. The work of critical reflection, to some extent, is left to specialized seminars and, if one is so predisposed, to legal scholarship. Nevertheless, there is something about Intellectual Property, and especially Copyright, that seems relatively immune from sociopolitical critique, compared to, for example, Criminal Law or Property Law, where categories of race, gender, class, and sexuality are almost impossible to ignore.

What prompts this book are a number of things: first, a resurgence of interest in Loïe Fuller's heritage as a pioneer of modern dance, as well as a continuing fascination with the details of Josephine Baker's, George Balanchine's, Martha Graham's and Katherine Dunham's lives, as evidenced by the virtual cottage industry of their biographies; second, except for, for example, Kevin Greene's work, a lack of a sustained critical examination of connections binding copyright, choreography, and critical race theory in law-related academia. The choreographic inheritances of Fuller, Baker, Balanchine, Graham, and Dunham are important to map because these constitute crucial sites upon which negotiations on how to package bodies of choreographic works (both of the choreographer and the performer, as racialized and gendered). Such negotiations are staged, reflective of larger social, political, and cultural tensions, as revealed by the differential treatment in the reception of copyright claims.

More importantly, the study of intellectual property still seems principally insulated from critical studies of culture, as if intellectual property (and in particular, copyright protection), and in this case, choreography were spawned, fully formed, independent of historical, political, and cultural forces. Like all legal "innovations," the evolution of choreographic works from being federally noncopyrightable, unless they partook of "dramatic" or "narrative" structures, to becoming a category of works potentially copyrightable under the 1976 Copyright Act, is a fascinating story. The principal historical markers that demarcate the temporal borders this book uses are the American copyright landmark cases, specifically in relation to choreographic copyright. These begin with *Fuller v. Bemis* (1892),[3] which established the precedent for why choreography was not copyrightable (at least not until the 1976 amendment of the Copyright Code). The second is *Horgan v. Macmillan II* (1986),[4] which established the template for what type of choreography is not only copyrightable but also fully protected from infringement. The third is *Martha Graham School v. Martha Graham Center III* (2006),[5] which affirmed the findings of *Martha Graham School v. Martha Graham Center II* (2004),[6] and opened up the legal possibility that choreographic works are not necessarily the intellectual property of their creator—thus loosening the connection between choreographer and choreographic works. Though temporal boundaries can be laid out for copyright case law, geographical and national boundaries are more porous, especially when one deals with something like dance choreography, as to what is "American," and is always and already rooted in a global context. Thus, Fuller's attempt at seeking copyright protection in the United States has to be contextualized against her success in Paris as the "Goddess of Light." Similarly, Balanchine's attempt to forge a "purer" form of classical ballet, using untrained American bodies, has to be understood against the backdrop of his Russian background. Correspondingly, some of Graham's modernist experiments have to be contextualized as responses to her travels to South America, funded by grants. Along a parallel track, Dunham's ethno-choreography has to be analyzed in relation to her anthropological fieldwork in the Caribbean and, like Fuller and Baker, Dunham's stardom in Europe. The other significant factor to keep in mind is that choreographic innovation far outpaces what copyright law "fixes" as copyrightable, so there is often a significant time lag between actual choreographic production and presentation, and copyright protection, if protection ever even becomes possible.

Nevertheless, crucial to this evolution of the relationship between copyright and choreography, in my view, drawing from Cheryl Harris' 1993 *Harvard Law Review* article, is the development of whiteness as status property—both as an aesthetic and cultural force, and eventually, a legally accepted and protected form of property. Harris argues that historically, US law has "accorded 'holders' of whiteness the same privileges and benefits accorded holders of other types of property."[7] This book is an extension of that argument, but equally important to map are gender and class, especially in relation to the star system. Thus, to enhance Harris' characterization of "whiteness," I also employ Kimberle Crenshaw's "intersectional model" of critical race theory, showing that race, gender, and class are interrelated, rather than isolated factors, in the negotiation of agency and identity.[8]

Yet probably the most directly relevant, to the approach I take, is Kenneth Nunn's critique of Eurocentrism, as enshrined in law.[9] There is much in Nunn's critique of Eurocentrism that resonates with this critique of whiteness as property, especially his astute observation that "[i]t is the core cultural dynamics of Western societies that produce social structures in which male traits, material possessions and white racial characteristics are so highly privileged."[10] Finally, Richard Dyer's work on "whiteness," although it has been employed more for film studies, would also be of interest, because of the theatrical nature of performance dance, and its use of lighting to enhance visual illusion.[11] Given La Loïe's collaborations with early film *auteurs* and their experiments with light and black and white film, as well as Graham's own experiments with film, light, and shadow, Dyer's approach has a particular relevance.[12] Similarly, Balanchine's choreography for Goldwyn's *American in Paris*, an updated *Swan Lake*, in which the beauteous white nymph, Zorina, emerges from a pool at a garden party, to surrealistic effects, showed a brief flirtation with an experimentation with light reminiscent of Fuller.[13] It is noteworthy that all the figures I discuss in this book—Fuller, Baker, Balanchine, Graham, and Dunham—experimented with film, in different ways, either as a commercial, artistic, or in Dunham's case, even as a preliminary documentary mode for her anthropological studies—and all of these figures (at least in their commercial or artistic forms) displayed, or were framed by, the kind of white aesthetic Dyer critiqued in his work.

In addition, just as significant to observe is the fact that I use "big names" in the history of dance to chart this relationship between copyright and choreography. This is because the nature of copyright law, as we shall see, mimes the modern attitude of elevating one rare individual—an authorial figure, or "creator"—who forges something "radically new" and "revolutionary"; the method this book employs, therefore, simply traces and mimes that "logic" to uncover its tensions, its hesitations, and its anxieties.

Thus, located within the context of my larger project, "whiteness" is really about having property (both tangible and intangible), being privileged enough to be considered an "artist" (i.e., one having the "genius" necessary to create something "original" as opposed to something merely "derivative"), and consistently being protected by the law in a seemingly "neutral" process. All these certainly implicate an analysis of the assumptions about "authorship," "creativity," and "property" behind American Copyright Law, as it has evolved, mirroring the potentials and tensions of its historical moorings.

The key questions this book grapples with are:

1. What does one mean, as a rough heuristic, by a "white aesthetic," and a "nonwhite aesthetic"?

2. How did race and gender, and to some extent, class, figure into Fuller's and Baker's choreographic and improvisational legacies?
3. Why did Balanchine's choreography succeed at gaining full copyright protection, where Fuller's failed?
4. What accounted for the more refractory stories of success, in terms of copyright and choreography, for the cases of Graham and Dunham?
5. In brief, what possible new directions of inquiry could emerge from this study?

Literature Review

Whiteness, Property Law, and Critical Race Theory

Debates about race and racial identity in addition to discussions regarding property rights and ownership have dominated much public discourse in the United States. In "Whiteness as Property," Harris argued that racial identity and property are deeply interrelated concepts. Harris analyzed how whiteness, initially constructed as a form of racial *identity*, evolved into a form of *property*, historically and presently acknowledged and protected in American law.[14] Harris tracked the origins of whiteness as property in the parallel systems of domination over African American and Native American races, out of which emerged racially contingent forms of property and property rights. "Even in the early years of this country, it was not the concept of race alone that operated to oppress Blacks and Indians; rather, it was the interaction between conceptions of race and property that played a critical role in establishing and maintaining racial and economic subordination."[15] Harris tracked the theoretical genealogy of whiteness as property from its traditional, custom- and identity-based roots, to more modern theories that move across power relations, social expectations, and prestige.[16] "In a society structured on racial subordination, white privilege became an expectation, and... whiteness became the quintessential property for personhood."[17]

Harris argued that after the period of slavery and conquest, whiteness was constructed as the functional basis of racialized privilege—a type of status in which white racial identity provided the basis for allocating societal upward mobility and prestige, both private and public in character. "[T]he law has accorded 'holders' of whiteness the same privileges and benefits accorded holders of other types of property... [inclusive of] the exclusive rights of possession, use and disposition. Its attributes are the rights to transfer or alienability, the right to use and enjoyment, and the right to exclude others."[18] Eventually, these rules and practices became legitimated in law as a type of status property. "In constructing whiteness as property, the ideological move was to conceptualize white racial identity as an external thing in a constitutive sense...accomplished in large measure by recognizing the reputational interest in being regarded as white as a thing of significant value, which like other reputational interests, was intrinsically bound up with identity and personhood."[19] Thus, even when legal segregation was overturned, whiteness as property continued to operate as an obstacle to effective change as the system of racial classification operated to uphold systemically entrenched power, as evidenced in *Brown I* and *Brown II*.[20] Ultimately, Harris analyzed how the concept of whiteness as property persists in current perceptions of racial identity, exemplified in the law's misperception of group identity, and in the Court's reasoning and decisions in the arena of affirmative action, given *Brown I*'s and *Brown II*'s refractory heritage, in relation to dismantling white privilege.[21]

Acknowledging the complexity and mobility of racial construction in relation to power, Kimberle Crenshaw proposes an "intersectional" approach: one that takes into account how race, gender, and class, for example, are not isolated indicia of personhood and privilege, but operate as concrete foundations of power, which interact, much like variables.[22] Crenshaw's focus is less on whiteness and identity politics, than one of its counterparts, the experiences of violence lived by poor African American women, who are institutionalized through an accretion of norms.

> Many women of color...are burdened by property, child care responsibilities, and the lack of job skills. These burdens, largely the consequence of gender and class oppression, are then compounded by the racially discriminatory employment and housing practices often faced by women of color, as well as by the disproportionately high unemployment among people of color that makes battered women of color less able to depend on the support of friends and relatives for temporary shelter.[23]

Nevertheless, like Harris, Crenshaw points out the reductive quality of identity politics and its failure to grapple with the lived power differentials, institutionalized through legal practices and social norms. Crenshaw argues that the problem with identity politics is, at a basic level, that it "frequently conflates or ignores intragroup differences," which in turn "contributes to tension *among* groups."[24] The ironic aftermath is that the liberatory agendas of feminist and antiracist critique, rhetorically enacted in isolation from each other, serve to silence those who live intersectionally. "Although racism and sexism readily intersect in the lives of real people they seldom do in feminist and antiracist practices. Thus, when the practices expound identity as 'woman' or 'person of color' as an either/or proposition, they relegate the identity of women of color to a location that resists telling."[25] Using Harris' notions of "whiteness as property" and Crenshaw's "intersectional" approach, I track how the concept of whiteness, mapped alongside variables of gender, class, and nationality operated in the cases of Loïe Fuller and George Balanchine, and his estate, which mark the institutionalization of choreography as intellectual property.

Additionally, Kenneth Nunn outlines seven characteristics of Eurocentric (whitened) culture; briefly summarized, these seven characteristics are dichotomous reasoning, employment of hierarchies, analytical thought, objectification, abstraction, extreme rationalism, and desacralization. Five of these listed characteristics also emerge in this analysis of the history of copyright and choreography, instantiated, for example, in Fuller and Balanchine. These are as follows: (1) dichotomous reasoning[26] (here, emerging in the dichotomy between copyrighted/copyrightable material and noncopyrightable/public domain material: (2) employment of hierarchies[27] (here, in the elevation of copyrighted/copyrightable material as deserving of "protection" from unauthorized use, over noncopyrightable/public domain work); (3) analytical thought[28] (here, in the creation of "stars," who seem ethereally elevated above community connections as self-sufficient artistic divinities); (4) objectification[29] (here, particularly evident in the treatment of Josephine Baker); and (5) abstraction[30] (here, "distilled excretions of ideas take precedent over ideas in context,"[31] as evidenced, for example, in Fuller's spectacular world of illusion and noncorporeality, and Balanchine's fantasy world of hyperwhitened, impossibly waif-like ballerinas). However, Nunn's final two characteristics don't really fit this particular set of case studies: extreme rationalism and desacralization.[32] Dance, being an art form, rather than a science, probably resists both characteristics, substituting expressiveness for strict rationality, and the sacralization of the artistic, for secular desacralization. Nevertheless, Nunn's powerful critique of Eurocentrism buttresses this critique of whiteness as property, especially his astute observation that "law works to legitimate white institutions and practices by helping to place the imprimatur of universality on European practices and champion the desirability and inevitability of white dominance."[33]

Along a parallel track, Richard Dyer (in relation specifically to conventions of American Hollywood film and its aesthetics) observes that whiteness is associated with power, heterosexuality, virtue, cleanliness, godliness, wealth, ethereality (if female), and universality.[34] "Whiteness," within the context of American history, unlike nonwhiteness, has *often* (not always, as there are always exceptions) been treated as a monolithic pass to privilege, perhaps legally traceable to the "one drop rule"—where even just one drop of black blood was sufficient legal basis to exclude a person from owning property and to relegating them to the status of being property, resulting in a complex history of slavery.[35] Without devaluing these insights, the argument I make in this book is more nuanced: that whiteness as property, too, is a contested and negotiated site of social relation, rather than a fixed identity or "thing" that is owned. White privilege often maintains itself through an ambivalent posture of negation; it needs its "other" to distinguish itself, and to establish its superiority. Yet whiteness is not monolithic.[36] Furthermore, possessors of white privilege are not uniformly privileged in an automatic and unproblematic manner. Additionally, white privilege's underside is a fascination with, and envy of, that which is nonwhite, which it appropriates unto itself through its characterization of the "exotic."[37]

Of course, issues of race and privilege intersect with representations of gender and sexuality; however, because the artistic self-representations of the figures I study remain predominantly heterosexual (as does the legal point of view, though implicitly, in the background), the focus of this book remains predominantly on the complex relationship between sex and gender. In a groundbreaking observation regarding the interplay between performance and lived experience, which is appropriate to this analysis of performance and gender via dance choreography, Judith Butler remarked: "The act that gender is, the act that embodied agents are inasmuch as they dramatically and actively embody and, indeed, wear certain cultural significations, is clearly not one's act alone. Surely, there are nuanced and individual ways of doing one's gender, but that one does it, and that one does it in accord with certain sanctions and proscriptions, is clearly not a fully individual matter."[38] This notion of gender as performance is particularly true of the women of color, such as Baker and Dunham, though of course this is also present in Fuller's image as an ethereal goddess of light and Graham's initially "sexless" solo performances. This is because as women of color, despite their celebrity, Baker and Dunham had more limited access to whiteness as status property, compared to their white counterparts, Fuller and Graham. Though in all the women's cases, sex and gender trumped race, Fuller and Graham clearly were more empowered by both the cultural and legal systems than Baker and Dunham.

Baker and Dunham, unlike Fuller and Graham, were burdened by the colonial myth of the "Ebony Venus"—an ambivalent myth, beginning with Sara Baartman, enshrined in museum displays and iconized in popular culture. Thus, Ann Stoler's work on archives is important to some parts of this study because as Stoler noted, Parisian archives included cultural memories of Baartman's dissected genital "apron" as the trace that constituted her identity as a "Black Venus," thus forging and strengthening "codes of recognition and systems of expectation at the very heart of what we still need to learn about colonial polities."[39] Baker and Dunham (Baker more so than Dunham) were thus particularly subject to these codes of recognition and theatres of raced and gendered performance. Given these constraints, both women (and especially Baker) had to be, to some extent, complicit with their promoters and audiences in order to operate successfully as artistic and commercial entities. As we shall see in chapter 2, Baker, for example, employed several evolving performative strategies of image and identity construction, which both exploited, and were subject to, the raced and gendered expectations embedded in the "Ebony Venus" myth such as: exoticizing race and gender; reversing racial and cultural codes and meanings; displaying difference through nudity, cross-dressing, song, and dance; exploiting the images of difference; and universalizing the outcome to allow the performative messages to reach broader based audiences.[40]

Unique Features of this Book

Despite the plethora of biographical books on especially Josephine Baker, George Balanchine, Martha Graham, and Katherine Dunham, and of various anthologies on critical race theory, few critical manuscripts examining the lacunae connecting whiteness, copyright protection, and choreography exist. However, each of these related texts has some weaknesses this book attempts to avoid.

Some limit themselves purely to the study of nonwhite choreography created well before choreographic works became potentially protected by federal law. For example, for all its critical strengths, Anthea Kraut's *Choreographing the Folk: The Dance Stagings of Zora Neale Hurston*[41] focuses on Hurston's work in the 1930's when she produced theatrical concerts that depicted a day in the life of a railroad work camp in Florida that featured a "Bahamian Fire Dance" as the production's dramatic finale. Kraut, although she raises similar questions regarding ownership and artistry, limits her analysis purely to the significance and influence of Hurston's little-known choreographic work.

Some, despite the wealth of information they provide regarding the nexus between critical race theory and copyright, don't address choreography at all. For example, an essay in an anthology, Kevin J. Greene's "Papa's Got a Brand New Bag: James Brown, Innovation, and Copyright Law,"[42] provides insightful descriptions of how the history of copyright, in relation to music, reifies the familiar stories of innovation by African American musical artists, the perpetuation of racist stereotypes, and exploitation by the capitalist and "whitened" music industry. Greene has written extensively on this topic, but focusing principally on African American musical artists, not on choreographers and dancers.

A plethora of authors provide popular accounts of connections between choreographic creation and copyright protection but don't provide a detailed and nuanced analysis of the relevant cases, or of the raced, gendered, and sexualized dimensions of the biographical accounts of these key figures. For instance, Bernard Taper's *Balanchine: A Biography with a New Epilogue*[43] gives a popular account of how Balanchine's choreographic works were converted into intellectual property and became objects of ownership and dispute. However, it does not engage in depth with the cases, or the courts' reasoning, relevant to maintaining the border separating protected choreographic works from those in the public domain; neither does it reflect on the gendered, raced and classed dimensions of Balanchine's comparatively easier ascent into artistic immortality compared to the women I study in this book.

Along a parallel track, Ann Cooper Albright's *Traces of Light: Absence and Presence in the Work of Loïe Fuller*[44] provides an insightful scholarly account of Fuller's rise to stardom. Albright's book includes a section on the *Fuller v. Bemis* trial, during which Fuller sued one of her competitors for control over her "serpentine" dance. Albright's focus on Fuller's aesthetic of whiteness supports my thesis, but Albright fails to account for why Balanchine, partaking of the same aesthetic of whiteness, succeeds where Fuller fails, though the analysis of the performance of gender, race, and class in Fuller's theaters of light are frontal and central to her project.

On the other extreme, numerous critical race theory anthologies abound, such as *Critical Race Theory: The Key Writings that Formed the Movement*, edited by Kimberle Crenshaw, Neil Gotanda, Gary Peller, and Kendall Thomas;[45] *Critical Race Theory: The Cutting Edge*, 2nd ed., edited by Richard Delgado and Jean Stefancic;[46] and *Making Race Visible: Literacy Research for Cultural Understanding*, edited by Stuart Greene and Dawn Abt-Perkins.[47] However, while many of them harness various interdisciplinary perspectives, none of them coherently yoke together a consistent theory of how whiteness operates in cultural and legal worlds, in interaction with gender and class.

In contrast, the following are a few distinctive features of this book. First, as a general historical account, it draws from what Bruno Latour analogously characterizes as the "hot" sites (before clear rhetorical lines have congealed)[48] within which the relationships between copyright and choreography are forged—ranging across biographical and autobiographical accounts, legal cases, newspaper stories, and artistic visual interpretations, among others. Furthermore, it examines the co-construction of whiteness against its exotic "others," and shows that the resultant narrative is complex, rather than one of simple domination because women like Fuller and Graham, while having some access to white privilege as *white* women, were not automatically "entitled" to full access as white *women*, unlike Balanchine, who had access to the privileges of both whiteness and maleness. This is not to discount the focus on nonwhiteness, but it does emphasize that whiteness and nonwhiteness do not form a simple binary, but comprise a complex continuum that is constantly negotiated and mediated, not only through formal legal mechanisms but also through broader cultural forces. But the contrast between Balanchine and Dunham, for example, is striking, as it is clear that Dunham could easily have rivaled Balanchine in forging a body of choreographic works capable of commanding intellectual property protection, much as Balanchine's estate, and to a less successful extent, Graham's estate did. Part of the answer for why that did not occur is complex, as Dunham was herself a fairly complected black woman with the "whitened" credentials of an ethnographer-scholar, and there is some reason to believe that her physical attractiveness and closeness to a Caucasian standard of beauty led to refractory receptions of her performances and choreographic creations. Part of the answer, as well, is simple: Dunham, though she had some access to whiteness as status property, was very well aware of her liminal status, and as such did not push the issue of intellectual property ownership of her choreographic creations; furthermore, she passed away only in 2006, thus making it possible to defer the issue of the intellectual property ownership of her choreographic works to later in her life, when she now had the established renown of being the "Matriarch of Black Dance."

Second, as this book eventually shows, while there is a general type of whiteness that is privileged in relation to choreographic works (usually conflated with aesthetic abstraction), there are different types of "whitenesses," some of which appropriate aspects of the "exotic" or "nonwhite." Thus, this study differs from accounts of wholesale discrimination and exploitation unproblematically dichotomized along racial lines. What this book attempts to document are the hesitations, the complexities, the ambiguities, and not the easy generalizations.

Third, this book also argues that crucial to the formation of a successful form of "whiteness" in the development of copyrightable choreographic works was the development of a star persona—one delimited from a mass of "skirt dancers"; one able to conjure and embody the myth of the Ebony Cleopatra; one capable of drilling either light technicians or dancers into precise executors or quintessential embodiments of artistic visions; one with the reputation of "Genius," "Picasso of American Dance" or "Matriarch of Black Dance." The construction of celebrity is intimately tied with the privileging of whiteness as an aesthetic, as the history of Hollywood film shows.[49]

Copyright and Choreography: A Broad Historical Sketch

The US Constitution grants Congress the power "[t]o promote the Progress of Science and useful Arts, by securing for limited Times to Authors . . . the exclusive Right to their respective writings . . ."[50] The framers of the Constitution enacted this clause with what appears to be very little elaboration or contextualization at the Constitutional Convention. Many of the colonies had already embodied their position on the issue of copyright in their own statutes and constitutions prior to the Constitutional Convention and this direction was consistent with the direction many of the colonies had taken in relation to copyright.[51]

The overtly stated purpose of copyright was to promote the public good by encouraging the development of creative works by compensating the creator. Under common law and the 1909 Copyright Act, which was effective until 1978, choreography was ineligible for the protection of copyright *unless* it was "dramatic" or "dramatico-musical."[52] Thus, the 1909 Copyright Act enabled copyright protection for abstract musical works and paintings but left abstract dance, devoid of narrative, unprotected. Music and painting were unfettered from the requirement of being attached to story. Dance, however, did have to narrate a plot, in order to become copyrightable.[53]

Although choreography in the United States was denied federal copyright protection as such until 1978 (when 17 U.S.C. 106, the Copyright Act of 1976 was enacted),[54] the struggle to win property rights for dance choreography began, arguably, at least eight decades prior to that.[55] For example, as we shall see in chapter 3, Loïe Fuller, considered one of the "mothers" of modern dance, unsuccessfully sued one of her imitators in 1892 for performing an "unauthorized" copy of her "Serpentine Dance."[56]

Until 1978, the Courts, in their interpretation of the Constitutional Clause on Copyright, didn't find that abstract dance promoted "the progress of science or the useful arts"—a position held, for example, in 1867 in *Martinetti v. Maguire*.[57] In *Martinetti*, the choreography in "Black Crook," a play or "spectacle," was not abstract but it was dramatic.[58] There was clearly a substantial similarity between "Black Crook," deemed the original, and "Black Rook," the colorable imitation.[59] Nevertheless, the court found the dramatic part of the presentation "immoral" and as such, promoted "nothing useful" for the arts.[60] Thus, the court dismissively characterized the work as an "indecent ballet."[61] In the colorful language of the court:

> The Black Crook is a mere spectacle—in the language of the craft a spectacular piece. The dialogue is very scant and meaningless, and appears to be a mere accessory to the action of the piece—a sort of verbal machinery tacked on to a succession of ballet and tableaux. The principal part and attraction of the spectacle seems to be the exhibition of women in novel dress or no dress, and in attractive attitudes or action... To call such a spectacle a "dramatic composition" is an abuse of language, and an insult to the genius of the English drama. A menagerie of wild beasts, or an exhibition of model artistes might as justly be called a dramatic composition. Like those, this is a spectacle, and although it may be an attractive or gorgeous one, it is nothing more.[62]

There is no evidence indicating that the Court even saw the work in question. Relying purely on expert witness testimony, and in particular, on the statements of W. B. Hamilton, a well-known actor in Europe and America and stage manager of the Metropolitan, the court quickly arrived at the conclusion that: "the so-called play of the Black Crook has no originality, and that it consists almost wholly of scenic effects, or representations taken substantially from well-known dramas and operas."[63]

In the United States, because abstract choreography couldn't be protected by copyright until the enactment of the 1976 Copyright Act, Balanchine initially believed most of his works were ineligible for copyright.[64] As we shall see in greater depth in chapter 4, it was only in 1978, after a heart attack, that Balanchine, mistakenly believing that his ballets couldn't be bequeathed by will, sought the advice of an estate attorney.[65] To his surprise, the lawyer claimed that they could be protected by copyright, once registered and bequeathed.[66] Balanchine passed away five years later, on April 30, 1983.[67] Unlike his star persona, who bowed to no one, Balanchine's will acknowledged "that dance has always been created and handed down through personal contact," and bequeathed his ballets to his chosen heirs, Tanaquil LeClercq, Karin von Aroldingen, and Barbara Horgan, who created the Balanchine Trust.[68]

Balanchine choreographed over 400 ballets, most of them abstract and devoid of plot. These ballets were presented as abstract performances that enveloped the dancer and the audience in the performance rather than the plot.[69] In terms of being free of narrative form, Balanchine's ballets bore a kinship to Fuller's choreographic experiments.[70] Nevertheless, where Fuller failed, Balanchine (and his estate) succeeded. Part of the third chapter of this book is principally about how Fuller's failure in the legal arena was counterbalanced by her success in the popular arena. Ironically, popular cultural mechanisms arguably better preserved her legacy than copyright could. Chapter 3 also examines the ambivalent gains of being able to copyright choreography against the cultural–legal backdrop of whiteness as property. Prior to proceeding with the principal analytic sections of this book, I begin with a brief examination of why copyright and choreography in the United States have had such a refractory history.

The Difficulties of Copyrighting Dance Choreography

The US Copyright Act of 1976, in order to grant copyright protection to choreographic works, requires that these works be "fixed in any tangible medium of expression, now known or later developed, from which they can be perceived, reproduced, or otherwise communicated, either directly or with the aid of a machine or device."[71] However, dance choreography's improvisational and ephemeral qualities make it difficult to fix. Thus, correspondingly, Yeoh attributes the "paucity of case law on dance copyright" to its "ontological instability."[72] Similarly, Sparshott points to some of the reasons why the history of dance choreography in relation to copyright is thinly documented, pointing to dance's nonverbal representation and the scarcity of reliable records. "The lack of any reliable and generally accessible way of recording dance has given it a fugitive nature. It has rendered dances unstable, depending on generations of dancers whose uncertain memories are associated with their own styles and body habits."[73]

Copyright's history is bound up with printing and copying; given that backdrop, it is hardly surprising that dance, with its bodily based and oral traditions, is an anomaly.[74] In contrast, books are created in a manner that judges have no difficulty understanding—through the combination of words into phrases, and cumulatively, phrases into sentences, until "copyrightable" material emerges.[75] While choreography shares some of these properties, in terms of its building blocks, choreography differs from literary composition in that its fixation in a medium is separate from its creation.[76] Most choreographers have only a general idea, rather than an outline or detailed notes. Even if choreographers write down notes, these often are so incomplete that they do not rise to the level of being copyrightable.[77] Choreography is thus analogous to a living sculpture, whose final form gets fixed based on what transpires between choreographer and dancer, and the dancer's physical limits.[78]

Traditionally, dancers have relied on memory to conserve and pass on choreography.[79] Memory, clearly, is an unreliable method of fixation and of preserving choreography. Nevertheless, the dancers' memory, along with community norms, has been the traditional way in which the dance community has preserved dance, and prevented infringement, especially as the costs of litigation often preempt choreographers from suing. Noting that choreography is one of the least represented among the performing arts, Patry remarks:

> This very low figure [regarding the number of copyrighted choreographic works] corresponds to the legal literature on copyright and choreography, which repeatedly notes choreographers' decision not to rely on copyright and to instead develop their own "community" system of protection, protection believed to be better suited to choreography and providing better protection. The community system works in large part because of the concentration of choreographers in New York City, the tight-knit nature of dance companies, and the reputation within the community enjoyed by choreographers.[80]

Thus, choreographic works are created differently from most art forms that judges adjudicate in copyright infringement cases. Furthermore, the Copyright Office prefers forms of notations that are more precise and text-based, but are not necessarily perceived as the most effective by the dance community. For example, written notation systems, such as Labanotation and Benesh Notation,[81] are preferred for their precision and attention to detail.[82] Unfortunately, the costs of using these methods are prohibitively expensive: 20 minutes of Labanotation can cost up to $12,000.[83] Furthermore, the period of time required to notate the average ballet is "approximately 10,000 hours."[84] Film or videotape are possible to use as alternative methods of fixation but they have their own drawback: "[F]ilming, unlike labanotation [sic], cannot preserve the clarity and definition of the individual movements comprising the dance; a film, even running in slow motion, does not allow the viewer to separate the individual steps of a dance."[85]

Even more significantly, as the House Report to the 1976 Act made clear, Congress created a separate category for choreography, but it chose not to define what "choreographic works" mean.[86] The House Report claimed that the term's meaning was "fairly settled" and commonplace knowledge, not requiring definition.[87] *Maralasco* asserted that the "Register [of Copyright] has the authority to interpret the copyright laws and... its interpretations are entitled to judicial deference if reasonable."[88] Thus, the original *Compendium*, which described policy and procedure for Copyright Office staff, in relation to the 1909 Copyright Act, evolved; *Compendium II*, which replaced the original *Compendium*, was a manual produced by the United States Copyright Office, directed to policy under the 1976 Act, as amended.[89]

The earliest landmark federal case to address infringement of a choreographic work after the 1976 Copyright Act, *Horgan v. MacMillan*, as we shall see in chapter 4, used *Compendium II*'s characterization of "choreography."[90] Choreography, according to *Compendium II*, is "the composition and arrangement of dance movements and patterns... Dance is static and kinetic successions of bodily movement in certain rhythmic and spatial relationships."[91] The Copyright Office also specified that "[s]ocial dance steps and simple routines... such as the basic waltz step, the hustle step, and the second position of classical ballet" did not fulfill the requirements for copyright registration.[92] Nevertheless, the *Compendium* also qualified its regulations by stating that that these elements might be copyrightable if they were integrated into an "otherwise registrable choreographic work" and "may be utilized as the choreographer's basic material in much the same way that words are the writer's basic material."[93]

To close this general historical sketch, what emerges is the observation that the relationship between copyright and dance choreography remains in flux, sometimes in conjunction, and often in tense interplay. Unlike music and film or video, choreography has often been regarded as the invisible stepchild among the copyrightable categories. Although there are numerous factors that account for why this is, the critical factors this book focuses on are those that underlie the construction of whiteness as property, against the intersectional backdrop of race, gender, and, to some extent, class.

Organizational Schema

The organizational scheme of this book is as follows:

Chapter 1: "Introduction: Preliminary Remarks." This chapter functions principally as an explanation for the scope of the book (including key questions), and the various methodologies it employs. It also covers a brief review of other approaches explaining why copyright and choreography have had such a refractory history.

Chapter 2: "Comparing an Aesthetics of Whiteness and an Aesthetics of Nonwhiteness." This chapter functions as a general schema in order to map out how whiteness functions as status property in relation to choreographic works. It is a general heuristic for mapping what constitutes a white aesthetic (which tended to be copyrightable) and a nonwhite aesthetic (which tended to be noncopyrightable), in the history of American dance from the late 1800's to roughly the mid-2000's.

Chapter 3: "Loíe Fuller, 'Goddess of Light,' and Josephine Baker, 'Black Venus': Non-narrative Choreography as Mere Spectacle." This chapter examines Loïe Fuller's (1862–1928) rise to stardom in Paris as "La Loïe" and her failure to secure copyright protection in the landmark trial, *Fuller v. Bemis* (1892). It also comparatively examines Josephine Baker's (1906–1975) equally phenomenal rise to becoming Europe's "Black Venus" and examines why, if she had dared mount a claim for copyright protection for her dance improvisations like Fuller, such a claim would have failed even more miserably, despite her celebrity. Crucial to the differences between the conditions of possibility within which Fuller, as opposed to Baker, could attempt to claim ownership of her choreographic works was her possession of an aesthetic of whiteness and of whiteness as status property, even if her sex and gender trumped her whiteness.

Chapter 4: "George Balanchine, 'Genius of American Dance': Whiteness, Choreography, Copyrightability in American Dance." This chapter recounts George Balanchine's (1904–1983) acquisition of the reputation of being a "genius"; his lawyer's successful conversion of his choreographic works into copyrighted material via a will, and his estate's eventual successful protection of his choreographic works from infringement in a protracted legal battle that ended in 1986 (*Horgan v. Macmillan*). Crucial to that success was Balanchine's establishment of an aesthetic of whiteness, through his ballets, as the template of copyrightable American dance, and his possession of white (male) privilege as status property.

Chapter 5: "Martha Graham, 'Picasso of American Dance,' and Katherine Dunham, 'Matriarch of Black Dance': Exoticism and Nonwhiteness in American Dance." This chapter reviews Martha Graham's ascent to stardom as a white woman capable of forging her own choreography, while appropriating the look of the "exotic" and rebelling against the conventions of ballet. It also analyzes how the Second Circuit eventually justified divesting her estate of control over her choreographic works, in direct contrast to Balanchine's estate, in another long and bitter battle (*Martha Graham Sch. & Dance Found., Inc. v. Martha Graham Ctr. Of Contemporary Dance, Inc.*) (2006). The chapter also briefly analyzes Katherine Dunham's establishment of a "black ballet" as a "Matriarch of Black Dance." However, although she was very much Balanchine's contemporary and in some instances, co-innovator of choreographic works, unlike Balanchine, she did not receive credit for some of her choreographic works, despite their immense commercial success, let alone copyright protection. Like Graham, Katherine Dunham (1909–2006) was considered "exotic"—but less because she assumed exotic personae onstage through makeup and choreography, but because as a woman of color, she was comparatively light skinned and was closer to the Caucasian ideal, as opposed to someone like Pearl Primus, whose dark skin, larger frame, and more muscular movements were considered more "authentically" black than Dunham. Dunham's "black ballets" probably came closest to finding a fusion between an aesthetics of whiteness and an aesthetics of nonwhiteness, despite the problem of "colorism"[94] that persists. Nevertheless, like Graham, her choreographic creations have not achieved the kind of copyright protection Balanchine's ballets have. Crucial to that difference, once again, is the interplay between race and gender, in the determination of who has access to whiteness as status property.

Chapter 6: "Moving into New Directions: Cunningham and Ailey." I close with a comparison and contrast between Merce Cunningham and Alvin Ailey because such an approach is instructive, when trying to understand how race, gender, and in the case especially of Cunningham, sexuality intersect with kinesthetic conventions of choreography. Copyright law takes a back seat in this chapter because unlike Fuller, Balanchine, and Graham, there are no law suits contesting choreographic ownership. That absence of legal squabbling itself deserves some scrutiny, as it illustrates how Cunningham (and his lawyers) probably learned from the examples (and mistakes) of Balanchine's and Graham's estates, and how Ailey, following a similar approach as Dunham, succeeded in establishing unambiguous legal ownership of his choreographic work, even at the young age of 22. Cunningham and Ailey were allies in their revolt against classicism and the dominance of ballet; they created hybrid forms of dance, combining both white and nonwhite elements of choreography. Cunningham subtly problematized conventional depictions of heteronormative masculinity: the aesthetic he developed remained safely within the whitened realm of "high art" with its emphasis on technique. In contrast, though Ailey achieved the distinction of being more than a "black performer" to become an internationally recognized "American choreographer," his predominant depictions of gender relations remained safely within the heterosexual realm despite Ailey's private life. While Cunningham experimented with integrating avant-garde art and cutting-edge technologies into his predominantly abstract works, Ailey preferred to return to the basics of theatrical staging, focusing on simpler lines, emotional expressiveness, costuming and lighting, and connection with popular audiences. Cunningham's inclusion of new technologies, such as magnetic tape, film, and video, into his choreography, probably strengthened his claim to choreographic ownership, because of his overcoming of the usual copyright hurdle of fixation, and probably increased the perceived originality of his work. In contrast, Ailey's preference for more conventional means of staging, devoid of, or at least without the deliberate inclusion of new technologies or new methods of fixing choreography, probably helped bolster the impression, at least among traditional dance aficionados, rather than the public, that in general, Ailey's work was "less original" than Cunningham's. Nevertheless, in both men's cases, masculinity trumped race or sexuality in terms of access to whiteness as status property.

Chapter 7: "Conclusions: Quo Vadis?" This chapter comparatively tracks how whiteness as status property, mapped in relation to gender and class, operated in the cases of Fuller, Balanchine, Graham, Baker, Dunham, Cunningham, and Ailey. It also includes new directions that could be explored, such as a further refinement or nuancing of Cohen Bull's description of an African aesthetic drawing from African-centered scholars such as Kariamu Welsh-Asante. In addition, additional inquiries that examine the legacies of Isadora Duncan and Ruth St. Denis—drawn against the evolving relationships binding whiteness, choreography, and copyright—would enhance this study. Furthermore, detailed comparative analyses of the dance legacies of Ted Shawn, Merce Cunningham, Arthur Mitchell, and Alvin Ailey would further round out this inquiry into the intersectionalities of race, gender, and sexuality, with a focus on masculinities. Furthermore, more far-reaching ramifications, such as the differences between the smooth or standard dances of competitive ballroom dance, which partake of an aesthetic of whiteness, and the Latin or rhythm dances of DanceSport, which use an aesthetic of nonwhiteness, could be explored, both in terms of choreographic and copyrightable possibilities. Additionally, on a parallel but different track, initial explorations of how the conflicts and hurdles that haunt attempts to use copyright law to protect the intellectual property rights of indigenous peoples (especially their expressions of folklore, inclusive of folk dance) mime the problems that plague nonwhites' access to whiteness as status property. These are only some of the many ways in which this research could be further deepened.

Chapter 2

Comparing Aesthetics of Whiteness and Nonwhiteness in Relation to American Dance*

Introduction

In this introductory chapter, I begin, preliminarily, with a simple binary, opposing an aesthetic of "whiteness" and "nonwhiteness" only because it is analytically useful to start this way. I am not trying to exhaust what a "white aesthetic" or a "nonwhite aesthetic" mean; this is a pragmatic set of parameters, set up, not to forge absolute definitions but to function as a general heuristic. One can begin to appreciate the chiaroscuros, the *sfumatos*, the complex shading across categories, after one has established, at least in principle, the extreme ends of a spectrum. After I have characterized these categories, I begin to problematize the neat schematization—which I do in later chapters, in keeping with what the individual stories and historical data allow—because my purpose is neither to essentialize these categories nor to moralize about the inherent superiority of one aesthetic over the other or even to form a "documentary" description of the "fundamentals" to these two general aesthetics. Nor do I see it as my task, in this book, to "correct (moral) problems."

My concern is first principally analytic, which means what I strive to do is understand how cultural constructions (not factual or genetic categories), as historically grounded, often systematically and invisibly privilege some categories and not others. Certainly, moral implications and potential activist projects could flow from this analysis. But these are not at the forefront of this project. My first impetus, as a legal scholar, is this: it is an attempt at a genealogy of how a whitened aesthetic (and a very specific one at that) hardens, in law, to become the authorized form—the copyrightable form, as opposed to its other(s). I am not against examining moral implications, but they are not the focus of this study. If they were, then I would use a very different approach and a different set of theorists—overtly moral theorists, for example, Levinas, Kant, Gandhi, maybe even Fanon, etc., who use a different set of tools and arguments—to make those kinds of arguments effectively. I am well aware and appreciative of the activist bent that is possible, because of this study. But this study simply begins the process of getting there; it makes no pretensions at having forged absolute answers—particularly in relation to what a nonwhite aesthetic is, especially given the historical and legal record, much of which is steeped in whiteness, rather than its others.

Thus, what I focus on, in this preliminary chapter, is a working schema, established in order to explore intersections linking critical race theory, copyright, and a certain period of American dance (the late 1800's until roughly 2006), not an attempt at totalization or an overtly "morally" driven project. Moral questions, while they are important, are simply part of the destination, subtly embedded, but not at the forefront. An analogous way of describing the principal thrust or spirit of this book is to frame it in Habermasian terms: as an exercise in reasoned discourse within the public sphere.[1]

These constructions (whiteness/nonwhiteness; masculinity/femininity) do not stay stable, but like living organisms, evolve, in relation to each other, sometimes cross-fertilizing to produce new strains, which in turn either spawn new variations or are reabsorbed back into the preexisting classification (and hierarchy) of terms; my principal task is to try to illustrate that dynamic. To understand how "whiteness" is a "property" as much as an "aesthetic," one must plot, to the extent one can, how systems function to produce these differences, in operation, as property is not about "things." Property is about relations between or among entities (some of whom are persons) regarding the management of relations concerning the use and ownership of these "things"—some of which are intangible, such as whiteness. The larger metaphysical questions of what is "property" (especially "intellectual property") or what is "art" elude mechanical reductions, and I do not see the task of this project as finding an absolute answer to such questions. My task is much humbler and more limited in scope.

This chapter, in specific, focuses on:

(1) within the context of American dance, a preliminary sketch of what a "white" aesthetic looks like—and how it functions to demarcate what

passes as "artistry" (as opposed to what is "not art") during a certain period of the history of American Dance, as the template for what passes as copyrightable begins to form. I focus mainly on the twentieth century as this period is crucial in the formation of what is distinctively "American" and "modern" in dance. It is also the period in which dance choreography becomes an independently listed legally copyrightable category, rather than being subsumed into being a certain type of "dramatic work," requiring a narrative to be legally protectable as "intellectual property." In the context of my larger project, "whiteness" is really about having property (both tangible and intangible) and having others recognize that entitlement; being privileged enough to be considered an "artist" (i.e., one having the "genius" necessary to create something "original" as opposed to something merely "derivative"); and consistently being privileged by the law in a seemingly "neutral" process, simply because law does not exist in a historical and cultural vacuum. As Joseph Singer points out: "Property law concerns the relations among people regarding the control, use and transfer of valued resources."[2] This is simply an extrapolation to more "intangible things" and to the relations creating or barring access to these "intangibles." All these certainly implicate an analysis of the assumptions about "authorship," "creativity," and "property" behind American copyright law, as it has evolved, mirroring the potentials and tensions of its historical moorings.

In keeping with the development of the theoretical schema of what I mean by "whiteness" (which is derived, to some extent, from Richard Dyer's well known account—but one that goes beyond film representations), in the larger project, I also focus in greater detail on describing how whiteness articulates with issues of gender and class in relation to the questions regarding whom copyright laws have traditionally protected, and what has counted as "intellectual property" that can be set apart from the "public domain" on "legitimate grounds." Crucial to this larger project are as follows: (a) ballet's primacy and persistence as the principal "body vocabulary" in American dance; (b) Balanchine's vision of the hyperwhitened ballerina as the still-reigning aesthetic model against which other dance body types are mapped (and the drama of his attempting to marry and thus control all the women who embodied this ideal); and finally, (c) Balanchine's unparalleled legal success and cultural legacy compared to the ambiguous gains of two equally talented white women, Fuller and Graham. I do this analysis in depth in chapter 4.

(2) As Jacques Derrida,[3] Michel Foucault,[4] Simone de Beauvoir,[5] and Luce Irigaray,[6] among others, have taught us, given how hegemonic discourses can only function against their less privileged "others," an analysis of how "whiteness" (both masculine and feminine) operates against its nonwhite "others" is also crucial. And as Derrida in particular teaches us, a system

of privilege works on setting up unproblematic dichotomies: white versus nonwhite, where nonwhiteness, a broader and inevitably vaguer category, is necessary in order to shore up the inherent superiority of the privileged term.[7]

(3) For this chapter, my focus is also on characterizing, as a general heuristic,—not one aimed to exhaust or totalize definitions—what I mean by "whiteness" or "nonwhiteness" as an aesthetic in American dance recognizable as such, more importantly, by lay audiences and courts and not so much by specialized dance critics or experts in dance ethnography—during the context of the times in which these particular aesthetics took specific form. Gender imbricates with race in this cultural imagination of a "white" versus a "nonwhite" aesthetic. Nevertheless, the aesthetic frame, for this period, remains staunchly heterosexual much as class divisions inherent to those frames remain essentially stable—particularly as stabilized by legal decisions concerning what "furthers the progress of the arts."

Establishing "Whiteness" in American Dance: Balanchine's Aesthetic

Richard Dyer's canonical account of "whiteness" associates it with power, heterosexuality, virtue, cleanliness, godliness, wealth, ethereality (if female), and universality.[8] Yet what does this description mean, in terms understanding how bodies function as "texts" in dance and choreography? Is there such a thing as a "white" aesthetic, and if so, how is this aesthetic embodied and communicated to an audience acculturated to reading bodies styled and staged specifically to enact this aesthetic?

As dance historians and ethnographers tell us, the quintessential dance form that comes closest to Dyer's characterization of a "white" aesthetic in dance is ballet. Historically, the origins of ballet are traceable to the European courts of the sixteenth and seventeenth centuries. During the Renaissance, ballets were featured as part of lavish political spectacles in which the quality of movement and body carriage (or deportment) were viewed as visible manifestations of inner moral states, status, political authorization or resistance, and even divine association; that is, many ideals and conventions of the chivalric code became refined into aesthetic principles. Crucial to the production, consumption, and professionalization of this art form was the theatre of class and privilege.

> For the largely upper-class audience, going to the ballet was a social event of great importance; being seen at the theater by the right people was as

important to some spectators as the stage spectacles they went to see. But the core of the experience remained the dancing of skilled professionals who were applauded for their feats of expressive and athletic grace.[9]

For example, Louis XIV's 1672 founding of the first ballet academy led to the evolution of a complex process of schooling in bodily techniques, the production of illusion and spectacle, and the professionalization of performers trained to enact these bodily scripts.[10] By the early-nineteenth century (the romantic period in ballet), the body vocabulary (and aesthetic), that persists even in today's ballet, had congealed. Crucial to this aesthetic is the emphasis on an erect, uplifted spine, with an unbending torso, with shoulders pulled up and back—a clearly aristocratic bearing meant to embody courtly ideals. This close association between "classical" ballet training, corporeal discipline, and (moral) "purity" continues to be extolled by various contemporary dance theorists. As Selma Jean Cohen notes:

> By "ballet" let's say we mean what is usually considered its quintessential style, classical, if by "classical" we mean pure. Lincoln Kirstein [Balanchine's patron] once defined style as a moral virtue manifested in the conquest of untidy egotism; ballet as "a clear if complex blending of human anatomy, solid geometry and acrobatics, offered as a symbolic demonstration of manners . . ." . . . Adrian Stokes suggested deftness and economy or neatness; Edwin Denby cited lightness, elevation, and ease. Kirstein qualified: "clean and open, grandiose without affectation, noble without pretension."[11]

Yet even more powerfully enduring was forging the convention of an illusion of weightlessness—a prerequisite especially for ballerinas, whose technical virtuosity was geared towards the Romantic sensibility: "to express the beauty of the spirit that transcends the flesh."[12] Indeed, popular lithographs of famous ballerinas in Romantic ballets such as *La Sylphide* and *Giselle* not only show them *en pointe* but actually depict them as floating above the earth, their feet bare—symbolizing both the aspiration of freedom from constraints, and the colonial sensibility of "expansion, exploration, and exploitation."[13] Interestingly, these romantic ballets were called "white ballets" (named after the ballerinas' revealing yet elegant tutus fashioned from white gauze).[14] Nevertheless, that ideal of ethereality or even noncorporeality, linked with a look of feminized hyperwhiteness, is one that not only persists, but even reaches an extreme in Balanchine's ballets, as we shall later see.

Technically, that illusion of feminine ethereality is created by the cultivation of a full-180 degree turn-out; that is, ballet students are required, early on, to stand, heel to heel, with their feet forming a perfectly straight line, thus providing a stable base for the five basic foot positions that serve as the foundations for more complex movements,[15] combining foot positions and arm styling with shapes of the entire body and physical movements, such as *plié* (bend), *tombé* (fall), *glissade* (slide), *relevé* (rise). More precisely, "the turn-out," which begins with the feet but culminates in the rotation of the legs in the hip socket, manifests what Cohen describes as the principle of *en dehors*—of being directed outwards, for maximum specularity.[16]

Historically, this outwardness was directed frontally in keeping with what Havelock Ellis has termed the "social discipline"[17]—a set of conventions shaped by European hierarchical class mores. Much as European conventions of painting reveal whose gaze matters—the patron's—so did the staging of the ballet centralize towards a focal point: the sovereign's gaze. When the ballet moved from the ballroom to the theatre, the royal box became the central axis, inhabited by the royal presence. Thus, "[t]he ballet dancer's turnout from the hips (which ensures maximal opening of the body toward the front), the strongly frontal orientation of ballet staging, even the proscenium stage itself can be traced to the European stage tradition that directed the performance toward the sovereign in attendance."[18] Even if there is literally no sovereign who persists, there is a clear classed dimension in relation to who sits where in relation to the stage, and such a seating arrangement is aligned not only with being able to see the stage, but also to be seen as occupying that space.

This stance of outwardness—of openness to the gaze—could become vulnerability save for the aristocratic bearing of the chest and the proud erectness of the body. "In the full classical style, the entire person appears in extroversion—open to other bodies, open to the surrounding space. But not vulnerable, because the rib cage is held erect, confidently; the arms seem buoyantly lifted away from the body, the head appears to float atop a long, vertical, relaxed spine."[19] *En dehors* embodied is a clearly artificial—one could say "unnatural"—deportment; there is nothing useful or "ordinary" about it; it exists only in the theatrical world of ballet, which is designed as an "extraordinary" world, and its only usefulness resides in its facilitation of this aesthetic of whiteness.

A vital element of this aesthetic of whiteness, as we have seen, is the creation of an illusion of weightlessness, interpreted as ethereality, for the female form. For male dancers, however, weightlessness is interpreted differently—as aligned "with verticality and with reason, since it relates to the height of the placement of the center of gravity in the body."[20] Even more significantly, weightlessness in the male form is an expression of power, control, and mastery. While women are required to maintain the illusion of appearing to virtually floating off the floor, men are required to maintain the appearance of clean, muscular virtuosity. As Cohen observes:

> Male dancers, including those who excel in elevation, seldom produce an appearance of sheer lightness, for the man more often stresses vigor and firmness of stance and tread that show him to be in command of the situation...The attack is strong but not heavy. Further, it never intrudes on, never distorts, the clean line of the movement.[21]

There are other aesthetic elements, characteristic of the balletic body vocabulary, which Cohen draws attention to: a clarity of line; a goal orientedness or efficiency of movement, with no extraneous effort discernible; a thorough—one could say martial—discipline of the body.[22] These elements are just as required for the individual dancer, as they are for the coordinated movements of the *corps de ballet*, which requires a military precision with a seeming effortlessness. For example, as Cohen points out, "Balanchine's *Le Tombeau de Couperin* depends for much of its effectiveness on the dancers' precision in maintaining a series of intricate designs of lines and semi-circles and waving paths."[23]

Crucial to the balletic aesthetic is the concealment not simply of effort, but in the very effacement of physicality. Starting at a very young age, ballet dancers spend hours practicing, drenched in sweat, muscles pushed to their limit, with the ever-present danger of injury looming (or lived with) as they strain to partner seamlessly. Yet during the performance, the audience colludes in the effort to preserve the aesthetic illusion, politely ignoring any inadvertent sound of footfalls. Indeed, to preserve the appearance of weightlessness, Balanchine cautioned his dancers not to reveal any anticipatory breaks in a choreographic sequence that might foreshadow a major turn or spin.[24] An anecdote about one of Balanchine's classes illustrates the premium Balanchine placed on this component of a balletic aesthetic.

> [Balanchine] had the [dancers] line up and go separately across the room in a sequence combining a gliding step, a leap, an intermediate step, and another leap. When Violette Verdy had done this, he called her back and had her try it again, telling her that she must push forward on the glide, not rest on it. Miss Verdy, who was dressed in a bright-blue sweater and black tights, with her golden hair in a shining topknot, nodded eagerly as she listened. As she went through it again, Balanchine cried at the start of second leap, "Stay in the air!" and incredibly, she seemed to obey this impossible command, hovering momentarily in space like a hummingbird. There were gasps of appreciation from the other dancers. Balanchine nodded, the faintest trace of a smile on his lips. "Tha...at's right," he said. "You're getting it."[25]

Balanchine's choreography was described as "neoclassical" precisely because it drew from this set of conventions and this type of body vocabulary. His innovations lay largely in further clarifying, speeding up, and sharpening technique by focusing his dancers' attentions to " 'the smallest parts of our bodies'; he showed them how a slightly misaligned instep or an imprecisely curled index finger could destroy the beauty of a step or pose."[26] Under Balanchine's tutelage, a more athletic, faster and sharper style of doing ballet emerged—one even more resistant to gravity, but with the cool, "hard edges" of a modern aesthetic, which is part of why Balanchine is recognized as a pioneer in American modern dance. "In the classroom [Balanchine] exhorted his dancers to lift their legs ever higher, even at the expense of perpendicular body alignment; he taught them to spring into jumps large and small by pushing off from the mid-metatarsal, not from the heel, as had been practiced for centuries."[27]

Another crucial element to Balanchine's choreography, which appeared to contribute to the perception of the "purity" of the lines of his work, was Balanchine's devotion to the music to which he choreographed sequences of movements. To render clear what he called the "shape" of the notes, he sometimes chose to set more steps to a single phrase (thus increasing speed), or at other times, recombined the steps in unexpected ways, appearing to render the steps in "slow motion," but actually making the subtleties more central to the movement.[28] Like Marius Petipa, Balanchine's principal choreographic thrust was synchronizing the structure of movement with the structure of the musical score, reminiscent of the classical view that architecture is frozen music and has the same carefully controlled structure. Balanchine proclaimed,"The structure of a ballet must be tight, compact, like the structure of a building; good ballets moved in measured space and time, like the planets."[29] Robert Gottlieb, one of Balanchine's biographers, recounts one of Martha Graham's remarks about the process of watching Balanchine choreograph during their joint venture, *Episodes*. "It is like watching light pass through a prism. The music passes through him, and in the same natural yet marvelous way that a prism refracts light, he refracts music into dance."[30]

Institutionally, ballet reflects the hierarchical class system that spawned it. Dancers are ranked carefully according to experience and ability, and despite the apparent glorification of the female form as embodying the very essence of ballet, the "puppet-masters" backstage, the ballet masters and choreographers, remained male, and Balanchine is the quintessential example of that stature of privilege in American dance. Given the power and prestige Balanchine possessed at the peak of his creative abilities, it is hardly surprising that it is his aesthetic vision of the hyperfeminized (that is, hyperwhitened, immortally young, ethereally slim, and long-limbed) ballerina that came to be forged as the required "look" of the "authentic" female ballet dancer. One of the quintessential embodiments of this aesthetic was one of Balanchine's wives: Tanaquil Le Clercq. "Long, slender, and extremely supple, [Le Clercq] could give piquant accents to Balanchine's hip-protruding postures and angular body designs; in her demeanor, she was by turns chic, comic and teenage casual."[31]

One of the anecdotes about Balanchine's transition from Russia to the United States was his rejection of even Alexandra Danilova, one of his former lovers and principal dancers, at the age of 27 and in her prime, as "too old" for the new American ballet company he intended to form. Bernard Taper, one of Balanchine's biographers, matter-of-factly observes that extreme youthfulness—even more so than its European progenitor—was part of Balanchine's envisaged aesthetic for the new American ballet company he intended to create from scratch:

> At that time [Balanchine rejected her expectant inquiry into the new American company he was forming] Danilova was twenty-seven years of age. She was just reaching her peak. Ahead of her were to be more than twenty years of glory and adulation... So it is understandable that Balanchine's words left her fuming. The fact was, however, that compared with the ballerinas Balanchine planned to employ, the twenty-seven-year-old Danilova did, indeed, seem venerable.[32]

Ballet, given its origins, as Cynthia Jean Cohen Bull pointed out, already hyperemphasized the sense of sight;[33] ballerinas are trained to produce good lines through endless mimicry and repetition via the use of mirrors. A ballerina lives in the constant glare of being visually compared to a hyperfeminized, ethereal ideal; she must never be allowed to age or to deviate physically from the idealized norm. Neither must she appear mortally histrionic; her general demeanor, as the most important symbolic figure of the ballet, must be one of coolness and detachment, much like the smooth and linear composition of the ballet. Balanchine discouraged his ballerinas from falling into "Gisellitis"—a brooding and affected sentimentalism that tainted the "purity" of the lines he wished to create, using their bodies.[34] For Balanchine, emotion was already integrated into the choreography; all he required, particularly from his ballerinas, is that they be "cold angels."[35] This is a characteristic very much in keeping with Nunn's characterization of whiteness, privileging rational thought over body, as it is the choreographer's abstract vision that dominates the ballerinas' bodies, viewed as Galatea-like matter to be sculpted by a balletic Pygmalion.

Furthermore, choreographers design movement with a great deal of spatial precision and the *corps de ballet* must not only move in unison but execute identical lines, against which a principal dancer or soloist may display a stylistic uniqueness, such as phrasing as movement slightly differently, to set herself apart, but only within very strict and highly visual parameters. Though music plays a crucial dimension, it is important that the musicians who generate the music be rendered invisible by locating them in the pit; while the sense of touch is paramount to a *pas de deux* between principal dancers, that sense of touch is always already interpreted in visual terms. The audience, schooled in these conventions, shares the same expectations regarding what constitutes a "good" balletic aesthetic.

> [F]or the dancer, the edges and lines of the body as perceived by a viewer became paramount. Students who do not possess a "good line," that is, a slender, long-limbed body which can form geometrically proportioned shapes, know that they will never be successful performers and are told so by teachers and administrators of professional schools. They may enjoy studying ballet, but they know they do not "have the body"—the physical appearance—to be a "real" (professional) ballet dancer. While having the body by no means provides sufficient basis for success, it is the necessary prerequisite.[36]

Ballet, thus, is most like film in this area. It is meant to be consumed principally at the visual level, and as such, appeals to the most disembodied, and the most "rational" of the senses. And its gendered dynamic remains unabashedly heterosexual, with a strict demarcation of masculine power from feminine ethereality along with a clear visualization of "ideal" male and female body types. There is, in other words, a strict distribution of gendered "duties" or properties appropriate to sexed male and female bodies in relation to each other. Although homosexual relationships can also reproduce the masculine–feminine dichotomy, these are not usually iconized, aesthetically, the way the heterosexual model is, in dance. This gendered dynamic and aesthetic illusion is especially evident in lifts.

> Lifts demand the participation of both dancers, the woman in many cases jumping with great energy and holding the position of her body in the air as the man catches her and utilizes the momentum of her movement. Yet the ballerina looks as if she does very little, the lightness of her upper torso and arm motion in particular (as well as her slender body and her ability to balance on the point of her foot) conveying weightlessness, airiness. The *danseur*, in contrast, appears solid, stable, either firmly connected to the floor or propelled from it by virtue of his own strength. Paradoxically (magically), in many classical *pas de deux* in particular, the nearly disembodied female provides the primary image of the dance, while the fully embodied male nearly disappears from sight. As spectators, our eyes confirm the reality of the unreal, the fantastic disembodiment of the body.[37]

Thus, we arrive at the point at which we began. Ballet, as the iconic example of a "white" aesthetic in American dance, displays many of the characteristics Richard Dyer observed in American Hollywood film. Hierarchy, virtue, rationality, linearity, heterosexuality, and noncorporeality are crucial components of ballet, as a "whitened" dance form.

In Balanchine's work, one can find traces that seem to authorize him as America's premier guardian of these traditions. For example, Suki Schorer, who had danced one of the *pas de deux* sequences in Balanchine's *The Four Temperaments* remarked that the key to understanding the choreography in that piece is to visualize the danseur as "manipulating... totally controlling the girl. The boy should appear to be strumming—playing—some harp or cello. The girl is like an instrument."[38] That remark, expressed by a ballerina, reveals how even women can be swept into fully acquiescing to, and embracing, an aesthetic that potentially commodifies women as instruments to be used by men.

Perhaps even more tellingly, Balanchine's infamous remark that "Ballet is woman" earned him the wrath of many feminists, who interpreted his work as the ultimate expression of a patriarchal order aestheticized to reduce women, *a la* Laura Mulvey, to mere objects of the male gaze.[39] And certainly, Balanchine referred to Suzanne Farrell, his ultimate muse, as "my Stradivarius."[40] The observation underlines the power of the choreographer and ballet master in relation to the dancers, both female and male, upon whose bodies he wrote his choreographic texts. And such a hierarchy of power is inherent to the production of the kind of "superhuman" aesthetic characteristic of ballet—as an art form whose origins lie in a Eurocentric aristocratic system; an art form clearly "whitened" when mapped in relation to its other correlates.

A View of Nonwhiteness in Relation to American Dance

Preliminary Remarks

To begin to wrestle with what a "nonwhite" aesthetic is in American dance, one must return to one of the most fundamental distinctions in American culture, which, in dance as an art form, still remains at the culturally imagined binary between "black" (African) versus "white" (European) culture.[41] Legally, of course, within the United States, this dichotomy finds moorings in the "one-drop" rule: that one drop of black blood, no matter how light (or close to white) one's complexion is, is sufficient to classify a miscegenated child as black—that is, as property, or later, as someone "different" to enough to treat as essentially a separate species. As Brenda Dixon Gottschild observes:

> Asians and Latinos have their own colonial and postcolonial crosses to bear; yet all peoples subjected to Europeanist influences grew up with comparable myths surrounding black inferiority and white superiority. I speak... of a black/white axis of difference because this is the line of difference across which all peoples of color must choose sides: are you light enough to pass for white? Are you a white Latino? As an Asian, can you assimilate and become white? If you are of mixed ethnicity (well, aren't we all?), will you list yourself as white or black?[42]

In attempting to describe what a nonwhite aesthetic might look like, Cynthia Jean Cohen Bull[43] chose "traditional Ghanaian dance" as *one* of ballet's counterpoints,[44] probably largely because she wished to return to a radical opposition to ballet: one imaginatively unfettered from the trauma and history of slavery, attempting to reach back into deep African roots—a project not too different from Katherine Dunham's project in its aspirations, but with marked differences as well, as we shall later see in chapter 4.

I use traditional Ghanaian dance, building from Cohen Bull's description of it, purely as such: as a culturally imagined counterpoint reflective of a nonwhite aesthetic. It is important to preface these remarks by admitting that there are different types of "whitenesses" as there are different types of "nonwhitenesses." Just as Balanchine's interpretation of ballet is only one among many interpretations of ballet, Cohen Bull's imagination of traditional Ghanaian dance is one representation among many of a black aesthetic. Similarly, "nonwhite" does not have to mean only "black." The schema begins this way because it is fundamentally genealogical in the Nietzschean sense and begins with a mapping of morals: in the history of American dance, Balanchine's vision of what is "pure" in ballet has become the dominant paradigm of whiteness/"art"/the copyrightable. Culturally, the white–black dichotomy is one of the primal founding myths of American culture because of its history of slavery, and this same dichotomy extends to the realm of the cultural valuation of dance. Part of the reason why imagining a counterpoint to Balanchine's vision is important is that especially given the history of copyright in relation to choreography, no such correlate existed, particularly during the time period when this template was being forged. My use of Cohen Bull's schema is thus partly rhetorical, partly imagined—set up to visualize what Nietzsche would call one possible "healthy" and "nonreactive" counterpoint to the dominant paradigm.

The continuum I mean to set up, as a preliminary way into the material, has to begin with relatively identifiable ends of the spectrum, even if these points are initially conceptually simplified. This is a rough schema, meant as a heuristic—a guide to further exploration. I realize, of course, in following Cohen Bull's lead, I face the Scylla and Charybdis of anyone who attempts this kind of work: that of appearing to either essentialize all African dance, thus losing essential specificities that characterize African dances, or just as badly, and perhaps essentially the same thing as the prior danger, to elevate Ghanaian dance, one specific regional type of African dance, into some kind of universal paradigm of all things African. None of these, of course, I intend to do. In addition, the reference point of the system I genealogize, given its historical and cultural moorings, is whiteness—and as such, anything constructed in relation to whiteness, even in opposition to it, is always already is implied in relation to it. I cannot escape that dynamic, if I am to begin with a critique from within, which is what I believe is the more difficult and in the long run, the more effective approach. A critique from the outside is easier to mount, but it can also be more easily dismissed or marginalized—ghettoized (that is, allowed to exist, but only under "special parameters" as an isolated phenomenon, culturally tolerated out of political correctness but still relegated to the margins).

This is not to say that white culture, no matter how dominant, is hermetically insulated from its "others"—far from it. Appropriation without giving credit, particularly to women of color, is a common pattern of this hegemonic system, especially in the history of American modern dance. Thus, while modern dance allowed for white women to represent "the universal body" (as in Martha Graham's "sexlessness"), "the black body could only represent a black body," even if inadvertently extending the assumptions of minstrelsy.[45] This is evidenced, for example, in Graham's appropriation of Native American culture in, for example, *Primitive Mysteries* (1931), or Balanchine's treatment of Dunham in their "collaboration" on *Cabin in the Sky* (1940), as we shall see in chapter 4. Dunham's remarks in an interview regarding her possible influence on Balanchine, as a result of their having "co-choreographed" *Cabin* are instructive, not only for their content, but also for their rhetorical savviness, as we shall later see. She said, carefully:

> I think there was a meeting of the Georgian freedom of expression and the Georgian heat, you know, that he found a response to in the whole black element...

> In other words, I would see him dance or choreograph, and I would not see the blatant use of the pelvic girdle..., but I would feel behind it an affiliation with it. So I got to really appreciate him, that point of view. So I'd say that some of our things put us at ease, let him do things he might not have done otherwise. I do think the freeing of the pelvic girdle, I think he sort of was relieved to see it on the stage.[46]

I follow Cohen Bull's analysis, as a preliminary analytic schema for the following reasons. First, Cohen Bull is an established dance ethnographer and has a clear description of what she views as the crucial characteristics of what she considers "traditional" (and not simply contemporary) Ghanaian dance; the parallel to Balanchine's vision of ballet is apt, precisely because like Balanchine's recasting of classical ballet into its modern form, it has both traditional and contemporary elements. Second, her analysis, precisely because it sets up such a distinctive contrast to ballet, is rhetorically useful to me, in terms of charting how or why ballet is set up as a reference point to its "others," among which a certain type of aesthetic, instantiated, not totalized, by her description of traditional Ghanaian dance is. And in order to understand the particular time period that I am studying, that apparent unproblematic dichotomy—one rhetorically constructed and mythologized—is important to chart, before one can attempt to explode or deconstruct it.

Third, that kind of critique is not specific to this type of study. As we shall see in chapter 4, Dunham herself faced this kind of critique in her reinterpretation of her memory of her ethnographic studies into performance. The point of using Cohen Bull's interpretation of what she calls "traditional Ghanaian dance" in this preliminary chapter, is less to create a literal documentary description of Ghanaian dance (and even less so about forming absolute generalizations about all African dances), than as a rhetorical way to imagine a vibrant alternative to Balanchine's interpretation of classical ballet. This is an admittedly rough sketch, in order to set up the later discussions of Josephine Baker's and Katherine Dunham's nonwhite aesthetics, which partake of some characteristics of this rough (and probably idealized) sketch, and deviate from it in others.

Cohen Bull's Interpretation of Traditional Ghanaian Dance as an Example of One Nonwhite Aesthetic

For Cohen Bull, if sight is the predominant sense cultivated by the ballet, hearing is the sense most acutely appealed to by traditional Ghanaian dance, with its emphasis on the rhythmic interrelationship of different drums with each other, and the symbiotic relationship between the sound of the drums and the undulations of the dancers and the audience.[47] For unlike ballet, which is tied to an artificial world, screened from the ordinary world and the *hoi polloi*, traditional Ghanaian dance is tied up with lived experiences of being part of a community. "Most Ghanaians learn the dancing of their own village and often those of neighboring villages, or, if living in a city, learn the traditional dances of their family, neighbors, and friends."[48] Again, unlike ballet, where the ballet master's vision dictates the dancers' movements, instructors remind students to "say the drums in your mouth"[49] and to be aware and responsive to all the rhythms, communicating with and through the music, forging connection with the community of fellow dancers and the audience. Thus, in Cohen Bull's description of traditional Ghanaian dance, the notion of "individualistic" movement is antithetical as a good dancer is first and foremost one who learns to listen and observe—not moving in silence (separated from the music) or isolation (separated from the group). Neither is it "free-form" as the movement, much like classical ballet, is tied to the music; the connection between movement and music is not arbitrary. Although there is some room for variation, analogous to classical ballet, a good dancer must seek to integrate into a larger whole.

> "Self-expression" does not appropriately describe these individual statements, because they are explicitly musical-choreographic in nature, shaped so as to enhance the entire performance. The experience of dancing and playing realizes and creates social values: flexibility within clear formal structures, participation by everyone, attentiveness of each individual to the group, maintenance of a sense of overall balance. The kinesthetic is tied to social relationships.[50]

Again, unlike ballet, where an erect torso must be coordinated with toe and hip alignments to create the illusion of seamless weightlessness, as Cohen Bull describes it, traditional Ghanaian dance typically involves isolated undulations of body parts, whether they be the limbs, hips, shoulders, ribs, or head; ballet's emphasis on an elevated spine, erect torso, and upward-directed legs and toes is displaced by a virtual democracy of body parts, free to undulate separately, in keeping with the rhythms of the drums and bells.

To attempt to give a label to this different kinesthetic dynamic—one so radically different from ballet, Cohen Bull uses the word "Africanist," not "black." For her, "Africanist" movement appears grounded, and the body vocabulary is polycentered, in keeping with polyrhythmic music. However, this does not mean there are no rules and anything goes. "From the Africanist perspective, movement may originate from any body zone, and two or more areas of the body may simultaneously serve as centers of movement. Africanist-based movement is also polyrhythmic. The feet may maintain one rhythm while torso, legs, arms dance to the beat of different drums."[51]

Thus, for Cohen Bull, in keeping with this polyrhythmicity of drums and democracy of body parts, the unison among dancers is not strictly visually controlled and there is room for some degree of improvisation. Dancers mime and interact with the pattern of "apart-playing"—where drums sustain one pattern in cross-rhythm to another, "retain[ing] their pattern vis-à-vis the bell part but do not sound in unison with it or with other drums, except on isolated beats,"[52] while still coming together to form a polymetered beat. While there are leaders, such as a master drummer or lead dancer, who can signal the start of a new pattern, precise uniform miming is not a requirement, and the audience is expected to join in, moving some body part(s) in a manner that complement/s the general rhythms. "[W]hile dancers may appear unified, they seldom produce an exact spacial [sic] unison because the emphasis of their movement lies in rhythmic, dynamic action rather than on achievement of a shape or line, as in ballet. Within the general framework of a step, one may let an arm swing slightly higher or lower or emphasize a movement more or less percussively—in other words, one may improvise subtly within a tight rhythmic and spacial [sic] framework."[53] Solo work is allowed within this framework, but this is created in response to an invitation by others, either by dancers momentarily stopping to watch, or a master drummer calling out to a particular dancer to perform.[54]

In other words, for Cohen Bull, unlike ballet, where the choreographer's vision constitutes the controlling overall script, here, whatever script emerges does so in interaction with the musicians, dancers and audience, who are not strictly demarcated from each other either in role or function or spatial configuration. "He or she (or in some cases, a pair of dancers) performs in the service of the group, playing with variations in response to the group's encouragement. Thus, choreography becomes shaped by the rhythmic interaction of many people, rather than by a choreographer's vision (as in ballet)."[55]

Similarly, therefore, although professional dancers of traditional Ghanaian dance exist, for Cohen Bull, the gulf between the skill level of the professional and the nonprofessional is not as extreme as in the ballet; she concludes that this does not necessarily mean professional performers of traditional Ghanaian are generally less skilled than ballet professionals.[56] What it does reflect is that "the general level of dancing and musical ability in Ghana ranks very high in comparison with the general level among most populations in the United States, for instance."[57] In other words, what is an immense, often class-based gulf in dance education in the United States is simply a continuum in Ghanaian culture.

Similarly, although there are gender distinctions in traditional Ghanaian dance, these are not as tightly demarcated as in the world of ballet. For example, though quick slashing gestures and percussive accents are requirements for the men's war dances, in general, in many group dances and also in partnered male–female dances, "everyone does the same movement, that is, movement within the same rhythmic and spatial parameters varied according to each individual's style, regardless of gender."[58] Again, unlike the idealized balletic body that must remain eternally young (especially for the ballerinas; *danseurs* can be sometimes be literally aging Don Quixotes, as Balanchine unabashedly was, in relation to Suzanne Farrell—but he is the exception, not the rule), the dancer of the traditional Ghanaian dance does not have to be young,[59] the way Balanchine's prima ballerinas had to be: older dancers can be recognized, "without condescension, as skilled and subtle performers."[60]

Brenda Dixon Gottschild differentiates between being young (an attribute highly prized by Balanchine) and youthfulness or "ephebism" (which is valued as part of what she calls an "Africanist aesthetic").[61] An *ephebe* (the ancient Greek word for a youth or young person) is not a literally young person, but one who displays power, vitality, attack, drive, and flexibility[62]—traits that more mature dancers can possess along with the sophistication that experience brings. Robert Farris Thompson describes ephebism as "the phrasing of every note and step with consummate vitality."[63] For Gottschild, in terms of a kinesthetic body vocabulary, ephebism "implies a supple, flexible torso, bending knees, and the ability and willingness to go down in order to be lifted up, literally and metaphorically: a flexibility that allows one to go with the flow and roll with the changes (of the dance, of life itself)."[64] It thus goes without saying that unlike ballet that has very strict parameters concerning the professionalized dancing body and movements that are "proper" to particular sexes, traditional Ghanaian dance seems, comparatively, more open to physical differences in body types and different modes of interpreting the rhythm of the music, which is principally percussive.

Similarly, the organization of space in traditional Ghanaian dance differs radically from the harnessing of space in ballet. The proscenium in balletic productions clearly demarcates who is a performer, to be looked at, and who is the audience, who does the looking. It is a more "linear" or hierarchical way of organizing space, such that it is clear from where the sovereign's gaze/the gaze of the most powerful patron is supposed to emanate. In contrast, traditional Ghanaian dance's "circular" organization of space around a group of percussionists allows for a permeability between spectator and performer, and also the coexistence of multiple choreographies in motion, and multiple perspectives, from which these performances may be viewed or engaged with, in participation. "Frequently there is more than one 'performance' going on simultaneously. No one person is capable of knowing/seeing all that is going on at a particular moment in time.[65] But this is not to be mistaken for chaos (a cultural bias emanating from those who see linear structure as superior to other possible alternatives). Instead, this is a democracy of structure that is characteristic of Africanist-based performance modes."[66]

Finally, whereas ballet as a European classical (white) dance form, attempts to erase the body using aesthetic illusion, to make it seem a manifestation of pure Spirit (or Reason), an Africanist (nonwhite) aesthetic appears to accept what Gottschild labels "contradictions"[67] (from the point of view of the Enlightenment tradition) embracing, rather than dichotomizing, body and mind/spirit. Thus, whereas ballet disciplines the body, making it a pliable vessel of the choreographer's vision, an Africanist aesthetic embraces the principle of "embodied wisdom,"[68] accepting the possibility that something other than Reason or Spirit, in the European Enlightenment tradition, inspires dancers to move (not simply a choreographer who orchestrates overall movement). Sheila Walker describes African dance: "that the spirit dances in/through the bodies of its believers is an affirmation and celebration of the fact that the universe is a dynamic process-in-motion, rather than a static entity."[69] Thus, if Balanchine's (whitened) aesthetic for his ballerinas in particular, demanded being a "cold Angel," then, in contrast, an Africanist (nonwhite) aesthetic requires of its dancers in general, whether male or female, embodying "The Cool"—a body stance that integrates energy with composure or "hotness"/engagement with "coolness"/detachment. Gay and Baber, for example, describe "the cool" in African dance and ritual as both spiritual and corporeal: a "soul force" that integrates "energy, . . . fiber, . . . spirit and flair."[70]

To summarize, Brenda Dixon Gottschild poetically outlines what she views as the key elements of an "Africanist" (which, following Hilliard-Nunn's lead, I could rename a "black") dance aesthetic:

> Bare feet in solid contact with the earth; the ground as a medium to caress, stomp or to make contact with the whole body (whether with serpentine, supplicatory, or somersaulting movements); a grounded, "get-down" quality to the movement characterized by body asymmetry (knees bent, torso slightly pitched forward . . .); an overall polyphonic feel to the dance/dancing body (encompassing a democratic equality of body parts, with the center of energy, focus and gravity shifting through different body

> parts—polycentric; as well as different body parts moving to two or more meters or rhythms—polymetric and polyrhythmic; articulation of the separate units of the torso (pelvis, chest, rib cage, buttocks); and a primary value placed on both individual and group improvisation.[71]

White/Black Bodies in Relation to White/Black Aesthetics

I began with giving a general description of how a white and nonwhite aesthetic may be characterized, in terms of kinesthetic movement, historically based conventions of production and reception, gendered roles of performance, and body types preferred by (Balanchine's vision of) ballet and Ghanaian African-dance. Yet is white skin (along with other implicitly "whitened" characteristics, such as the ethereally thin and long-limbed body type Balanchine preferred and properly pointed toes) necessary for a ballet ("white") aesthetic? And is having black skin (along with other implicitly "nonwhite" characteristics, such as having a more "muscular" body, and having more "pronounced" exotic-erotic body parts, such as breasts and buttocks, and more "heel") necessary for a "black" or "nonwhite" aesthetic?

The initial and certainly traditional answers, particularly for ballet, are clear. African American women, especially those with dark complexions, were usually not hired, especially during the 1920's–1930's, no matter how skilled they were because their skin color would "break the uniformity" of the *corps de ballet*. Brenda Dixon Gottschild recounts a particular autobiographical incident that illustrated how racism had so radically penetrated the ballet aesthetic that it was used, unabashedly, as a justification for turning away a dancer for even just a small part in a ballet—much as the establishment of the Rockettes had used the same "hook" as the basis to hang their preformulated rejections of many talented darkly complected applicants.

> Still auditioning and still a neophyte dancer, I had an unsettling experience with choreographer Pearl Lang. I responded to her call, not for a featured role but to work as a pick-up in a small chorus of four dancers. I was informed, after auditioning, that I could not be used because my skin color would "destroy the unity of the corps."...It struck me as ironic and frustrating that dancers could live in fantasy worlds, be Wilis or princesses, goddesses or witches, but black-skinned dancers in a dance based on a Greek-inspired theme would be detrimental to some principle of unity.[72]

In another of her books, Gottschild writes a "biohistory" of Joan Myers Brown, her determination to pursue her dream as a black ballerina, and her successful establishment of the Philadelphia Dance Company (Phildanco, the trademark name), one of the few American black ballet dance troupes. Phildanco paved the way for other nonwhite dancers to enjoy lucrative careers and form successful nonwhite dance companies, such as the Alvin Ailey American Dance Theatre and Jiri Kylian's Netherlands Dance Theatre, on Broadway as well as in Europe.[73] It is important to note that for Joan Brown ("JB," her preferred name) as for the many talented black ballerinas whom she trained, dancing ballet was neither a rejection of ballet's "white" aesthetic nor a rejection of her nonwhite racial heritage. Rather, it was a rejection of the traditional ballet aesthetic's banishment of nonwhite bodies from its enclave. Gottschild quotes Vanessa Thomas Smith, one of the renowned ballerinas of Phildanco, and then contextualizes that statement, not as an internalization of racism but as a rejection of it. "So I got to feel that again in the ballet, and it's the same feeling I have now when I teach these girls in class... 'Aaaah! that's [sic] when I decided I was exquisite and that I was pretty and that I was lovely and that I was all these—that I was precious, lovely, angelic'—and, you know, all of the words that come when you think of a young lady doing ballet."[74] Gottschild interprets Thomas Smith's statement as a successful mastery of her image in both black and white worlds, rather than as indoctrination into a hegemonic white aesthetic. For Gottschild:

> Once again, we see the Du Bois talented-tenth concept at work, for, above all, the ballerina represents a European ideal. To the degree that black women master the genre, they become masters of their own image in both the black and white worlds. And it is important to read this information in context: to be a black ballerina is not a simple rejection of one's African and African American heritage but, instead, a challenge and victory over those who would say, "Stay in your place; your body and abilities are not capable of doing this." It's an embracing of our full heritage—black and white—just as white Americans can see fit to embrace black genres.[75]

But despite this heroic and triumphant portrait, Gottschild's biohistory of JB's story does not flinch from showing how the racial system worked not simply to exclude all African Americans (or force separate white versus black realms), but also to divide African American dancers in terms of the lightness of their complexion (and their physical proximity to the European ideal). Ananya Chatterjea, in her Afterword on Gottschild's biohistorical account, characterizes Gottschild's account as a Foucauldian project that genealogizes a complex and plural narrative of the flows of power, authorship, and artistic possibility.

> It is not just the black-white divide that creates exclusions; the racial hierarchy labors through the ways in which race and class collude and the color-caste system weeds out darker-skinned dancers from the lighter-skinned ones. There is also Philadelphia's constant antagonism with New York City, the reputations that accrue to the two different cities and the opportunities they offer to dancers. These then further complicate the way struggles over funding, reception, and the management of never-enough resources cut across the dance world, differently, across the decades.[76]

And indeed, it is interesting that ultimately, Phildanco's eventual forging of a unique and commercially successful dance identity seems not to have been based on a black ballerina's successful integration into a white aesthetic, but on the centrality of the black *danseurs*, who were, in the beginning, untrained football players. These initially untrained male dancers were given more muscular and powerful moves (because they could not move like conventional ballet *danseurs* since they did not have the training) producing a more masculine aesthetic (even more "muscular" or "powerful" than their white counterparts but less refined in technique). Thus, correspondingly, the ballerinas, to match the danseurs, had to be given stronger and more masculine lines as well. And this became the successful signature look of Phildanco. JB, in an interview with Gottschild, reminisced:

> That set the style for Phildanco because those guys couldn't dance! They had no training, and Harold worked those guys so they looked good. Now, the girls were all trained. The momentum he gave them was all very masculine. He wasn't giving them pirouettes and tour jetés. No: he was giving them stuff where they looked [here she makes angular, "masculine" body gestures] you know, *so people always talk about Phildanco's men were always so strong. So anybody I hired had to fit into that mold and that's kind of how I kept it. I like the big, strong men—that look—and I tell the guys if I wanted all girls I'd hire all girls. You gotta be a man on my stage*... [Gottschild's emphasis].[77]

In some ways, Phildanco's success at forging a successful identity as a ballet company turns the classic white aesthetic on its head. For no longer is the ethereal ballerina the principal focus; rather, it is the more muscular and physically prominent body of the *danseur* around whom movement is designed. However, in order to preserve the (heterosexual) contrast between male and female bodies that the balletic aesthetic requires, black ballerinas, even if they had been trained classically, had to adapt to more muscular and angular lines. Correspondingly, black *danseurs* were placed under increasing pressure to prove their strength and masculinity compared with their female counterparts. Deborah Manning St. Charles, in an interview with Gottschild, recalled: "Harold Pierson instilled that in [the men], constantly, constantly: You must be a man on stage: the women jump this high, [then] you have to jump this high [namely, higher]."[78] This aesthetic illusion of powerful black masculine heterosexuality had nothing to do with reality, as many of Phildanco's prominent male dancers were homosexuals, and JB provided a nondiscriminatory dance haven for them.

> The question of a dancer's homosexuality, bisexuality, or heterosexuality was of little interest to [JB]. She was building a dance company, and it was a signature professional image that concerned her. Being "manly" was an onstage aesthetic device, not a demand on the male dancer's personal life. For JB, it was about the ballet tradition of the male dancer supporting the female—being the one to lift her, both literally and figuratively.[79]

Without detracting from Joan Myers Brown's and Phildanco's numerous accomplishments, it is important to note that ultimately, the "successful" look the company forged—partially out of accident, partially out of necessity, partially out of careful cultivation—fitted easily into racial and sexual stereotypes. The "powerful" and "muscular" movements, racialized as "natural" to black bodies aesthetically styled as heterosexual in their pairing, were very much in keeping with the segregated worlds of "white" and "black" ballet.

Related questions thus surface: is it possible for a black skinned dancer/choreographer to take "whitened" elements, or for a white choreographer to adapt elements from a nonwhite aesthetic, and to break completely free of the white-versus-nonwhite aesthetic dichotomy and more importantly, its hierarchy of power? Even here, the answer seems persistently difficult because categories of "whiteness" and "nonwhiteness" remain stubbornly dichotomous, largely because of a persistently hierarchical cultural valuation.

When Alvin Ailey combines African American elements of dance with ballet, that is not black "appropriation" because nonwhites, marginalized in the dominant culture, are in no position to "appropriate;" the best they can do within the hierarchy, as Dunham does, as we shall see in chapter 4, is come closer to a "whitened" ideal—and even that is a refractory process, both advantageous and disadvantageous. When Arthur Mitchell, like JB, founds a ballet company of black dancers performing white-based balletic technique, their productions remain secondary to "white" productions. And black dancers, even when they innovate, tend to be generally praised as dancers, not as choreographers (i.e., authors/creators/owners of dance movements understood as "property"). When black dancers organize successful dance companies, comparisons maintain the racial splits, as if it were inconceivable to cross racial lines. Gottschild recounts an interview with JB, during which JB bristled with animosity:

> In *Standing at the Edge, We Dance,* a video about Phildanco made by Carmella Vassor in 2001,... [JB] mentions that someone asked her, "What makes your company different from Alvin Ailey?" Her response: "What makes my company different from Eliot Feld or Paul Taylor?!" Again, the dance world seems not so much to democratically self-select but to dictatorially segregate by continuing to categorize along racial lines.[80]

When Balanchine uses one black *danseur,* like Arthur Mitchell, precisely because he views black skin as part of a "costuming" aesthetic, does that break the hegemony of the whiteness of his aesthetic? When Balanchine incorporates a nonwhite element, such as a contraction, in his remake of *The Firebird,* which features a native American ballerina, Maria Tallchief, as its principal dancer, does that make the overall trajectory of his *oeuvre* less "whitened"? And when Martha Graham makes contraction and release her principal body vocabulary, does that make her dancing less "white"? When she uses black and Asian dancers in her choreography, as *mise en scene,* against which her agency, as choreographer-principal dancer is displayed, is she any less "whitened" (or "masculinized" in relation to her dancers) than Balanchine? Are there concrete senses in which Fuller, Balanchine and Graham partook of whiteness-as-property/privilege in ways that were inaccessible to their nonwhite performer/dancer/choreographer contemporaries, such as Josephine Baker and Katherine Dunham?

As a counterpoint, Josephine Baker, like Loíe Fuller, was an American expatriate with working-class origins who achieved iconic success in Paris. Both women took Paris by storm as aesthetic inspirations, but why was Fuller's aesthetic as a goddess of light kept sharply demarcated from Baker's aesthetic as a "Black Venus"? How was it that it was Fuller who dared mount the first copyright lawsuit over choreographic creation as her intellectual property, while such an option was never possible for Baker, despite her equally iconic status? And as a further contrast to Balanchine, how is it that Katherine Dunham, with her academic and scholarly training as both an anthropologist and dancer from the University of Chicago, and ethnography-based choreography derived from her fieldwork in the Caribbean, has not achieved the kind of choreographic immortality associated with George Balanchine, her less academically trained contemporary, and with whom she collaborated on "negro ballets"?

These are difficult questions, requiring careful analysis, not in an abstract sense, but in a nuanced, genealogical manner, tracking the complex intersections between their private lives, their public personae, their improvisations/choreographic creations, and how their different audiences interpreted their dance movements in relation to their skin color/racial affinity/racial costuming. I engage these questions in the next chapters of this book.

What emerges from this chapter is a clearer template of whiteness as an aesthetic. Thus, describing the dynamic of whiteness versus its others from within this relationship, the characterization of what is "not white" remains deliberately looser as that is always the way whiteness as status property has functioned historically, especially in both dance choreography and law. Privilege often operates precisely by clarifying who is at the top of the hierarchy, but keeping the category of who is not privileged and why, fuzzy as Derrida has taught us through his deployment of critical techniques of deconstruction.[81]

From the point of view of someone like Dunham, as I shall show in chapter 4, the moral thrust and the activist strain are at the forefront. While certainly American culture draws heavily from nonwhite elements (not simply Africanist or Negro or black culture but other cultures as well—Asian, Indian, etc.), the legal perspective, especially in the realm of aesthetics, lags far behind that cultural appropriation and in some cases, synthesis. And the black–white divide remains the paramount category with which to grapple, despite the onslaught of postmodernism in other areas of study; law, like the hard sciences, remains staunchly impervious, despite some courses on this topic in some law schools. Copyright in particular is and has remained whitened, especially during this time period I am studying, when the template for what is choreographically copyrightable was forming.

The parameters of this study covers roughly the late-nineteenth century to 2006, legally—not what is currently available choreographically at a cultural level.[82] While many developments have occurred, for the most part, copyright has remained, in relation to choreography anyway, staunchly and resiliently white, even as choreography, as an art form, has evolved beyond the black–white binary.

Chapter 3

Loíe Fuller, "Goddess of Light" and Josephine Baker, "Black Venus": Non-narrative Choreography as Mere "Spectacle"*

Introduction

In the first part of this chapter, I examine how Fuller's failure to obtain copyright for her "Serpentine Dance" lay rooted in how her whiteness was offset by the class origins of burlesque theatre as well as legally enshrined doctrines concerning the primacy of narrative over simply "decorative" or "abstract" subject matter. In contrast, as the fourth chapter of this book shows, Balanchine had no problems with acquiring copyright protection partly because he was already so effectively integrated into the upper-crust elite of American ballet that his vision of the hyperwhite, anorectically thin ballerina became the iconic "natural" look of the ballerina in the United States. According to one commentator, Balanchine himself stated that the skin of a ballerina should be the same color as a "peeled apple."[1]

It is hardly surprising, in some ways, that where Loïe Fuller failed, Balanchine (and his estate) succeeded, despite the equally "abstract" nature of his ballets. Certainly, the larger historical narrative about Fuller, Balanchine, and the refractory relationship between copyright and choreography is not reducible only to "whiteness." Nevertheless, the construction of whiteness as status property in relation to the complex relationship between copyright and choreography is a factor that is in sore need of serious examination.

Fuller's Serpentine Dance

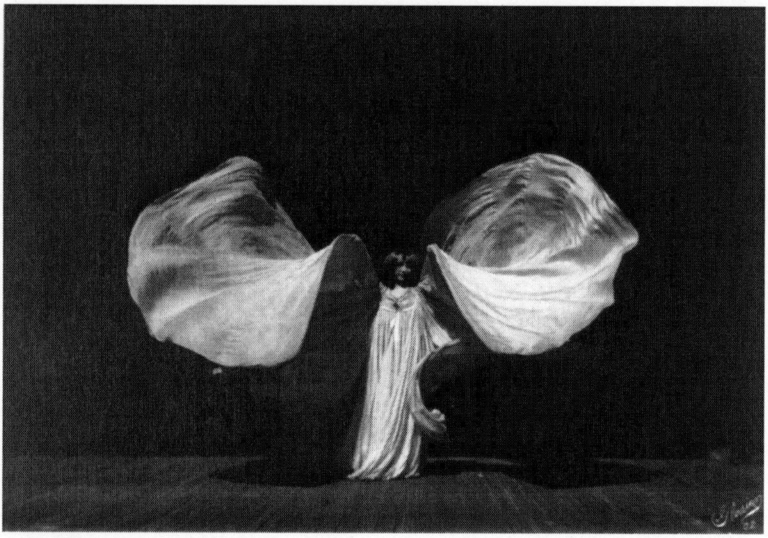

Figure 3.1 Public Domain Image of Loíe Fuller's Serpentine Dance. From the Library of Congress. http://www.loc.gov/pictures/resource/cph.3b37279/.

The Genesis Stories and Legal Precedent

In her autobiography, *Fifteen Years of a Dancer's Life*, Fuller narrated how she was inspired to create what eventually became her signature and a quintessential *art nouveau* motif. While touring in a new play, *Quack M.D.*, Fuller was instructed to create a scene in which she would appear to be hypnotized. She described what appears to be the *bricoleur*'s holy grail: a fortuitous conjunction of improvisational resourcefulness and just the right materials, at the right time. Fuller grabbed a long skirt sent to her from India by acquaintances; she pulled the waist of the skirt up to just underneath her breasts, creating an empire-waist gown made of very light and diaphanous material.[2] What happened next is one of the iconic eureka moments of modern dance history.

> [Framed against] pale green light[,] Dr. Quack made a mysterious entrance and then began his work of suggestion . . . I endeavored to make myself as light as possible, in order to give the impression of a fluttering figure obedient to the doctor's orders.

> He raised his arms. I raised mine. Under the influence of suggestion, entranced—so, at least, it looked—with my gaze held by his, I followed his every motion. My robe was so long that I was continually stepping upon it, and mechanically I held it up with both hands and raised my arms aloft, all the while that I continued to flit around the stage like a winged spirit.
>
> There was a sudden exclamation from the house: "It's a butterfly! A butterfly!"
>
> I turned on my steps, running from one end of the stage to the other, and a second explanation followed: "It's an orchid!"
>
> To my great astonishment sustained applause burst forth.[3]

Like all myths, there appear to be several versions of the serpentine dance "genesis" story. In another version, while Fuller was playing around, in front of a mirror, with a "voluminous white skirt" she had received from an "admirer," she had a vision: "With dramatic lighting, she could create fantastic, evanescent, suggestive shapes onstage by agitating swaths of silk from underneath with a pair of hand-held wands."[4]

Nevertheless, what is clear is that Fuller, in order to achieve iconic status, had to become elevated to pure "whiteness"—an ethereal abstraction—a fairy of light and illusion, an archetypal descendant of the Greeks, devoid of corporeality. Her onstage persona mesmerized audiences. Whirling around on a glass platform, lit by as many as 14 electric spotlights whose colors kept metamorphosing, she held up voluminous fabrics billowing about her in three-dimensional evocations of flowers, butterflies, and flames. The illusion was powerful enough to inspire and enthrall poets (Mallarmé and Yeats), painters (Toulouse-Lautrec and Whistler), and scientists (Pierre and Marie Curie).[5]

For example, below is one of the ecstatic reviews of one of Fuller's performances:

> Suddenly the stage is darkened and Loïe Fuller appears in a white light which makes her radiant and a white robe surrounds her like a cloud. She floats around the stage, now revealed, now concealed by the exquisite drapery which takes forms of its own . . . She is Diana dancing in the moonlight with a cloud to veil her from Acteon, She is a fairy flitting about with a cloak of thistledown. The surprised and delighted spectators do not know what to call her performance. It is not a skirt dance, although she dances and waves a skirt. It is unique, ethereal, delicious. As she vanishes, leaving only a flutter of her white robe on the stage, the theater resounds with thunders of applause.[6]

But that description is of La Loïe at the pinnacle of her artistic career, when she had achieved the celebrity of being the "inventor" of the serpentine dance, even if she failed to establish copyright ownership to it when she sought an injunction against Minnie Renwood Bemis in 1892. Despite her lack of formal education, Fuller displayed a sense of compositional acumen and business-savvy when she "asserted that [because] she originated the dance, and ... having ... copyrighted [it], [the serpentine dance] was her exclusive property."[7] Thirty years old, plump, and hardly the conventional beauty, Fuller, knowing that her theatrical career and financial stability hinged on her ability to control ownership of the serpentine dance, attempted what was then unconventional. She turned to the legal apparatus for protection against copyright infringement, rather than relying on community norms within the dance community.[8] Yet in an opinion that has become much quoted, Judge Lacombe of the New York Circuit Court dismissed Fuller's serpentine dance as unworthy of copyright protection because of its lack of "narrative" or "dramatic" content.[9] In his opinion, the district court judge held:

> It is essential to such a composition that it should tell some story. The plot may be simple, it may be but narrative, or a representation of a single transaction, but it must repeat or mimic some action, speech, emotion, passion, or character, real or imaginary. When it does its ideas thus expressed become subject of copyright. An examination of the description of the complainant's dance, as filed for copyright, shows that the end sought for and accomplished was the illustrating and devising of a series of graceful movements combined with an attractive arrangement of draperies, lights, and shadows, telling no story, portraying no character, depicting no emotion. The mere, mechanical movements by which effects are produced on the stage are not subjects of copyright. Surely this dance described here conveyed and was devised to convey to the spectator no other idea than that a comely woman illustrating the poetry of motion in a singularly graceful fashion, and while such an idea may be pleasing, it can hardly be called dramatic. Motion ... denied.[10]

This opinion became virtually enshrined as the legal basis for denying dance choreography (or anything that was merely "spectacle" or "decorative") copyright protection. Thus, in *Glazer v. Hoffman*, a similar copyright infringement suit praying for injunctive relief involving a dispute between competing magician-performers over ownership of a magician's sleight of hand performance, Judge Chapman cited *Fuller v. Bemis* as legal precedent for dismissing the case.[11]

> The case of *Fuller v. Bemis* involved an infringement complaint. The act consisted of a stage dance illustrating the poetry of motion by a series of graceful movements, combined with an attractive arrangement of drapery, light and shadows. While the idea may be "pleasing," said the Court, it is not such a dramatic composition as to bring it within the meaning of the copyright act. See *Barnes v. Miner*, 122 F. 480 (C.C.S.D.N.Y. 1903);

> *Dane v. M. & H. Co.*, 136 U.S.P.Q. 426 (N.Y. 1963). We therefore conclude that the plaintiff below failed to bring his act or performance within the terms of the Federal copyright statutes.[12]

What the judges' opinion do not explicitly address is Fuller's (and by extension, Martinetti's) class status as a vaudeville performer and their proximity to the purely "popular," merely "illusory," or "decorative" forms of entertainment, such as belly dancing, for example. In 1892, within the context of the infringement case against Bemis, Fuller's identity as a white woman, and her entitlement to white privilege, were trumped by her working class status; she was simply one among many dancing girls of vaudeville theatre.

From Skirt Dancing To Art Nouveau: The Rise of Loïe Fuller

Despite Fuller's eventual commercial success at branding herself an "original," skirt dancing (from which her serpentine dance sprang) was already very much in vogue in the popular variety entertainment circuit, crossing the Atlantic Ocean from England to the United States. Letty Lind, one of the popularizers of the skirt dance, was a celebrated star of the Gaiety Theatre, a London music hall known for the "Gaiety Girls," a nineteenth-century British version of the Radio City Music Hall Rockettes; she was also one of the celebrities Fuller replaced in some productions, in 1889, prior to becoming "La Loïe."[13] Along a parallel track, Flitch characterized the skirt dance as a "compromise between the overly academic ballet of the time and the more outrageous step-kick dancing, such as the can-can (le chahut) or its English derivative, the 'ta-ra-ra-boom-de-ay.'"[14] Thus, the skirt dance uneasily straddled the realms of vulgarity and the "grace of flowing drapery, the value of line, the simplicity and naturalness of Greek dance."[15] As it evolved, the skirt dance "became increasingly associated with the burlesque, an excuse to flaunt what was hidden underneath the skirt."[16] As a choreographer, Fuller's genius lay in her appropriation of the general aesthetic of the skirt dance, to "whiten" it beyond its burlesque, working-class roots to become an iconic image of Art Nouveau. Fuller's serpentine dance, at the height of her artistic career, became immortalized through Mallarme's poetry as a metaphor for a powerful, abstract expressiveness beyond language and corporeality.

> To understand that the dancer is not a woman dancing, for the juxtaposed causes that she is not a woman, but a metaphor summarizing one of the elementary aspects of our form, sword, cup, flower, etc. and that she does not

> dance, suggesting, by ellipsis or élan, with a corporeal writing that would necessitate paragraphs of prose in dialogue as well as description to express, in the rewriting: poem disengaged from all writing apparatus.[17]

Ugly Duckling, Fairy, and Orientalist Temptress

One fascinating feature of Fuller's ascent to stardom is that she was an unlikely candidate for celebrity, and there was a large divide between her stage persona, and her image offstage. According to Rhonda K. Garelick, offstage, Fuller clearly had no formal dance training, little natural grace, and no fashion sense.[18] That is, in real life, as opposed to artistic performance, Fuller did not embody the hyperwhitened feminine (exotic) ideal that had captured the hearts and imaginations of Europe's intellectuals.

> To say [Fuller] was unglamorous is an understatement. Her round face, wide blue eyes, and short, stout body gave her a cherubic rather than sultry look. And at thirty, Fuller was nearly of retirement age for a music-hall dancer of that time. Offstage, she dressed haphazardly in oversized clothes, kept her hair in a tight bun, and wore little round spectacles.[19]

Fuller herself tearfully recounts how the fissure between her stage presence as a supernatural incarnation and her reversion back to an ordinary woman, backstage, led to a little girl's fearful recoil from her. To preserve the illusion, Fuller pretended to be "the fairy's" emissary.

> The mother and child found their way to my dressing room…
>
> The child's eyes opened wider and wider. The nearer I came the further she shrank away…
>
> "No, no. That isn't her. I don't want to see her. This one here is a fat lady, and it was a fairy I saw dancing."
>
> …
>
> I said to the child:
>
> "Yes, my dear, you are right. I am not Loïe Fuller. The fairy has sent me to tell you how much she loved you and how sorry she is not able to take you to her kingdom…She told me just to take you in my arms and give you a…good kiss for her."
>
> At these words, the little one threw herself into my arms…[20]

For as long as Fuller remained in her role as the quintessential disembodied symbol of artistic whiteness, both the public and her critics were forgiving of her idiosyncrasies, and tended to treat her as something in between "a female version of Thomas Edison, a mad scientist lady,"[21] and a chaste, sexless, and "proper" creature, despite her open lesbian relationship with her live-in companion of 20 years, Gabrielle Bloch, "a Jewish-French banking heiress who dressed only in men's suits."[22] Again, this points out the difference between performance space and lived experience, and the demarcation between the two, which is crucial to the maintenance of the illusion of the hyperwhitened feminine ideal. For as long as Fuller did not flagrantly try to deviate from her adored image onstage (as the embodiment of quintessential feminine whiteness as an abstract ideal), her celebrity was unchallenged. This is crucial because again, it illustrates how tenaciously culture tends to preserve its aesthetic idols, especially the cherished one of "the [universal] eternal feminine"—within the context of the times, implicitly raced as white.

To illustrate one attempt, by Fuller, to escape her own image as the (abstract) "Goddess of Light," Fuller's most memorable artistic failure appears to have been her first staging (1895–1896) of Salomé, the quintessential seductress.[23] Everything about the Salomé production seemed radically at odds with the tried and tested recipe that had made Fuller a success in her serpentine dance numbers. Unlike her earlier productions, where all she seemed to need was blank, black space, which she then filled with color, movement, and sound, here, she collaborated with George Rochegrosse, a popular salon painter, who did the costumes and set, inclusive of a "perspectival view of Jerusalem on a backdrop."[24] Nevertheless, one feature of her earlier performances was kept, in terms of press coverage: the *New York Times* heralded her use of underlighting for dramatic effect and her "expressive" treatment of the well-known story.[25] That is, her genius at experimenting with light remained unchallenged, despite the deplorable reviews she got for her performance, not as a disembodied hyperwhitened "Goddess of Light" but a flesh and blood historical figure: Salome.

Unfortunately, Fuller's genius at self-promotion and artistic projection this time backfired, largely because of her earlier success. Her hyperwhitened ethereal image, as status property, became devalued by her self-unveiling as a woman of flesh and blood: slightly corpulent, and prone to all fleshly weakness and imperfection. Jean Lorraine's acid expression of disappointment over Fuller's rendition of Salome reveals how deeply invested the Parisiennes had become in Fuller's hyperwhitened artistic illusion: "One perceives too late that the unhappy acrobat is neither mime nor dancer; *heavy, ungraceful, sweating* with make-up running at the end of ten minutes of little exercises, she maneuvers her veils and her mass of materials like a *laundress using her paddle* [italics added.]"[26] The reference to Fuller's thighs, a synechdoché of her class origins, and her "exotic" status as an American foreigner, were not uncommon in Paris.[27] But it was not until then that Fuller's "Yankeeness" became a diatribe dripping with contempt and condescension, when Lorraine wrote: "Luminous without grace, with the gestures of an English boxer and the physique of Mr. Oscar

Wilde, this is a Salomé for Yankee drunkards."[28] As long as Fuller did not deviate from the image projected by her serpentine dance performances, Fuller's Americanness, was a source of "exoticism;" when she did, she was severely punished by both critics and popular audiences.

Perhaps even stranger is Fuller's restaging of the Salomé pantomime in November 1907 titled *La tragédie de Salomé.* The program notes combine what was then a typical blend of Greek and Orientalist themes, visualized through a series of studio head shots of Fuller decked in "Egyptian-looking" wigs.[29]

Admittedly, there was a great deal of difference between the 1895 and 1907 productions, with significantly more preparation, both in terms of choreographic planning and the use of lights.[30] Reputedly, in the third tableau, at the climactic moment of the "La danse du paon," Fuller unveiled an iridescent tail of large feathers, which she could transform into a fan. Albright reports that this outfit was comprised of "4,500 peacock feathers...along with other equally impressive statistics such as [Fuller's] use of 650 lamps and 15 projectors to create 10,240 watts of candlepower."[31]

Fuller's second *Salomé* rendition thus attempted to bring together her genius in lighting artistry with another foray into a more "expressive" and less abstract artistry. Though the result was generally hailed as a "feminist" triumph, what emerges is that Fuller's "expressive" version of Salomé was also an attempt to return to the more traditional seductive stereotype—which was the "other" of the image for which she was glorified, as a white woman who could hide her body underneath the spectacle of cloth and the illusions of brilliant light.[32] What is also clear is that Fuller, onstage, even as the quintessential possessor of whiteness as status property, nevertheless remained fascinated with the imaginative reworkings of an Orientalist or nonwhite "other." La Loïe, having achieved the immortal status of a hyperwhitened goddess of light and abstraction, in her Salomé productions unveiled white envy of, and fascination with, constructions of nonwhite mortal Otherness. This is a theme that runs through this book—that those who are privileged bearers of whiteness remain fascinated with nonwhiteness, and attempt to appropriate it for their choreographic creations, with varying degrees of success, as we shall see. And this tense interplay between a white aesthetic, and its nonwhite others, is important to the development of choreography and what becomes copyrightable in the history of American dance.

La Loïe's Legacy

Despite (and probably because of) Fuller's defeat in her copyright infringement suit against Bemis, she left behind an impressive collection of scientific patents, especially in terms of lighting and set design. For example, three of Fuller's best-known inventions were registered with the US Patent Office between 1893 and 1895; these were her "Garment for Dancers," her "Mechanism for the Production of Light Effects" (a device for underlighting), and her "Theatrical Stage Mechanism" (a design for a mirrored room).[33]

Nevertheless, Fuller's choreographic legacy ironically seemed best protected, not by copyright, but by her effective acquisition of celebrity through the smart marketing of her image as La Loïe, the originator of the serpentine dance. To show how successfully Fuller had acquired ownership of a hyperwhitened form of popular artistry, Albright claims "Fuller had even more imitators than Madonna on an early 1980s karaoke night."[34] As Fuller's reputation grew, so did the legions of imitators. Yet that proliferation of faux-serpentine dance copycats only served to bolster Fuller's uniqueness as La Loïe. Where copyright failed, popular cultural mechanisms of the creation of stardom, through the generation of multiple copies, rather than their prevention, succeeded in cementing Fuller's legacy. That is, where whiteness as an aesthetic failed to be copyrightable (probably largely due to sexism and negative class associations), whiteness as an aesthetic remained supreme culturally and within the star system, as status property. Fuller herself perceptively commented in an interview:

> There are 500 . . . little misses—who can twirl a few yards of muslin and bob in and out of the focus of a limelight, but twirling a few yards of muslin and playing at touch with the limelight—any girl who is given to kicking her toes at all can do that—do not make a skirt dancer. To be an artist at your business calls for a life's experience . . . I leave nothing to chance. I drill my light men, drill them to throw the light so, or so, and they have to do their business with the exactitude of clockwork . . . Theme, style, time, all differ in one dance from another.[35]

What emerges from the interview excerpt is not only Fuller's confidence in the unassailability of her position, but also her awareness of what it takes to move from being an interchangeable popular dancing girl to being a respected artist. Instead of focusing on the physical labor of dancing, she emphasized the conceptual aspects of composition; rather than focusing on the disciplining of her body, she stressed the command over her supporting crew and the technical aspects of production. In so doing, Fuller rhetorically kept her dance legacy within the realm of the abstract and noncorporeal: the whitened realm of privilege. Though Fuller flirted with Orientalist themes in her Salomé productions, as Garelick remarks, this seems like a "sanitized 'borrowing' . . . because Fuller seems too high-tech, too asexual, too white, and too 'unforeign' to be compared to such 'exotic' and scantily clad dancers as the era's popular Algerian troupe, the Ouled-Nayl."[36]

Well before Balanchine successfully copyrighted his ballets as intellectual property, Fuller had begun the process of rhetorically converting dance choreography from simply popular entertainment, which is not protectable, into "art," which is eminently copyrightable. Fundamental to Fuller's (and eventually Balanchine's) project was the association of abstractness (noncorporeality) with the aesthetic of whiteness. As the first chapter of this book briefly shows, the history of copyright in relation to dance choreography, has been like a tango: one of repulsion and attraction. Yet one point of significant tension and equipoise in this tango has often been that invisible (though normative) fulcrum: the social and legal construction of whiteness as status property. In Fuller's case, the aesthetic precedent was unassailable in the realm of popular culture even as the attempt to set legal precedent failed. The first part of this chapter has been aimed at mapping some of the traces of whiteness as status property, both culturally and legally, in Fuller's theatre of light. The second part deals with Baker's nonpossession of whiteness as status property, despite her immense celebrity.

Josephine Baker: Refracted Traces of A Nonwhite Aesthetic in American Dance[37]

Introduction

My task in this section of the third chapter is more focused on studying one concrete example of a historically grounded nonwhite aesthetic possibility glimpsed through the example of Josephine Baker (1906–1975). This section, in specific, focuses on sketching, within the context of American dance, an understanding of how one distinctive type of a "nonwhite" aesthetic has historically played out. The larger backdrop of this project requires analyzing how race tracks on to what becomes regarded as the work of an "artist"/choreographer (thus deserving protection as legal property), as opposed to what is "not art" (that is, simply "popular entertainment" or purely "improvisational" work). I analyze mainly the twentieth century because this period is crucial in the formation of what is distinctively "American" and "modern" in dance, and though Baker's stardom, like Fuller's iconic dancing status, resounded most strongly in France, the cultural currents that flowed from their dancing legacies undeniably helped shape what eventually became regarded as distinctively

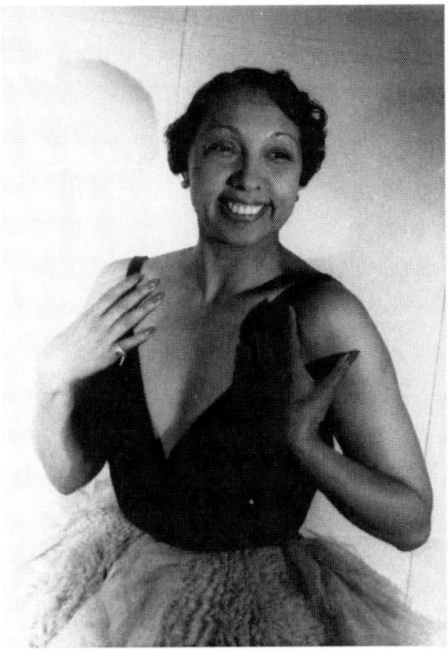

Figure 3.2 Public Domain Image of Josephine Baker, circa 1938. From the Library of Congress. http://www.loc.gov/pictures/item/2004662545/.

"American" and "modern" and what eventually became legally delineated as "private property." The twentieth century is also the period in which dance choreography becomes an independently listed legally copyrightable category, rather than being subsumed into being a certain type of "dramatic work," requiring a narrative to be legally protectable as "intellectual property."[38]

For this section, my principal focus is on one distinctive example of "nonwhiteness" as the precursor of aesthetic possibilities in American dance. Gender imbricates with race in this cultural imagination of a "white" versus a "nonwhite" dance aesthetic, much as postcolonial imaginings of a "primitivist" and "exotic" other (in the case of Baker), refracted through the prisms of stardom and image making, form a complex narrative. But the aesthetic frame, for this period, remains staunchly heterosexual much as class divisions inherent to those frames remain essentially stable. An additional layer of nuancing appears to be how comparatively darkly complected Baker was, and how closely she embodied the colonial fantasy of the "Black Venus"—which appeared to have resulted in ambivalences that both privileged her and discriminated against her.

Josephine Baker: Icon, Idol, Trickster

To attempt to even write about Josephine Baker is a monumental task because Baker's life is so multifaceted and has been reviewed through different prisms, numerous times.[39] For the purposes of this section of the chapter, I focus purely on Baker's legacy as a dancer who choreographed her own work, much of it as a soloist, much like Martha Graham and Loíe Fuller, but who is remembered very differently in the history of American dance, largely because of her race. I do not discuss Baker's philanthropic efforts at adopting a "Rainbow Tribe"[40] (similar to Angelina Jolie and Brad Pitt's adoption of orphans of different races) nor her activism, leading to her being a member of the French resistance against the Nazis[41] and the FBI's developing a secret file on her because of her political activism in the United States;[42] neither do I discuss Baker's numerous love affairs with men and women, both black and white,[43] and her admiring association with the Peróns, especially Evita, of Argentina.[44] These extend far beyond the scope of this book and are not relevant to the questions I ask concerning the construction of what a nonwhite aesthetic in dance might look like, as historically instantiated.

Jean-Claude Baker, who, though not among the 12 "official" members of Josephine's "Rainbow Tribe," was 14-years old when he first met Baker and eventually became one of Baker's close friends and confidants;[45] Jean-Claude became so devoted to La Baker that it was he who legally adopted her name. Jean-Claude begins his "second mother's" biography with the following words:

> "*Quel cul elle a!*" What an ass! Excuse the expression, but that is the cry that greeted Josephine as she exploded onstage in "La Danse de Sauvage." (Sixty years later, her friend and sometime lover, Maurice Bataille, would say to me, "Ah! *ce cul*... it gave all of Paris a hard-on.")[46]

The succinct, explosive expression captures an inkling of the complex combustion of shock, adoration, fascination, and disgust that greeted Josephine Baker's star-making performance, as an "Ebony Goddess," at the Théâtre des Champs-Élysées during the opening of La Revue Nègre on October 2, 1925.[47] The dance was supposed to be a reenactment of a story well known to Paris: Pierre Loti's novel about the seductive "native" girl, Fatou-gaye, and the French explorer, Jean Peyral.[48] But the result was a love affair between the exoticized image of Josephine Baker as a "Black Venus" and colonialist and scopophilic Paris.

Josephine, clad only in a belt and collar of feathers and flat-heeled black shoes (an odd costume for a "savage"), entered strapped onto her fellow dancer, Joe Alex, who was barefoot and just as scantily clad as Baker.

But it were as if Alex were simply part of the tableau as all eyes were on Josephine. "So strong was the impression she gave of nudity that keen-eyed Janet Flanner would remember her as having appeared with only one pink feather between her legs."[49] Jean-Claude Baker himself uses images that compared his adoptive mother to animals, but he does so, sharing the same fascinated colonialist lens with which Paris ogled Josephine's nearly nude black body—and most especially, her *derriere* (a body part especially specularly racialized, as we have seen in the first chapter of this book). "First, you feel sorry the lovely animal is dead, the shape of the body is so perfect, the color, the stillness. Then she starts to come alive, the muscular body begins to move, the music begins to pound."[50] Phyllis Rose recounts Baker's entrance, as a black female body displayed for visual consumption, as immediately and overtly sexually charged: "Baker was upside down and had her legs splayed."[51] For Paul Regnier, the "*Danse de Sauvage*" was "barbaric... naughty... a return to the customs of the dark ages... [Josephine accomplished] a silent declaration of love by a simple forward movement of her belly, with her arms raised above her head, and the quiver of her entire rear."[52] Baker, in her own autobiographical memories of the event, uses language reminiscent of a Dionysian *bacchante*:

> Driven by dark forces I didn't recognize, I improvised, crazed by the music, the overheated theater filled to the bursting point, the scorching eye of the spotlights. Even my teeth and eyes burned with fever. Each time I leaped I seemed to touch the sky and when I regained earth it seemed to be mine alone.[53]

Baker's own narrative of the event therefore seems to reinforce the stereotypical depictions of black womanhood as "naturally" savage, sexualized primal body. Nevertheless, part of the complexity in trying to analyze Baker's rise to stardom is not only Paris' projection of its colonialist and voyeuristic fantasies on her then-19-year-old black body, but also Baker's own multiple and revisionary accounts of her story.

Baker stepped into a series of historical confluences that launched her into stardom as the "Ebony Venus," the "Black Venus, the "Jazz Empress," and like Fuller (though as the "other of the other," using Michelle Wallace's expression[54]) other "luminous" expressions that idealized her as the essence of Black Womanhood.[55] Terri Francis succinctly details the genesis and power of the commercialized and publicly imagined myth of Black Womanhood, which T. Denean Sharpley-Whiting has described as the "the Black Venus narrative."[56] As Francis notes:

> [W]hen Baker debuted in Paris in 1925, she walked into a preexisting role that had been previously "interpreted" by Sartjee Baartman on stage as

> "La Vénus hottentote," Laura as the black female figure in Edouard Manet's 1863 painting Olympia and Baudelaire's writings inspired by his Creole mistress, Jeanne Duval—as well as the American jazz bands and other performers that date back to the nineteenth century.[57]

But where Francis sees continuity of the term "Black Venus" in relation to Sartjee Baartman and Josephine Baker, Brenda Dixon Gottschild sees contrast:

> If Sara Baartman is at one end of the primitive spectrum, then Baker is at the opposite end. Both were objects of the white male gaze, ensnared in the primitive trope, but one [Baartman] symbolized abjection and the other [Baker] agency. Baartman represented the (overtly) desexualized [as an exhibited scientific specimen], gross Other: oversized, static, de-energized. Baker was marketed as a moving target of a sexual object: lithe limbs, fast-footed steps, animated face, and most of all, a brilliantly active ass.[58]

But while Gottschild celebrates Baker's business acumen and guile, the parameters within which Baker could exercise that agency were strictly circumscribed within the culturally and literally archived term,[59] "Black Venus," as Baker herself recognized in her coauthored autobiography with her fourth husband, French bandleader, Jo Boullion: "According to another reviewer, I was a 'black Venus.' It was true that everyone seemed to love me, but I heard no talk of marriage. Venus, yes. But the black part didn't seem to help."[60]

Somewhat more analytically, Rose conjectures that Baker's frenzied improvisational "stomach dance" as probably derived from moves related to the belly dance: the Shake, the Shimmy, the Mess Around—all of which were popular with New York black jazz dancers in the 1920's.[61] Rose's biography is distinct from most of the other biographies because she focuses on the probable genealogy of many of Baker's dance moves. Benetta Jules-Rossette made similar observations: "During [Baker's] early performances of the savage dance, Baker creatively combined elements from American popular dances—the Charleston, the quadrille, strut of the cakewalk (which became Baker's chicken dance), and the black bottom—with improvised acrobatics and her own inspired high kicks and contortions."[62]

Baker, in the shrewd exploitation of the myth of her "natural" closeness to animals, as well as a "natural" dancer, liked to say that she learned how to move by watching kangaroos in the St. Louis Zoo, and from the odd, unpremeditated angles of ragdolls.[63] However, applying Judith Butler's observations concerning the complexities of the performance of gender (and heteronormativity),[64] Baker's gendered and raced autoethnographic fictionalizations were as much a part of the public persona she performed as an image she internalized. As Benetta Jules Rosette observes (which mimes, but does not replicate Kenneth Nunn's insights paraphrased in the first chapter):

> As ways of speaking about one's perceived and desired location in the social world, identity discourses express virtual states of existence. These discourses are affirmations, rather than statements of fact, that link individuals to larger collective identities. In complicity with her promoters and audiences, Baker employed five performative strategies of image and identity construction: (1) exoticizing race and gender; (2) reversing racial and cultural codes and meanings; (3) displaying difference through nudity, cross-dressing, song, and dance; (4) exploiting the images of difference; and (5) universalizing the outcome to allow the performative messages to reach a larger audience. These strategies emerged gradually and with varying degrees of sophistication.[65]

Indeed, what Rose unearths is how Baker's "natural" movements were very much rooted in American popular "street" dances,[66] which Baker first learned in St. Louis—movements perfected through years of practice, hammered in by the compunction of trying to leave behind a life of poverty and abuse. As Rose remarks:

> By the time she was thirteen, Baker had built up an enormous repertoire of moves. She knew them so well that when she started to dance professionally, it could look like she was making it all up as she went along. But underneath the seemingly total spontaneity were known steps and dances—the Mess Around, the Itch, Tack Annie, Trucking—and years of daily practice. When she seemed unstrung, there had been the most careful preparation. Even her eye-rolling was something she worked at.[67]

Rose's mention of "eye-rolling" is important, as it recalls a feature of Baker's performance that has not been as iconized as much as Baker's "Black Venus" image. On the same night that Baker closed the show with her "banana skirt" number, she had appeared earlier in an androgynous clowning routine, complete with blackface: seemingly, the very antithesis of the hyperfeminized "Black Venus." Baker herself quoted a review from the newspaper, *Candide*, regarding Baker's performance at the *Revue Nègre*.

> At one point a strange figure in a ragged undershirt ambles onto the stage looking like a cross between a boxing kangaroo and a racing driver. Josephine Baker. Woman or man? Her lips are painted black, her skin is the color of bananas, her cropped hair sticks to her head like caviar, her voice

> squeaks. She is in constant motion, her body writhing like a snake...She grimaces, crosses her eyes, puffs out her cheeks, wiggles disjointedly, does a split and finally crawls off the stage stiff-legged, her rump higher than her head, like a young giraffe.[68]

Despite the distinct contrasts between the clowning number and the "banana skirt" number, the analogies to "exotic" animals remain, much as the myth of "naturalness" remains intact—all stereotypic and iconized features of the dancing black female body. Yet the clowning number very clearly locates Baker's rootedness in American black vaudeville traditions rather than in some universal principle of "naturalness" that she spontaneously tapped through an untutored and undisciplined body (another cultural "myth" regarding blackness as "exotic").

This is the initial version of the aesthetic Baker's dance career initially steps into: it is culturally prefabricated and had deep historical roots in the French collective psyche. The only agency she had, in that context, was to exploit it by playing up to it and magnifying it, making her "real" life and her performed life mirrors that reflected these desires back to her adoring public. Her rise to stardom was facilitated by the ease with which she could remake herself to suit this public image and a bargain was struck: for so long as she could perform to this scopophilic gaze and maintain the illusion, even in real life, she could be a goddess, albeit a "black goddess."

But as in the way of all stardom, this is a moment that could not be maintained, as the adoring public is fickle and needs constant entertainment. In order to remain "the same"—as an "exotic" sexualized object of fascination—Baker would have to remake herself constantly. And a key component to Baker's many transformations was her consistent "whitening" as a wild child civilized into Parisienne culture: a "Black Cinderella" (though minus the Prince Charming part, in terms of her real life; she did not lack love affairs, but she did not marry a Frenchman (and receive a French passport) until 1937, when she married (without formally divorcing her prior American husbands, Willy Wells or Billy Baker) businessman Jean Lion, from whom she formally divorced in 1941).[69] This process of transformation took place both personally and professionally,[70] as Baker moved from being a nude body dressed by fashion and costume designers, a dancing body scrutinized by the press and used, venerated and maligned by artists and critics, an illiterate body incapable of expression or communication in French, to becoming an icon of fashion whom designers showered with free outfits, a star who could sell dolls made in her image and shill makeup to darken one's skin, and an idol who could command how her autobiography was written. In the prior sentences, I have chosen the rhetorical emphasis on being a body acted upon, to becoming a specular projection of the star system, with care.

The later Baker is less a dancing body that projects the illusion of nudity than a clothed body that projects an illusion of Europeanized sophistication. Baker grew increasingly "whitened" by the star system not only metaphorically but also literally. She also became increasingly preoccupied with, and better skilled at, costuming herself. As Jules-Rosette observes:

> "From the lessons learned in her early touring days with the Dixie Steppers...Baker brought the cosmetic processes of masking and blackening up, minstrel-style. Once in France, she became obsessed with both natural (lemon juice, milk, and flour) and artificial skin-lightening products. Skin, hair, costume and cosmetic changes were critical to the Baker mystique."[71]

Interestingly, compared to her siblings, Baker was fairly complected (which meant little to her family, given her class origins, and probably worked against her in her mother's eyes, as a constant reminder of her dalliance with a "spinach"—an olive-skinned Spaniard, unlike her siblings, who were fathered by a muscular, dark-skinned black man who married Josephine's mother despite the earlier illegitimate pregnancy[72]). However, compared to the other black girls who performed at the Revue Négre, Baker happened to be darker in complexion. But France, unlike America, preferred darker complected girls—at least, at that point in time when Baker and other "lighter" colored black performers arrived in Paris in 1925. As Baker and Chase recount: "The public would, by and large, have preferred the cast to be more black, resembling Africans right off the boat. Because of this, the very light-colored Hazel Valentine was forced to apply black body makeup, an act she and the other high-yellow girls considered a supreme degradation...."[73]

However, by 1927, a scant few years later, Parisiennes began to show signs of boredom and discontent with Baker's now-predictable acts until Baker extemporaneously berated them, and reminded them of how they had initially warmly welcomed her:

> "Are you still French?" she asks.
>
> She has won them back, they applaud her next song, partly to make up to her for the rudeness she has been shown...Josephine can't fool herself, her welcome has not been so warm.[74]

In order to remain an object of fascination, Baker had to conform to another colonial fantasy: the fantasy of the colony educating and civilizing its savage colonies. Part of the process of "whitening" her appeal was not only in terms of her costuming and grooming, but also the narrative motifs she had to repeatedly portray on stage and on film. And one of those narrative motifs, in addition to the "Black Cinderella," was the "Black Madonna"—the black woman with a pure heart who sacrificially gave up her true love, always a white man, to his true love, paradigmatically a white woman. During her brief stint into film, Baker recycled many of her signature dance routines, now glamorized, woven into the narratives of the Sacrificial Black Cinderella. Papitou in *La Sirène des tropiques* (1927), ZouZou in *ZouZou* (1934), and Aouina in *Princesse TamTam* (1935) are all examples of this Self-Sacrificing Black Cinderella: a primordially "savage" woman who is "saved" by civilizing forces and displays the power of this influence by denying her savage nature as primal body.[75] As Jules-Rossette recounts:

> [Pepito] Abatino [Baker's then-manager-lover] carefully crafted the narratives to appeal to what he perceived as French tastes, making sure that the exotic heroine would return to the empire of nature, retain the ties to her primal trappings, and exhibit self-sacrifice amid the glamour. The connection of cinema to the representation of colonial exotica was perfect for Baker, who portrayed seductive narratives caught up in civilizing dramas with romantic twists.[76]

Concluding Remarks: Baker and Fuller Compared

The principal irony of Baker's rise to stardom is Europe's attempt to reinvigorate its civilization and to return to its "dark" roots via the commercial adoration of Baker. This process revealed nothing more than France's/Europe's own ambivalent projections, writ large in order to engage in a temporary dalliance with its erotic "uncivilized" Other. "Combining animal sexuality with glamour, Baker was the stranger within who introduced Europeans to a 'lost' strangeness within themselves, to be recuperated as a fantasmatic *objet a* that perfected the European subject himself by simultaneously reaffirming his superior completeness and licensing his temporary departures from civilized propriety into the fantasy of erotic abandon. Thus Europe was 'blackened,' but only to reaffirm its whiteness."[77]

Choreographically, the roots of the "authentic Africanist" dance style Europe venerated were African American street dances magnified through Baker's hyperbolic and flamboyant exaggerations. More precisely, they lay in Baker's spontaneous improvisational reinterpretations of popular

American "street" dance steps because there are indications that she probably was temperamentally predisposed against the kind of structured repetitive flow formal choreography requires;[78] even Balanchine, when teaching her, chose not to teach her "choreography" than simply provide a backdrop for her. "In 1936 Balanchine shared credits with Robert Alton for dances in the *Ziegfeld Follies*... In the *Follies*, Balanchine provided an exotic background for Josephine Baker's dark beauty and daring costumes without tampering with her pulsating jazz routines."[79]

In some ways, Baker's case parallels Fuller's: both rose from American working-class origins, were principally self-taught, and yet managed to capture the European imagination as artistic Goddesses—Fuller as an icon of light and ethereality,[80] Baker as an idol of nonwhiteness and hypersexualized embodiment. But whereas Fuller managed to achieve patents in her name for her inventions for her staged productions,[81] there are no such documents attesting to Baker's "ownership" of her "intellectual property." Although Fuller preceded Baker by several decades, there is no indication that Baker ever attempted to demarcate the artifacts and traces of her artistry as her personal property the way Fuller had done,[82] through both Fuller's successful patent applications and her unsuccessful bid to claim ownership over the "Serpentine Dance" through copyright. If any intellectual property protection were even conceivable for Baker, trademark protection or perhaps even publicity rights, based on the commercialization of her image as a celebrity with a distinctive mark (e.g., through a doll that resembled her and walnut oil that was sold specifically to darken Parisian skin), would probably have been her best bet. Rose recounts that at the height of Josephine's stardom during the Fall of 1926:

> There were Josephine Baker dolls, costumes, perfumes, pomades... In Paris women's hair was slicked down like Josephine Baker's and to achieve this look, they could buy a product called Bakerfix... Women who, the summer before, had still been protecting their white skin from the vulgarity of sunburn now put walnut oil on their skin in lieu of weeks in the sun.[83]

But in terms of choreographic protection, like Fuller, Baker's claim to ownership of her choreographic improvisations, if she had dared to mount such a claim, would have failed, not simply because it would probably have been dismissed, like Fuller's claim, as pure "spectacle"[84] but also because, given her performances' overt eroticism and closeness to vaudeville traditions and "popular" dance steps, her claim would probably also have been roundly dismissed as "obscene,"[85] lacking originality, and not "promoting the advancement of science and the useful arts," which is the principal objective of patent and copyright protection.[86]

Even more problematically, improvisation, because it is not movement fixed in a replicable flow, is not copyrightable. Interestingly, even today, steps derived from "popular" or "folk" dances are not protectable using copyright. These remain in the public domain and are not protectable. Hardly surprisingly, as Richard Schur argues:

> By construing... [the creative works of marginalized people, such as African Americans] as mere folk tales, intellectual property law has allowed dominant culture to plunder traditions and forms of African Americans and other minority groups... [Thus,] intellectual property laws have consistently favored those white individuals who wrote down, composed, drew, or marketed the story over those African American individuals who lived or experienced it.[87]

Much of this is grounded in copyright's rootedness in Eurocentric conventions, which set apart the "genius" required for an individual artist/author/choreographer's work to be protected as private intellectual property from the merely "popular" entertainment or "folk" conventions that no individual can take credit for. As Anthea Kraut observes, "[t]he exclusionary formulation of 'choreographic work' certainly seems to inscribe an elitist hierarchy between 'high' art and 'low,' a hierarchy that has historically been racially coded."[88] It is not surprising that intellectual property law, in general, tends to privilege "whitened" dance forms, such as ballet, because there are clear choreographers who author the lines and movements using the bodies of dancers, who are as "raw material" shaped/posed/"created" by choreographers.

Copyright law creates a binary between private property (usually individually owned and exploited) and the notion of a "commons" (usually not owned by any individual and free for use by all in the community, such as "street dancing"). Historically, "[c]opyright law matured in the classical era of liberalism, which formally enshrined the ideal of the abstract individual freely exercising his or her creative capacity protected by a neutral system of natural rights, the most important of which was the right of property."[89] The converse to these clearly delineated individual rights is the amorphous "public domain," which is "usually equated with the non [-] propertied general welfare of the common people of a particular nation-state or, more generously, with the larger welfare of the undifferentiated global community as a whole."[90]

Yet what that binary hides are precisely the assumptions behind copyright law and its historical origins. Much as patent law requires an inventor, copyright law requires an author. Additionally, both scientific invention and the creation of literary texts (as copyright's origins lie in the attempt to protect the production of books) became regarded as testaments to the creativity and "genius" of a particular individual. Within the context of eighteenth-century England (which forged the philosophical foundations of US copyright law), a book rose to becoming "the intellection of a unique individual,"[91] rather than a product of mastering the rules of craftsmanship. Because a book is a particular embodied or "fixed" expression of the author's unique mind, originally expressed, it is private intellectual property; thus, the right to exploit this identifiable piece of property belongs purely to this unique individual. Yet as James Boyle points out, such an idealized view of authorship "blinds us to the importance of the commons—to the importance of the raw material from which information products are to be constructed."[92]

Dance choreography, because it is both embodied and seemingly so ephemeral (particularly during the 1920's), already faces an uphill battle, in terms of copyright protection.[93] Hardly surprisingly, given this binary between the whitened realm of "genius" and the nonwhitened realm of "mere folk traditions," "improvisation—especially improvisation derived from "popular" street dances that do not share the whitened aesthetic characteristic of more established dance forms, such as ballet, tends to become discredited as "not original." But as Kraut points out, the legal binary is one difficult to sustain in the practice of designing/learning choreography, especially within the nonwhite traditions of jazz and tap. "'Social dance steps' and 'simple routines,' however, routinely migrate from recreational arenas to the for-profit theatrical stage…, raising questions about when bodily movements that occur both onstage and off- might constitute a 'choreographic work.'"[94]

Given this historical context, had Baker attempted to follow Fuller's example, her claim would probably have failed. Nevertheless, traces of a nonwhite aesthetic, even if hyperbolically rendered a spectacle through colonialist and commercialist lenses, can be glimpsed through her dance legacy. As Dayal remarks:

> [Baker's] legacy may not be that of a profoundly subversive and parodic cultural activist. And in purely aesthetic and technical terms, her performances may not have been as precedent-setting as the performances of Katherine Dunham or Ruth St. Denis or Isadora Duncan. But no one can deny her immense performative breadth or the role she played in the "blackening" of the European cultural scene. Nor can it be denied that her presence in that scene brought to the fore how intimately "blackness" was sutured to the construction of modern white European subjectivity.[95]

Chapter 4

George Balanchine, "Genius of American Dance": Whiteness, Choreography, Copyrightability in American Dance*

Introduction: Establishing an Aesthetic of Whiteness

This chapter deals with Balanchine's successful gaining of copyright protection, which becomes a self-perpetuating system through which his estate (through the Balanchine Trust) now maintains ownership over his choreographic works. Unlike the majority of choreographic productions, Balanchine's balletic choreography became sharply delimited from the communally accessible public domain.

George Balanchine (1904–1983), born Georgi Melitonovitch Balanchivadze[1] in St. Petersburg, Russia, came to the United States in 1933, in acceptance of Lincoln Kerstein's invitation.[2] Born from a wealthy, mercantile Jewish family, Kerstein (1907–1996) dreamed of creating a world-class ballet company,[3] and thought Balanchine was the most promising candidate to choreograph pieces for such a new company.[4] At Balanchine's behest, Kerstein also funded the founding of the American Academy of Ballet in 1934.[5] After several ballet companies directed by Kirstein and Balanchine dissolved, the New York City Ballet was born, inaugurated with a performance on October 11, 1948.[6] Under Balanchine's leadership as its ballet master and principal choreographer, the company evolved to become one of the most reputable ballet companies internationally.[7]

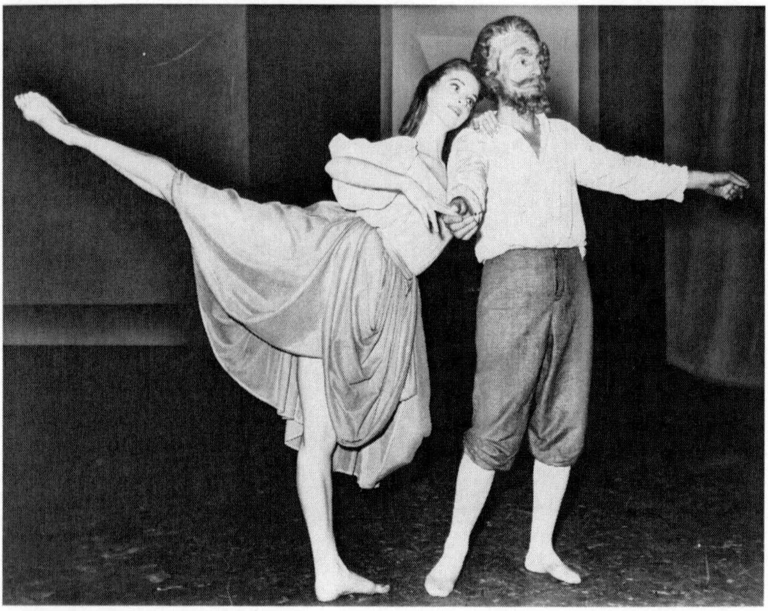

Figure 4.1 Public Domain Image of George Balanchine and Suzanne Farrell. From the Library of Congress. http://hdl.loc.gov/loc.pnp/cph.3c29045.

Many biographies of Balanchine abound, all of which are extremely complimentary. Robert Gottlieb compares Balanchine to other "geniuses," like Shakespeare and Mozart, who composed with "amazing fluency and ease."[8] Gottlieb's portrait of Balanchine captures the master choreographer's iconic stature in superlative, semi-divine terms—one who did not need "divine inspiration," but simply worked, pragmatically impervious to all external factors. In Gottlieb's eyes, Balanchine, the artist, towered above the contingencies of the human condition.

> Always, he adjusted himself to the immediate situation, whatever it was: big stage or little stage; large cast or small; money or no money; ballet, musical comedy, film or television. He was a leader, a model—both a supreme artist and a brilliant executive. To his dancers he was everything. To other choreographers he was a figure of awe. As Twyla Tharpe has put it, "Balanchine is God."[9]

In comparison, Bernard Taper[10] describes Balanchine, despite the heavy Russian accent that persisted throughout Balanchine's life, as a quintessential American—eclectic, adaptable, shrewd, and aware of the commercial nature of his craft—traits he shared with Fuller. In Taper's biographical portrait, Balanchine saw himself more as a craftsman than an artist. "When [Balanchine] spoke of what he did, he compared himself to a chef, whose job it was to prepare for an exacting clientele a variety of attractive dishes that would delight and surprise their palates, or to a...good carpenter, with pride in his craft."[11]

Despite the variance in portraiture, what is clear is Balanchine's total command over his dancers. It was as if he were the puppet master, and they, the wooden objects, into whom he breathed life, rendering them immortal vessels of eternal emotions and passions. As Taper remarks, "In [Balanchine's] cosmogony, dancers were like angels: celestial messengers who communicate emotions but do not themselves experience the joys and griefs of which they bring tidings."[12]

Balanchine's creativity seemed inextricably bound up with his romantic life, and he is legendary for having married many of his muses—at the height of his creative powers, they were always young dancers under his mentorship, always still unformed, like Galateas waiting to be sculpted into being by a balletic Pygmalion. For example, Balanchine, at 41, married the 21-year-old Maria Tallchief, whose exotic dark looks made her resemble a Mayan princess; he said he was charmed by her Indian heritage, and even remarked that by marrying her, he was becoming truly American, reminiscent of how John Smith married Pocahontas.[13] The Orientalist and patriarchal undertones, as well as Balanchine's complete identification with the romantic image of the American frontiersman, are clear, in that revealing remark. Equally clear is Tallchief's acceptance of his paradigm.

> [Tallchief] stood in awe of Balanchine. He was the master. She had said that she was astonished when he proposed, for he had not previously showed any lover's ardor, and when he turned his eyes on her, in the rehearsal hall, she had not been aware that these might be melting glances he was bestowing, but was rather painfully conscious of all the flaws he must be noting. There was no thought of refusing him, just as in the rehearsal hall there was no thought of refusing to attempt whatever he demanded of her.[14]

Balanchine's creative and personal pattern clearly worked itself in cycles. Like a painter or sculptor, these young muses-pupils represented both the reality and potentiality of his art—their limits were the limits of his creations. Like Michelangelo, he would then patiently awaken the ethereal forms he saw asleep in their young, mortal frames, still rough and uncut (as Tallchief, unlike his other dancers, still had some "flesh" on her when he started working with her). And they, in turn, submitted, serving him faithfully, and then when age or infirmity began to take their toll, made way for the next muse; it was unthinkable that they would rebel as they were grateful to have been made artistically immortal, for a few years, by the master choreographer. "That one woman should be supplanted in this role by another in the course of time had begun to seem by then, as with Picasso's succession of wife-mistess-models, an outward manifestation of the constantly renewed youthfulness of the artist's creative powers."[15]

Balanchine's marriage to Tallchief lasted for five years, and then was annulled. The legal grounds for annulment stated were that Tallchief wanted children, and Balanchine did not. The general perception seemed to be that this was simply a legal pretext to end the marriage, but it is also clear that Tallchief, during her later marriage to a Chicago businessman, did have a child; equally clear is Balanchine's preference that his dancers "suppress the urge to procreate" because "[a]ny woman can become a mother... but not every woman can become a ballerina."[16]

Balanchine married and divorced four women: Tamara Geva, Vera Zorina, Maria Tallchief, and Tanaquil Le Clercq. All the women were dancers, and under the aegis of his choreographic mentorship, blossomed into stars. Although Balanchine could never exercise as much control over Geva and Zorina, by the time he was in his forties, Balanchine was well established enough to become a virtual artistic god. During that period, the women he married (Tallchief and Le Clercq) were also his artistic "property," for it is upon their frail, hyperwhitened frames, which he thoroughly commanded, that he "wrote" his ballets. With the complete integration of his personal and professional lives, through an artistic justification, Balanchine had total control over his wives; he is reported to have said "If you marry a ballerina, ... you never have to worry about whether she's running around with somebody else or anything like that. You always know exactly where she is—in the studio, working."[17]

Unlike Fuller, Balanchine did not have to work hard at establishing a virtual trademark—the name "Balanchine" had by then come to signify both a certain classical purity of line and a hyperwhitened feminine aesthetic, as his ballets tended to glorify women with these kinds of physical attributes.[18] Unlike Fuller, Balanchine did not have to work hard to distinguish his art form from the burlesque because ballet's classical and regal heritage already distinguished it from the realm of "mere spectacle," devoid of any moral or artistic higher purpose.

Nevertheless, like Fuller, Balanchine also experimented with film, though his work in this medium was more in keeping with Hollywood's mainstream narrative style than Fuller's experimental work. For example, in Spring, 1937, Samuel Goldwyn contracted Balanchine to come to Hollywood and choreograph numbers for *The Goldwyn Follies*, its score to be written by George Gershwin.[19] Goldwyn hired the half-German, half-Norwegian blonde soloist with the Ballets Russes, Vera Zorina (Eva Brigitta Hartwig), to dance the principal role.[20] Balanchine had confided in a female friend, Lucia Davidova, that what he sought in a wife was not a "housewife," but "a nymph who fills the bedroom and floats out."[21] Elusiveness is a quality Balanchine romanticized: in his artistic world, the man sought, and the woman fled. And in Zorina, his dance-muse (and eventual second wife) for his most famous cinematic foray, the "Water Nymph" ballet, was perfect for the part, both artistically and personally: she was cool, guarded, disdainful, and emotionally unavailable.

Balanchine himself seduced Zorina with his vision of the updated Swan Lake concept:

> There will be marvelous, beautiful, big stage, round, with Greek columns on each side like Palladio; then, in the back, statue of big white horse. Poet comes and sees beautiful Undine coming out of pool... covered with beautiful white flowers... She dances with poet. Then big storm starts, wind blows like mad, and we discover her on the horse. Then the wind blows all her dress away and she slides slowly, slowly from the horse and in her little tunic and bare feet she goes back to lily pool, and slowly her body disappears in the water until only her head is visible, and then she puts her cheek on the water like a pillow and she is gone like sun disappearing in ocean.[22]

Here is the essence of Balanchine's artistic vision: a *mise en scene* drenched with classical referents (the column; the horse); a hyperwhitened muse, not of flesh and blood, but of the elements, who conspire in making her elusive; the ubiquity of whiteness, which adds to the visual ethereality of the muse. Though the eventual movie was shot in color, with Zorina swathed in gold, Balanchine's idealized vision had her clothed in white. This is an aesthetic that repeatedly surfaces in Balanchine's corpus. Personally, despite his artistic productivity, Balanchine was predominantly unhappy during his seven-year marriage to Zorina (who claimed to have felt "suffocated" by being "placed on a pedestal"),[23] and she eventually left him for classical-record producer, Goddard Lieberson.[24]

Nevertheless, at the height of his career, Balanchine delighted principally in transforming a natural-looking, uninhibited "tsoupolia,"[25] a concocted Russian word meaning a young chicken, into a disciplined, immortal swan, swathed in the aesthetic of hyperwhitened beauty. He succeeded in that project, essentially emotionally intact, with Maria Tallchief and Tanaquil Le Clercq. He had probably grown so accustomed to being able to convince his muses to marry him, out of artistic duty (and ambition), that when Suzanne Farrell came along, he was in shock when she resisted and married Paul Mejia, a young male dancer in the New York City Ballet, and left the company for a while, in protest against Balanchine's refusal to cast Meijia in the "roles [Mejia] expected and deserved."[26]

Suzanne Farrell (Roberta Sue Ficker) began her tutelage under Balanchine (whom she called "Mr. B.") when she was 16; her breakthrough occurred because then-prima ballerina Diana Adams became pregnant, and Farrell had to learn Adams' part for *Movements for Piano and Orchestra*, allegedly initially without music, and within days, for Balanchine and Stravinsky.[27] Violette Verdy, one of Balanchine's most "analytical" dancers remarked, "[T]he person who has come closest to surrendering to Balanchine is Suzanne Farrell. She has managed that kind of wonderful surrender that is also a glorification of self."[28] And indeed, Farrell herself, after describing what she remembered as a torturous rehearsal, filled with mistakes and lacking musicality because she was late from algebra class and did not have time to warm up before performing for Stravinski and Balanchine, remembered Balanchine's faith in her when she was ready to withdraw from the part. "I trusted him not to let me be a fool, but rather a tool, an instrument in his hands. In short, I trusted him with my life."[29]

What clearly emerged after Farrell's triumph in *Movements*, was Balanchine's increasing obsession with her, as evidenced in the pieces he created for her. *Meditation* was a highly emotionally charged duet in which an older man (danced by Jacques d'Amboise) conjures up a memory of a woman he had loved.[30] Two years later, Balanchine's three-act ballet, *Don Quixote*, left little doubt of his feelings for her.[31] Balanchine himself, now in his 60's, danced the part of Don Quixote, an old befuddled nobleman, who is inspired, cared for and tantalized by his beautiful servant, Dulcinea (played by Farrell), who symbolizes both purity and sensuality.[32] "[I]it was obvious that [Balanchine] that he was dancing not only with Farrell but for her. This was both a coronation (he called her an *alabaster princess*) [emphasis added] and a declaration of personal worship."[33]

Perhaps partly because of the poignant contrast between Balanchine's age and Farrell's youth and delicate beauty, Balanchine produced some of his most emotionally expressive works, crystallizing his hyperwhitened, impossibly frail feminine aesthetic (combined with an almost unnatural athleticism) as the norm for American ballet's prima ballerinas. Again and again, Balanchine cast Farrell as the chosen one in the white dress;[34] in 1982, when she had returned to the fold, and as Balanchine's health grew more tenuous, he chose to dress her again in white in a recreation of *Elegie*—a part she had originally danced in black in 1966.[35] Interestingly, even years later, Farrell's very rhetoric itself is steeped in Balanchine's culinary metaphors of choreographic creation and white aesthetic, when she recounted Balanchine's glee in pushing her to new physical and artistic limits. "This was... all very exciting for Mr. B. and myself, and he must have felt like the chef who first discovered that viscous egg whites could be transformed into a thick, light froth."[36] Nevertheless, Balanchine's legacy, casting the iconic hyperwhitened, waif-like look as the status property required for/to become prima ballerinas, is far more than artistic, as it has shaped copyright history as well.

Balanchine's Will: Converting Choreographic Works Into Financial Assets

Balanchine's creation of a will bequeathing his ballets as property occurred because of a conversation with a lawyer, Theodore M. Sysol, whom Barbara Horgan, Balanchine's personal assistant, had hired.[37] Balanchine, who had always lived in the present and never thought about the future, found out that upon his death without a will, his sole heir would be his brother who lived in Georgia, in the Soviet Union.[38] Appalled, Balanchine was determined not to let all of his possessions go, not so much to his brother, whom he had seen barely three times, but the Communist government, whom he suspected would claim everything.[39] Initially, Balanchine thought his ballets were "not worth anything," but the lawyer, knowing of the 1976 Copyright Act granting copyright protection to choreographic works, convinced Balanchine that the ballets could be bequeathed to Balanchine's selected heirs.[40]

Galvanized into action, Balanchine drew up detailed lists of his ballets (thus partially fulfilling the "fixation" requirement for copyright protection), as well as his other assets.[41] Balanchine signed the will on May 25, 1978; except for one minor modification, incorporated through a codicil on June 18, 1979, the will remained unchanged.[42] With that step, the world of dance choreography in relation to law changed forever: eventually, Balanchine's ballets, inclusive of its look of hyperwhitened, impossibly thin feminine beauty, became delimited from the public sphere as private property. The ability to control not only performances of the ballets, but also their "look" or representation, now passed into the hands of Balanchine's principal legaties: Tanaquil Le Clercq (his fourth and last wife, felled by polio at the height of her career, and from whom he obtained a Mexican divorce with the intent of pursuing Farrell);[43] Karin von Aroldingen (a prima ballerina who became a close Platonic friend to the aging choreographer after Farrell had rejected Balanchine's romantic advances);[44] and Barbara Horgan (Balanchine's faithful and devoted personal assistant).[45] Yet it would take years before the financial details, involving essentially the translation of things that belie financial calculation, such as balletic choreography, into raw dollar values that could be transmitted across generations, would be worked out.

The story of how the will produced choreographic intellectual property, which eventually became institutionally owned, is a fascinating and complex one, steeped in the contingencies of choreographic production, much of which is intangible. When the will was unsealed, it specified 113 ballets, to be bequeathed to 14 legaties, but not all of the ballets were still extant.[46] Approximately 75 were still potentially available for performance, and perhaps another six could be resurrected, with research.[47] The rest of the 425 ballets that Balanchine had prolifically created, now either no longer resided in the muscle memories of his dancers, or had disappeared with the passing of its dancers.[48]

Approximately 70 percent of the rights were willed to the three principal legatees.[49] Horgan and von Aroldingen were designated to share foreign royalty rights to all but 21 of the ballets identified in the will and media royalty rights to all but 25, including all rights to other ballets not specified in it (such as ballets created after Balanchine had signed the will).[50] Balanchine gave von Aroldingen sole rights to *Serenade*, *Liebeslieder Walzer*, and four other ballets in which Balanchine had designed principal roles for her: *Stravinsky Violin Concerto*, *Variations pour une Porte et un Soupir*, *Vienna Walzes*, and *Kammermusik No. 2*.[51]

Balanchine willed another ballet, *Brahms-Schoenberg Quartet*, to Barbara Horgan.[52] But Balanchine willed most of his choreographic intellectual property to Tanaquil Le Clercq, perhaps partially moved by his guilt over his abandonment of her, now saddled in a wheelchair due to a polio attack, in his Quixotic pursuit of Farrell. To his fourth wife, Balanchine willed all American performance royalty rights to 85 ballets, out of which about 60 were actually still viable.[53] None of Balanchine's other official wives, including his first common-law one, Alexandra Danilova, got anything. Taper, one of Balanchine's biographers, describes the complex distribution of choreographic assets:

> Other ballet bequests were Diana Adams (*A Midsummer Night's Dream*), Lincoln Kerstein (*Concerto Barocco and Orpheus*), Edward Bigelow (*The Four Temperaments* and *Ivesiana*), Betty Cage (*Symphony in C*), Mrs. André Eglevsky (*Sylvia Pas de Deux*, *Minkus Pas de Trois*, and *Glinka Pas de Trois*), Suzanne Farrell (*Meditation*, *Don Quixote*, and *Tzigane*), Patricia McBride (*Tarantella*, *Pavane*, and *Étude for Piano*), Kay Mazzo (*Duo Concertant*), Rosemary Dunleavy (*Le Tombeau de Couperin*), Merrill Ashley (*Ballo della Regina*), and Jerome Robbins (*Firebird* and *Pulcinella*).[54]

Such a wide distribution of assets would eventually require consolidation, if Balanchine's legacy were to survive, especially given that Balanchine left nothing for the New York City Ballet or the School of American Ballet—the immediate instruments for continuing to stage his choreographic productions.

It was only when Horgan actually had to deal with the IRS that the conversion of intangible choreographic productions into monetary values became an issue. How much was each choreographed piece worth? How long could one expect their value to last? Despite Horgan's initiative in depositing videotapes of many of Balanchine's ballets with the Copyright Office in Washington, to maintain control over them, as Horgan's first estate filing noted: "there has been no recorded case in which a choreographer's right to control his work, and thus, its value, has been protected by copyright."[55]

What resulted in response to IRS scrutiny was a masterful probate statement effectively arguing for keeping the tax on estate royalties as low as possible. A team from the law firm of Proskauer, Rose, Goetz & Mendelsohn, in consultation with Horgan, crafted the document.[56] Succinctly summarized, the document argued that because historically, choreographers' fees have been low, and dance audiences crave novelty, inevitably, the document predicted, the New York City Ballet would eventually become the forum of new choreographers; without Balanchine to refresh and renew his works, the Balanchine ballets would inevitably depreciate, and thus, the IRS could predict on no longer than five years of posthumous income for the choreographic works.[57] As to the actual itemized royalty breakdown, the document came up with a figure: "$190,691.37—precise to the penny and as close presumably as [Horgan and the law firm] dared come to Balanchine's [initial] dismissive 'Oh, they're [the ballets] not worth anything.'"[58] But the IRS agent disagreed, and after the requisite haggling over some ballets that could arguably last more than the predicted five years, all parties settled on an agreement: the official taxable value of the estate was pegged at $1,192,086; the federal tax was estimated at $300,562, and the New York State tax at $69,787.80.[59] In hindsight, it is now clear that the IRS agent "could well have justified increasing the assessment ten-fold" given the increased, rather than decreased, demand for performances of Balanchine's works.[60] But that is only part of the reason why Balanchine's estate now commands a fortune.

The consolidation of intellectual property rights in Balanchine's choreography occurred largely through the efforts of Horgan and von Aroldingen. The two women, following the advice of Paul H. Epstein, the attorney for Balanchine's estate, established the Balanchine Trust, into which they deposited the ballet rights that had been bequeathed to them, and invited other legatees to join them.[61] The goal, ostensibly, was to create order. "With fourteen legatees, the prospect of administrative chaos loomed, whereas a centralized entity could facilitate the licensing of the ballets, foster their dissemination throughout the world, and make sure that performances would be authentic and of satisfactory quality."[62] Patricia McBride and Rosemary Dunleavy joined the trust; Tanaquil Le Clercq chose not to, but requested Horgan, as trustee-administrator of the estate, to represent her. The Trust went into effect on March 30, 1987.

Nevertheless, tensions between the Balanchine Trust and the New York City Ballet Company continued to simmer. Using various legal theories, the board of the New York City Ballet Company tried to gain some control over Balanchine's ballets. One theory was that because Balanchine was actually an employee of the New York City Ballet Company, his choreographic productions belonged to the company, since he had done them on company time, and used company resources (i.e., the dancers).[63] Another theory was that the company was at least "owed" coownership of the choreographic productions.[64] Yet another was that the company had at least a proprietary (which Horgan humorously inadvertently renamed "predatory") right to perform these ballets as it desired.[65] Despite Randal J. Craft, Jr.'s (the New York City Ballet Company's board's counsel) seeking legal advice from two firms experienced in entertainment law and copyright law, the board's efforts to wrest some control over Balanchine's ballets were ineffectual.[66] After months of threats to sue, Horgan in turn threatened to hold a press conference; the board amicably dropped its legal claims.[67] Ultimately, painstaking negotiations resulted in a mutually satisfactory licensing agreement between the company and the Balanchine Trust.[68] Briefly described:

> The agreement recognized that the New York City Ballet was . . . entitled to special status and consideration. In return for a stipulated blanket fee, the five-year agreement gave the company the right to perform any or all ballets owned or represented by the trust. The company was also given the right to use Balanchine's name in fund raising—a right not allowed to other companies—and to limit and thus prevent competing Balanchine ballet performances by visiting companies. Equivalent agreements were worked out at the same time with Le Clercq and other legatees not represented by the trust.[69]

That licensing agreement expired in July, 1992, but appears to have cemented a lasting cooperation between the company and the trust as the agreement was quickly renewed for another five years.[70] To quote the board's Randal Craft's satisfaction with the agreement: "Anybody who wants to see the Balanchine repertory continue as a meaningful, coherent body of work has got to want City Ballet to continue to perform these ballets, and that's what we bank on. They [the Balanchine Trust and the legatees] . . . recognize that as well as we do."[71]

Horgan v. MacMillan: Choreography and Copyright Infringement

Since Balanchine's choreographic works were now legally delimited from the public domain, heirs of his intellectual property had to be vigilant to ensure that their newly acquired rights would not be violated. One such protective action, which resulted in a landmark copyright infringement case, *Horgan v. McMillan*,[72] was initiated in response to MacMillan's publication of a book, *The Nutcracker: A Story & A Ballet*, authored by Ellen Switzer, which had photographs of Balanchine's version of *The Nutcracker*.[73] The New York City Ballet Company's "official photographers" took the photographs, and the company, and its unions, as well as individual dancers, had granted permission to use the images.[74] Briefly summarized, Horgan, as the executor of Balanchine's estate, sought to block publication of the book by suing in the Federal District Court of New York on grounds of copyright infringement.[75] The district court ruled that because dance is an art of motion, still photographs, which capture static images, could not constitute copyright infringement, since they could not sufficiently capture motion and thus, could not provide a basis for infringement.[76] Undeterred, Horgan appealed and this time, won.[77] The appellate court held that the district court had applied the wrong test[78] and reversed and remanded.[79] According to Chief Judge Wilfred Feinberg, the correct test to apply is "not whether the original could be re-created from the allegedly infringing copy, but whether the latter is 'substantially similar' to the former."[80] The purpose of this section is to analyze both decisions,[81] not only in terms of their formal legal content, but also in view of their rhetorical construction. Ultimately, the chapter examines how the notion of whiteness-as-status property, while not overtly discussed by the Appellate Court, is a factor in the outcome of that decision.

Horgan I: The Reproducibility Test

The first decision, stated by District Judge Owen, is short and concise. Briefly, the judge began with a definition of what choreography is, in relation to the specific issue at stake: "the flow of steps in the ballet."[82] Since the still photographs in the book simply "catch dancers in various attitudes at specific instants in time[,] they do not, nor do they intend to, take or use the underlying choreography."[83] Thus, the judge concluded that the photographs, though "numerous,"[84] could not be used to recreate the staged performance, much as "a Beethoven symphony could not be recreated from a document containing only every twenty-fifth chord of the symphony."[85] Furthermore, the judge also concluded that Balanchine's right to be free from publicity was not being violated because of Balanchine's status as a public figure and because the judge did not get "the sense [that the book was]...published for trade and advertising purposes."[86] Finally, the judge delayed Horgan's request for a preliminary injunction because the plaintiff had "unduly delayed in seeking the claimed relief."[87] That is, although Horgan knew of MacMillan's intent to publish the book as early as May, 1985, the estate did not file a claim until November of the same year.

Rhetorically, *Horgan I*'s opinion is remarkable for its paucity. The judge very briefly described the ballet almost as if it were a run-of-the-mill production: "Each Christmas, the New York City Ballet features the ballet."[88] Furthermore, the judge attributed copyright credit for the production not only to Balanchine, but also Tsaichovsky (for the music), Rouben Ter-Arutunian (for the scenery and lighting), and Karinska (for the costumes).[89] Despite the nod to Balanchine's reputation as a "world-renowned choreographer,"[90] the judge clearly thought that the staging of a ballet production entailed far more than choreography, and thus, granting a blanket prohibition against any representational rights of the ballet might give Balanchine's estate too much control.

Horgan II: The "Substantial Similarity" Test

When the issue was revisited at the appellate level, the Court this time gave the facts a thorough review before stating the basis for its opinion of reversing and remanding. This time, photographers Steven Caras and Costas were identified, and the number of photos was specified: 60.[91] In addition, this time, the Court unambiguously condemned the lower court's decision as using the wrong legal standard, and "strongly" suggested that "any further hearing on the preliminary injunction be consolidated with consideration for the claim for permanent injunctive relief."[92] While the Court's instructions could be seen as simply maximizing efficiency, the emphatic phrasing used also showed the Court's determination to buttress its opinion as the final word on the matter.

Rhetorically, the facts as presented were set up to showcase Balanchine's dominance as an artist, and therefore, to justify more stringent measures in delimiting Balanchine's choreographic works apart from the public domain, which cannot be protected. The Court, citing Bernard Taper's biography,[93] now described Balanchine as a "genius," and an "artist of the same magnitude as Picasso."[94] This time, no mention was made of the artists responsible for costume design and lighting. Rather, the opinion cited Tsaichovsky[95] as the composer of the music used, along with two unprotected works (in the United States), as prior material from which Balanchine borrowed elements to create his ballet: E. T. A. Hoffman's nineteenth-century folk tale, "The Nutcracker and the Mouse King," and Russian choreographer Ivanov's earlier balletic rendition of the story.[96]

The Court did acknowledge that there was some dispute on the extent of Balanchine's "borrowing" from Hoffman and Ivanov,[97] but did not dally there. Instead, the Court immediately emphasized how the Balanchine rendition of the *Nutcracker* story, performed for the past 30 years by the New York City Ballet Company (with Balanchine as its director, ballet master and chief choreographer until 1983, when he passed away) had become a "classic."[98] In addition, the Court pointed out that both the New York City Ballet, and other companies, all pay royalties to Balanchine's estate,[99] showing the estate's dominance in the ownership of Balanchine's intellectual property. Finally, the Court gave a detailed account of how Balanchine's choreography came to be copyrighted, and how Horgan came to be one of his legitimate heirs and the executor of the estate:

> In December 1981, Balanchine registered his claim to copyright in the choreography of The Nutcracker [sic] with the United States Copyright Office. As part of this claim, he deposited with the Copyright Office a videotape of a New York City Ballet Company dress rehearsal of the ballet. Under Balanchine's will, which is presently in administration, all media, performance and other rights in The Nutcracker [sic] were left to certain legatees, including Ms. Horgan, who was his personal assistant at the New York City Ballet for 20 years.[100]

Rhetorically, the facts were already stacked up to show that Balanchine's choreography had already passed from the anonymous, nonpublished, unfixed realm of the public domain into the recognizable, published and delimitable realm of the copyrighted. The Court's description of the history of how Balanchine's choreographic materials became copyrighted emphasized the requirements for copyright protection: publication (through a 30-year history of well-known public performances by an internationally renowned ballet company, closely associated with Balanchine) and fixation (through the videotape, which was deposited with the Copyright Office). Finally, the reference to Balanchine's will, which had been unsealed and was being enforced by its appointed executor, personally handpicked by Balanchine himself, sealed the now-obvious argument that Balanchine's choreography legitimately deserved strong protection from infringement. Balanchine was no longer simply a "world renowned" choreographer, but more importantly, a "genius" comparable to Picasso. What better rhetorical proof was there that Balanchine's choreography, along its hyperwhitened feminine aesthetic, had now crossed into the whitened realm of status property?

Then the Court turned to outlining the facts of particular relevance to the issues on appeal. The photos germane to the dispute were the 60 photographs taken by Caras and Costas, which were interspersed with Switzer's description of the story, some parts of which were not visually portrayed. The Court drew attention to Caras and Costas' status as "official photographers," which in this context, using Horgan's description, simply meant that "Balanchine authorized them to take photographs of the Company, some of which might be purchased by the Company for publicity and related purposes."[101] Similarly, Switzer, a freelance journalist, had access to the performers (for her interviews in the book) only because an unnamed press liaison to the Company had granted Switzer permission and backstage entry to interview the dancers.[102] Finally, the Court also pointed out that Horgan and her counsel, after reading the galleys of the book, gave notice three times (April 3, April 15, and October 8, 1985) to MacMillan. The first letter asked MacMillan to withhold publication until "appropriate licenses" were in place.[103] The second letter advised MacMillan that Balanchine's estate was not willing to grant the licenses.[104] The third letter clearly indicated that publication of the book, in the estate's eyes, would constitute a "willful violation of the rights of the Estate."[105] Thus, the facts, as recounted by the Court, already delegitimated Switzer's text and Caras and Costas' photographs as "original" work that deserved protection because the only reason they were able to produce these materials was because they were given special dispensation by Balanchine's estate and its agents—and such permission was not meant to be abused. Furthermore, that Balanchine's estate had given repeated notice strengthened the argument that publication of the book was a flagrant and willful violation of the copyright owned by the estate.

From here on, the Court's remaining rhetorical task was simply to justify its decision for reversing and remanding. This time, the Court did not rely upon an arbitrary "intuition" about choreography entailing a "flow of movement" but instead cited, in depth, *Compendium II*'s (1984) definition:

> Choreography is the composition and arrangement of dance movements and patterns, and is usually intended to be accompanied by music. Dance is *static* [emphasis added] and kinetic successions of bodily movement in certain rhythmic and spatial relationships. Choreographic works need not tell a story in order to be protected by copyright.[106]

The Court's noting of "static and kinetic successions of bodily movement" opened the door for photographs infringing upon Balanchine's copyright because photographs freeze movement into still poses, which could, under *Compendium II*'s definition, be a protected element of choreography. Additionally, for supplementary guidance, the Court cited Section 450.01 of *Compendium II*, under "Characteristics of choreographic works:" "Choreography represents a related series of dance movements and patterns organized into coherent whole."[107] This characterization added justification for protecting the whole ballet, rather than segmenting it into parts (e.g., choreography versus music, costumes, lighting, etc.). Furthermore, the Court distinguished between either social dance steps, folk dance steps or individual ballet steps, which are in the public domain and can be used as raw material by anyone, and copyrightable/copyrighted material, such as Balanchine's choreography (and its hyperwhitened feminine aesthetic), which were set apart from the public domain.

Then came the crux of the matter. The estate claimed that the book was an unauthorized "copy" of Balanchine's work because it "portray[ed] the essence of the Balanchine *Nutcracker*."[108] Alternatively, the estate also claimed that the book was "derivative," meaning it was based on preexisting copyrighted work.[109] In contrast, the appellee, citing the court below, focused on Balanchine's reliance on prior-existing works already in the public domain and the photos' use of "nonchoreographic" aspects of the production, such as costuming and lighting.[110] Furthermore, the appellees echoed the lower court's opinion that because the central characteristic of choreography is movement, and a photograph only captures a fraction of an instant, "even the combined effect of 60 color photographs does not reproduce the choreography itself, nor does it provide sufficient details of movement to enable a choreographic work to be reproduced from the photographs."[111]

To resolve the dispute, the Court rejected the district court's test for infringement and substituted its own: "not whether the original work may be reproduced from the copy . . . but whether the alleged copy is substantially similar to the original."[112] That test, explained by Judge Learned Hand, was "whether 'the ordinary observer, unless he set out to detect the disparities, would be disposed to overlook them, and regard their aesthetic appeal as the same.'"[113] Furthermore, though the Court acknowledged that when the allegedly infringing material is in a different medium, "recreation of the original from the infringing material is unlikely if not impossible,"[114] the Court also firmly stated that that is not an automatic, affirmative defense.[115] Even more strongly, the Court cautioned that even a minimal amount of copying, if it were "qualitatively significant,"[116] could be sufficient to constitute copyright infringement, even if the original could not be reproduced from the copies. As analogies, the Court cited a hypothetical and two cases. The first was the "Gone with the Wind" hypothetical, phrased as a rhetorical question—that it would surely not be a defense against infringement that one could not reproduce the book from the movie.[117] Second, as instructive but not binding precedent, the Court cited two cases: the employment of short clips used in a film memorial to Charlie Chaplin was held to infringe full length films,[118] and the use of a mere four notes from a musical composition composed of 100 measures was sufficient for copyright infringement of the original.[119]

More crucially, the Court argued against a "limited" or literal way of viewing photographs as depicting merely a fraction of an instant. Rather, it argued for a more expansive interpretation:

> A snapshot of a single moment in a dance sequence may communicate a great deal... a gesture, the composition of the dancers' bodies or the placement of the dancers on the stage... A photograph may also convey to the viewer's imagination the moments before and after the split second recorded... The single instant thus communicates far more than a single chord of a Beethoven symphony—an analogy suggested by the district Judge.[120]

Using that standard, the Court found numerous examples of copyright infringement of Balanchine's choreography in Switzer's book. The Court identified photographs 30, 38, 42, 66–67, 68, 69, 74, 75, 78, 80, 81[121] as examples of photographs that "fr[oze the]... choreographic moment," thus "capturing a gesture," revealing "the composition of dancers' bodies," and the dancers' "placement" onstage.[122] Additionally, the Court took the time to explain, in some detail, why a two-page photograph of the "Sugar Canes," one of the troupes to perform in Balanchine's *Nutcracker*, was a clear infringement.

> One member of the ensemble is jumping through a hoop, which is held extended above the dancer. The dancer's legs are thrust forward, parallel to the stage and several feet off the ground. The viewer understands instinctively, based simply on the laws of gravity, that the Sugar Canes jumped up from the floor only a moment earlier, and came down shortly after the photographed moment. An ordinary observer, who had only recently seen a performance of The Nutcracker, could probably perceive even more from this photograph.[123]

Interestingly, the "ordinary observer," for both the ballet and the Switzer book, would have been a child, not an adult, as the target market for both were children. Nevertheless, the Court did acknowledge that a number of issues needed to be worked out: the "validity" of Balanchine's copyright (as the appellees questioned the scope of the applicability of Balanchine's copyright, which failed to mention preexisting material[124] from Hoffman, for example); the amount of "original" material in Balanchine's choreography (as opposed to Ivanov's) in both the New York City Ballet Company's performance of the ballet and the photographs;[125] and the confusion spawned by "the overlapping propriety rights of Balanchine's estate, the New York City Ballet Company, and the 'official photographers,' including defendants Caras and Costas."[126] Nevertheless, the Court ruled in favor of Balanchine's estate on the remaining issue (the injunction), and did not consider the estate's delay in filing for an injunction as rising to the level of laches and therefore a bar to a permanent injunction.

Horgan II thus completely reversed *Horgan I*. Where *Horgan I* effectively left Balanchine's estate with no control over photographic reproductions of the choreography, *Horgan II* left absolute control of photographic materials of Balanchine's ballets in the hands of Balanchine's estate. Indeed, it is difficult to think of an exception that lies beyond *Horgan II*'s characterization of the "substantial similarity" test as applied to Caras and Costas' photographs of the New York City Ballet's presentation of Balanchine's *Nutcracker* choreography. Balanchine's aesthetic of hyperfeminized whiteness in ballet thus becomes enshrined, both culturally and legally, as the paradigmatic case of the unimpeachably copyrightable. It is a (foreign) white male's vision of choreographic production (with its gendered and raced economy of performative duties) that becomes enshrined as the standard for copyrightability, or as the bearer of whiteness as status property in American dance choreography.

Fuller and Balanchine, and the Evolution of Whiteness as Status Property in Choreography

Fuller's and Balanchine's portraits as pioneers of American dance could not be more contrastively drawn. Fuller initially struggled to create an identity for herself as the creator of the skirt dance and to gain adequate financial compensation. Fuller also had to fill a variety of roles, in addition to choreographer and dancer; she created her own costumes, designed and patented the lights, planned the staging of the movements onstage, did her own self-promotions. Fuller attempted to gain copyright protection, only to have her work dismissed as "mere spectacle," devoid of any moral purpose that could further science or the arts.

In contrast, Balanchine, with his classical Russian training, had the financial support of Kerstein, and as such, skipped over many of the steps Fuller struggled through, to gain reputability. From the start of his move to

America in 1933, Balanchine had a school of pliant young dancers whose flesh and spirits he could shape to his choreographic designs without fear of them becoming his competitors, and a support staff who could take care of the other production-related tasks, such as lighting, costuming, and publicity. In addition, ballet, unlike skirt dancing, had a long-established tradition of being a dance form of the higher classes, regarded as a "classic" art form. Ballet, unlike skirt dancing, also had a long-established tradition of having a dominant, tyrannical male ballet master, which further cemented Balanchine's authoritative position.

This is not to say Balanchine did not undergo difficulty; his life appears to have been composed of successive seasons of feast and famine, with ballet companies ephemerally rising and expiring around him. Balanchine, unlike Fuller, lived for the present and was not bothered by the thought of his ballets passing into obscurity, much like beautiful butterflies that were spectacular at the height of their glory, but swiftly passed away. In contrast, Fuller's every act seemed focused on creating a memorial for herself that would withstand the test of time. Her savviness in negotiating legal hurdles (even submitting a detailed description of the skirt dance in her failed infringement claim), ironically, did nothing to ensure her success at acquiring copyright protection.

Given these differences in personality, it is ironic that it is Balanchine who succeeded where Fuller failed. Nevertheless, both Fuller and Balanchine were "stars," and part of the creation of their celebrity was their integration of a hyperwhitened aesthetic into their choreography. Fuller accomplished this through making her less-than-perfect body invisible, through the use of extended wooden wands, yards and yards of white silk, and the magic of lights. Balanchine accomplished the same task through hyperdisciplining his dancers' bodies, whom he carefully chose, to become the vessels of his artistic ideal: the embodiments of the all too romantic vision of the feminine-as-eternally-fleeing; young women chiseled down to such thinness so as to become virtually evanescent; marble princesses, with skins like "peeled apples," devoid of aging and infirmity. While Fuller produced no heir and until recently, was not recognized as a pioneer of modern dance, Balanchine's legacy, both culturally and legally, is now very well entrenched. Thus, Balanchine's estate not only commands the royalties to choreographic productions licensed to 150 ballet companies worldwide,[127] but now also possesses the trademarks of Balanchine's style and technique and even his name.[128] To be able to perform a ballet, a company representative has to have a consultation with the particular ballet's legatee concerning consent, terms, who should be recommended to do the staging, and any other special conditions; if the recommended stager does not think the company can do the work justice, the company will not acquire the license to perform it.[129] Finally, so absolute is the estate's control over Balanchine's choreography and even name that it now can also compel companies who perform Balanchine's ballets to include a trademark and licensing notice in their programs.[130]

In retrospect, the history of American modern dance, using Fuller and Balanchine as virtual bookends, in relation to the possession of whiteness as (artistic and legal) status property resembles Bruno Latour's characterization of the history of science as composed, rhetorically, of two phases: "hot science"/"science in the making," when the boundaries separating "real" science and emergent sciences are not yet fixed, and science in its "cold" phase/"ready-made science," when a science has now achieved respectability and authority.[131] Similarly, in Fuller's case, the boundaries separating "art" from the "burlesque" were porous, whereas in Balanchine's case, at least by *Horgan II*, balletic choreographic productions (not necessarily tied to narrative) were so clearly "art" that they could be passed on as heritable assets, and deserved broad legal protection as copyrighted materials. Crucial to the metamorphic process of making choreography copyrightable was the formation of the reputability of a recognizable aesthetic of whiteness, as imbricated with other factors, such as gender, class, race, nationality, and physical embodiment.

Another framework that could be of use, as an analogy, would be Kuhn's characterization of a "paradigm" (roughly translated, a worldview, requiring a problem-solving method and a community of practitioners)[132] and the shift across paradigms, such as the shift from the Creationist-Fixism to Darwinian Evolutionism. During Fuller's time, the dominant legal paradigm was that choreography of abstract works was mere "spectacle," devoid of anything that would further artistic or scientific advancements; by the time Balanchine was ready to pass on his balletic choreographic works as assets that his heirs could profit from, a different legal paradigm was in place. By the time Balanchine applied for copyright protection, his choreography, especially as steeped in traditions of classical ballet, already embodied the hyperwhitened aesthetic that began with Fuller's abstract expressionism, that it had already passed scrutiny as status property in cultural terms. Thus, the 1976 Copyright Act simply gave formal legal recognition to what was already an established cultural-artistic paradigm, steeped in a hyperwhitened aesthetic. The picture that results from this analysis, in broad strokes, is a proverbial tango between copyright and choreography—with a moment of repulsion instantiated in Fuller's legal rejection, and a moment of attraction instantiated in Balanchine's legal triumph. That tango between copyright and choreography continues in other areas.

Chapter 5

Martha Graham, "Picasso of American Dance," and Katherine Dunham, "Matriarch of Black Dance": Exoticism and Nonwhiteness in American Dance*

Graham's Artistic Immortality

Introduction

The significance of the prior chapter lies in that it is with Balanchine that choreography first gained copyright protection; it is thus important to understand why Balanchine succeeded where Fuller failed, even if they both partook of an aesthetic of whiteness (one of whose defining traits, as earlier chapters show, is abstraction). Furthermore, as I will show in the first part of this chapter, although Graham, following Balanchine, was able to gain copyright protection of her choreographic works, her estate, unlike Balanchine's, was not able to maintain control of her creations. The idea that ownership of choreographic works could be wrested away from the chosen heir of the choreographer was alarming to many in the dance community, and has resulted in dance circles and legal communities becoming more aware of contractual provisions and their effects.[1]

This chapter builds from the prior chapter, which analyzed how whiteness as status property functioned in Balanchine's rise to stardom as a "genius," enshrining his hyperwhitened feminine aesthetic as the iconic look of American modern ballet. That hyperwhitened aesthetic and Balanchine's authority as a white male ballet master helped delimit his choreography as copyrightable, and therefore, worthy of protection from infringement. The first part of this chapter discusses how Martha Graham's reputation as an "exotic" white woman helped cement her power as a choreographer. However, whiteness as status property functioned refractorily in her case, and unlike Balanchine's heirs, Graham's heir was unable to maintain unchallenged control over Graham's choreographic creations.

Graham's "Exotic" Whiteness

That Martha Graham rivaled Balanchine in reputational capital is not debatable. Her influence on modern dance has been compared to Picasso's on modern painting, Stravinsky's on modern music, and Frank Lloyd Wright's on architecture.[2] The list of her students reads like a "Who's Who" of modern dance; to name a few, Alvin Ailey, Twyla Tharp, Paul Taylor, Merce Cunningham.[3] She collaborated with equally successful

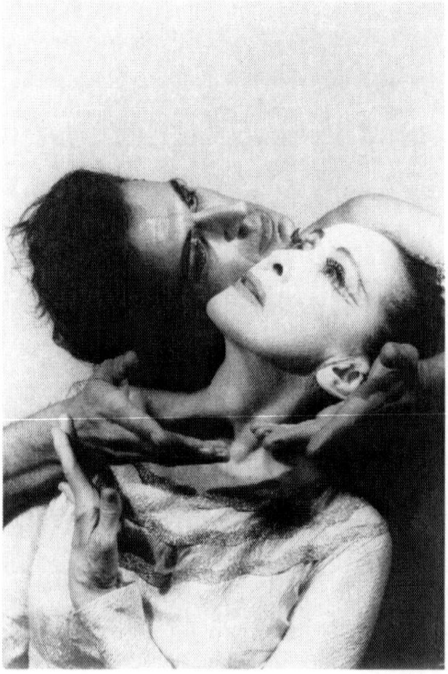

Figure 5.1 Public Domain Image of Martha Graham and Bertram Ross. From the Library of Congress. http://www.loc.gov/pictures/resource/van.5a52055/.

contemporary artists, such as composer Aaron Copland, sculptor Isamu Noguchi,[4] and ballet choreographer, George Balanchine.[5]

Like Balanchine, at the height of her powers, Graham had incredible control over her dancers. Actress Bette Davis, one of her former students, never forgot the incredible presence of her teacher: "I worshipped her. She was all tension—lightning. Her burning dedication gave her spare body the power of ten men."[6] Jane Dudley, another of her dancers, spoke of Graham as if she were an untiring army drill sergeant: "Martha was absolutely merciless. I never 'walked' [expended less than what is required for full performance] anything."[7] Yet Graham was also known for using shock tactics to achieve the effects she wanted, often using sexual sentences, sometimes charged with cruelty, to make a point.

> With one girl who was not doing one of the floor exercises correctly, she spread the girl's legs and said, "Some day a man will do this to you and you'll remember it." The girl was shattered and stayed away from class for some time. To another girl, who never seemed able to do as well onstage as she did in the studio, Graham said, "I won't have virgins in my Company. I don't care if you have to stand on a street corner to get a man."[8]

All these details are important to show that although Graham was a woman, she essentially occupied a very similar revered (empowered) space, in relation to the dancers she trained, as Balanchine generally did, in relation to his students. Graham was in effect masculinized (especially when her company was composed purely of women) relative to her dance troupe, and there was no essential difference, in terms of the authorial space she occupied (or the status she possessed as a white woman who created her own works), between herself and her dancers, as Balanchine, in relation to his. Whether or not one agreed with Graham's teaching methods, what was clear was that Graham disciplined and rigorously trained her dancers enough to become soloists, yet she ironically kept them in tightly bound formations that "ignored an individual dancer's special qualities."[9] In her ideal world, they were the tableau of highly ordered bodies that supported, surrounded, and showcased her genius and stardom.

Martha Graham was born in Allegheny, Pennsylvania in 1894;[10] she was the eldest daughter of George Greenfield Graham, a family doctor who had worked in a mental hospital, and taught his daughter that "movement never lies."[11] Graham was to take her father's insight regarding primeval emotions manifesting themselves through involuntary movement into an entirely new way of dancing—one radically opposed to the conventions of classical ballet. Unlike Balanchine's ballerinas who soared and defied gravity, Graham's dancers embraced the pull of gravity.[12] Ballerinas wore tight toe-shoes to keep them elevated, enhancing the illusion of their ethereality and weightlessness. In contrast, Graham's dancers danced barefoot and did not conceal their corporeality or the effort of movement; falling was simply one direction of movement for them.[13] Like her father, Graham was fascinated by the inner emotional landscape, which she sought to portray through angular, explicitly sexual, and even violently disjunctive movements. At the heart of her choreography were the principles of "contraction" and "release"—an enhanced study of the mechanics of breathing.[14]

Yet to understand why Graham became a legend, and how whiteness as status property functioned refractorily in the establishment of her legacy, one has to return to her roots as a dancer. Graham auditioned at the Denishawn School of Dance when she was 22—impossibly "old" for an aspiring dancer, especially one untrained in ballet. Outwardly, she did not seem destined for greatness: she was short, serious looking, and slightly plump.[15] Her idol, Ruth St. Denis, one of the founders of Denishawn, agreed to her enrollment purely for pecuniary purposes and relegated her tutelage to her husband, Ted Shawn.[16]

Fortunately, Shawn noticed and appreciated what St. Denis did not: not only Graham's fierce determination to succeed, but also her adeptness at mastering difficult choreographic sequences.[17] Shawn also helped cement Graham's reputation as an "exotic" white woman—that is, a white woman who could effectively masquerade as an "exotic" woman while remaining recognizably white. Shawn thought of Graham as a "beautiful but untamed little black panther;"[18] thus, Shawn cast Graham as Xochitl, an Aztec maiden whom a drunken emperor (Shawn) tried to rape.[19] Graham's ferocious and impassioned performance was a success (often leading to bruised and bleeding lips, for her leading men);[20] a star was born, and Graham's appetite for violently physical performances became part of her artistic identity.

In 1923, eight years after she had joined Denishawn, Graham was ready to leave the company, partly because St. Denis, the woman she idolized, had begun to view Graham as a competitor and had begun to, for a while, appropriate Graham's successful numbers for herself—even the part of Xochitl.[21] In 1923, Graham accepted a job with the Greenwich Village Follies and began to design and choreograph her own dances; she became a Broadway star overnight and earned $350 a week, which was a high salary at that time.[22] Nevertheless, Graham was unsatisfied by the constraints of the entertainer's route, and she longed for greater independence; there is a great deal of documentary evidence that Graham sought to insulate herself from any popular cultural influences and to differentiate herself as an "artist" rather than a "showgirl"[23]—a stance she was infamous for during her employment with the *Follies*, and which continued all throughout her career. Graham eventually accepted a position with the Eastman School of Music, which left her free to begin her experimentations in dance choreography with selected students.[24] Beginning with her Eastman students, Graham eventually founded the now famous Martha Graham School for Contemporary Dance in New York.[25]

Although Graham was eventually to rebel against her Denishawn roots, it is clear that many of her later choreographic creations still drew from Denishawn's fascination with the exotic, and its colonial imagination of the "mysterious" cultures of the Near and Far East, ancient India, and the Americas.[26] Nevertheless, this obsession with the East had nothing to do with what those ancient cultures were actually like and was a Romanticized mirage[27]—one "[s]umptuously costumed, bedecked and bejeweled, [drawing on] the 'lore of the ancients . . . wrap[ped] in clouds of sexy secrets.'"[28] Particularly as embodied in its central icon, Ruth St. Denis, the Denishawn style appropriated the mysterious but highly sexualized allure of the "exotic" and combined it with a hyperwhitened aesthetic similar to Balanchine's ideal. However, because Graham did not have St. Denis' "Northern European peaches-and-cream blonde" looks,[29] and her high cheekbones made her look, to Shawn, "exotic,"[30] Graham was the perfect vessel for the more primal, emotionally ferocious, physically demanding roles Shawn cast her in.

It is that hybrid identity of the "exotic" and "white" that Graham carried into her future roles as both performer and choreographer. Indeed, Graham's later creations drew from her interpretations of Native American, Egyptian, Cambodian, Indian, and Japanese dances.[31] And when she chose to cast herself in "nonexotic" roles, it was clear that she composed with herself at the center of the stage; as she began to struggle with aging, she reluctantly decided she could no longer hold center stage without the support of a surrounding cast of dancers, as in *The Triumph of St. Joan*, staged in 1951.[32] Like Balanchine, Graham fought ferociously against her mortality; it took a rebellion from her own dancers, demanding the right to perform without her, to finally begin to accept that her performing days were over.[33] In 1969, at the age of 75, Graham performed for the last time and reluctantly announced her retirement.[34] After that, her dances no longer had a strong central figure; Graham found it unbearable "to place in the body of another dancer the same movements and roles she once would have brought to life herself."[35] Yet she knew that to attain the legacy she desired (and to ensure the survival of her work), she would need to release her choreography to younger dancers.

The toll of giving up dancing, combined with her abandonment by her former husband and dance partner, Erick Hawkins,[36] along with years of alcoholism, made Graham sink into severe depression.[37] It was during this period of recovery from illness and depression (involving a series of relapses) that Ron Protas, a former Columbia University law student, with no theatrical or dance background, became indispensable to Martha.[38]

> From the day of the oxygen salvation, Protas made it his business to become indispensable to Martha, life-giving, life-sustaining... to be everything to her—her nurse, her dresser, her housekeeper... He became her business manager, her adviser, her counselor, her advocate... Protas was all.[39]

In 1972, three years after her last public performance, Graham announced that she was reemerging as director of her company.[40] Sadly, in her new reincarnation, Graham trusted no one but Protas, who proceeded further to isolate her from anyone who might have any influence on her.[41] Because of Protas' dedication to her, Graham decided to name him as her heir. She bequeathed to Protas the rights and interests to her "dance works, musical scores, scenery sets, [Graham's] personal papers and the use of [Graham's] name."[42] And this is where a three-year legal battle over ownership of Graham's works began. But such a battle was not possible without Graham's choreographic works being converted and fixed into valuable intellectual property, buttressed by her star power as a white "exotic" woman.

Martha Graham School and Dance Foundation, Inc. v. Martha Graham Center of Contemporary Dance, Inc.: *The Work for Hire Doctrine*

Graham's Dilemma: Funding Creativity

Graham, much like her teachers, Ruth St, Denis and Ted Shawn, found that artistic creativity needs a financial base. In 1930, Graham opened a dance school, which she operated as a sole proprietorship until 1956.[43] Yet opening the school did not prove a lasting solution; Graham still found herself trapped by the dilemma of whether to spend her time on financial and administrative affairs or on creative artistic experimentation. Graham turned to what must have seemed an ideal solution: she chose to seek funding from nonprofit corporations in the 1940's, thus freeing her from the worries of financing her art.[44] In 1948, the Martha Graham Center of Contemporary Dance ("the Center"), which was initially called the Martha Graham Foundation for Contemporary Dance, was incorporated.[45] Shortly thereafter, the Martha Graham School of Dance ("the School") was incorporated in 1956.[46] The Center and the School were essentially the same entity because they had the same board of directors, used the same facilities, shared bank accounts, and combined tax statements.[47] Simultaneously, both the Center and other nonprofits financed Graham's activities by "promoting and disseminating her technique and by raising and managing funds for performances."[48]

In 1956, Graham sold her sole proprietorship to the School;[49] simultaneously, she signed a ten-year (1956–1966) part-time employment contract to serve as the Program Director of the School.[50] The contract required that Graham simply provide the School with "one-third of her professional time,"[51] and specified teaching and administrative duties,[52] but not choreography. Because of additional subsidy from other nonprofit organizations, Graham was able to both teach and choreograph.[53] In 1966, the School renewed its ten-year contract with Graham, but this time, changed her appointment to Artistic Director, and due to financial contingencies, added new duties, such as choreographing new work, overseeing the repertory, rehearsing the company, and supervising the school.[54] The Center credibly testified that it is during this period that there was a tacit agreement between Graham and the board of directors that the Center owned any new choreographed pieces Graham produced, since choreography was listed as one of duties the contract specified; furthermore, Graham received a regular salary, with tax deductions withheld, as a regular employee.[55] Because her contract was renewed indefinitely in 1976, Graham remained the Artistic Director and Chief Executive of both the School and the Center until she passed away in 1991.[56]

The Effect of Graham's Death: The Battle over Ownership of Graham's Choreographic Works

After Graham's death in 1991, Protas was promoted from Co-Associate Artistic Director to Artistic Director of the Center, replacing Graham at the helm.[57] Seven years later, in 1998, Protas created the Martha Graham Trust ("the Trust"), to which he transferred the copyrights to Graham's choreographic works; the board did not contest the transfer though donors applied pressure on the board to dislodge Protas from his post.[58] Not long after, "Protas, . . . through the Trust, founded the [nonprofit] Martha Graham School and Dance Foundation ('S&D Foundation')."[59] The Trust licensed many of Graham's dances; in 1999, it granted the Center "an exclusive license to teach the Martha Graham technique, and a nonexclusive license to present live performances"[60] of Graham's choreographic works. As a condition of this agreement, Protas would step down from being the Artistic Director but remain a salaried employee, as Artistic Consultant, of the Center.[61] In 2000, Protas and the board vehemently disagreed regarding the viability of a new Artistic Director; and the Center's financial troubles deepened, forcing them to suspend operations.[62]

From 2000 to 2001, both Protas and the Center independently got copyright certificates of registration for Martha Graham's 30 choreographed works.[63] However, the S&D Foundation, controlled by Protas, was the exclusive American licensee for performances of Graham's choreography and the exploitation of the Martha Graham trademark.[64] Nevertheless, in 2001, the Center was able to reopen due to financial support.[65] Protas now launched a legal attack against his competitor for ownership over Graham's intellectual property. Based on Graham's will, he sought to enjoin the Center and the School from exploiting the Martha Graham trademark, using her dance techniques, and performing her choreography; even more emphatically, Protas sought a declaratory judgment that the Trust owned all the rights to Graham's dances, and the sets and jewelry associated with the performances of Graham's choreography.[66]

Briefly summarized, the central issue before the Southern District of New York was whether the Center owned any legitimate copyright to Graham's choreographic pieces.[67] Crucially, the court found that Protas had violated his "fiduciary duty of undivided loyalty to the Center and the School."[68] Yet most of the court's opinion hinged on whether Graham actually owned the copyright to her choreographic creations, and thus, could pass her ownership of these rights to her chosen heir, Protas. Ultimately, the district court ruled that by virtue of the contracts Graham had signed, the Center owned the copyright to 45 dances, while Protas' S&D Foundation owned the copyright to only one dance.[69] Regarding the remaining work, the court ruled that ten of the dances were in public domain and that nine were not yet published with the required notice; finally for five works, the court found that neither side had met the burden of proving the commissioner of the work (i.e., her employer) had intended that Graham reserve her copyright.[70]

On appeal, Protas claimed that the district court's decision was erroneous because none of Graham's dances was work for hire.[71] However, the Second Circuit affirmed most of the district court's opinion, finding that because the majority of Graham's choreographic creations were works for hire, the Center, and not Protas, owned the copyright to these works.[72] Nevertheless, the court reversed the district court's decision regarding the works Graham created between 1956 and 1965, finding that because Graham had simply been a part-time employee (with the creation of new choreographic works not one of her contracted duties), these particular pieces were not works for hire.[73] Additionally, the court reversed the ownership of one dance, *Acrobats of God*, granting that to Protas because he owned the renewal term of the copyright.[74] Ultimately, the court remanded the issue of determining ownership of seven dances published between 1956 and 1965 because two had been erroneously cited as unpublished.[75]

To determine whether Graham's choreographic pieces were works for hire, the Second Circuit applied the instance and expense test; in brief, the court held that Graham's status change from part-time employee to full-time employee rendered the choreography she produced from 1966 to 1977 works for hire.[76] By the same token, the dances created when Graham was Program Director, a part-time position, were not works for hire.[77] Although the court's reasoning seems logical, the court clearly had to struggle with justifying how the shift from part-time to a full-time status pragmatically changed anything, in terms of the "expense" prong (i.e., who had invested in/financed the development of the choreography); in both positions, Graham had access to the same dancers and rehearsal space.[78] Even more difficult to justify was the "instance" prong (who initiated or provided the impetus for the development of the choreographic works), which would require that the Center be the one that had insisted that the work be performed, and not Graham;[79] given Graham's leadership at the Center (and her passion for choreography as an end in itself), that was a position difficult to uphold.

It is striking that many of the arguments that wrested control over Graham's works away from her estate to the Center could equally have applied to Balanchine's estate, in its battle with the New York Ballet Company, and this is where it is Graham's sex that becomes a crucial factor, as revealed in the rhetoric of the courts' statements. Legally, such arguments, based on the 13 Reid factors (in brief, factors that help determine whether the person hired was an "employee" or an "independent contractor")[80] specified by the 1976 Copyright Act and upheld by case law,[81] focused on the degree of control the hiring party had over the "manner and means of creation"[82] of the work. The court's justification, that this is a situation where the employer would not "normally exercise control over the details,"[83] and that if any control exists, it "may be very attenuated,"[84] seems problematic. It is also difficult to imagine, given Graham's dominance (similar to Balanchine's), that at the time the contracts were signed, Graham and the Center intended to establish a clear master–servant relationship. Notwithstanding these issues, in conclusion, because of the court's interpretation of the work for hire doctrine, where Graham's estate failed to maintain control over her choreographic works, Balanchine's triumphed. Rhetorically, although the courts acknowledged that Graham was "extremely talented"[85] and a "great pioneer,"[86] they did not describe Graham's artistic stature as a choreographer in the same hyperbolic terms as they did, when describing Balanchine in *Horgan II*.[87] In other words, although the same arguments could have been made about the kind of relationship Balanchine had with the New York City Ballet, they were never raised in relation to his estate's claim of ownership of his choreographic works. The very idea of separating choreographic work from choreographer was inconceivable with Balanchine, as a (fully funded) white male ballet master, but it was possible, and actually rendered real, with Graham, a white female modern dance choreographer (whose artistic pursuits were always hounded by the threat of poverty). Nevertheless, crucial to the delimitation of both Balanchine's and Graham's choreographic works as intellectual property was their possession of whiteness as status property.

The next section examines whether Katherine Dunham, the "Matriarch of Black Dance," had access to whiteness as status property, given her liminal status as a highly educated anthropologist, with lightly complected skin and Caucasian features, and white husband. The answer is complex, as it is neither fully a "yes," nor an unambiguous "no."

Katherine Dunham: Matriarch of Black Dance

An Anthropologist with Hips

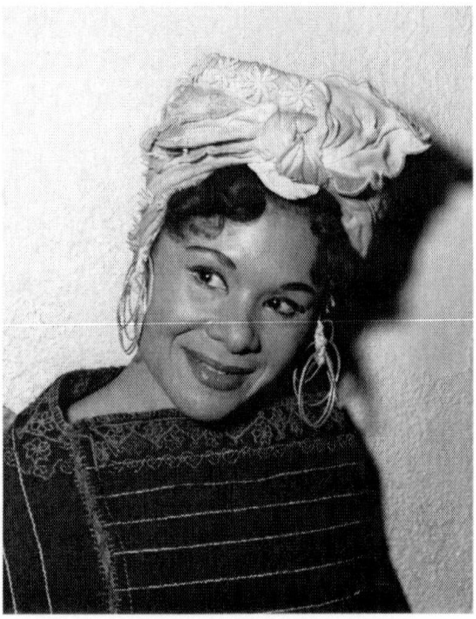

Figure 5.2 Public Domain Image of Katherine Dunham. From the Library of Congress. http://hdl.loc.gov/loc.pnp/ppmsca.05791.

Katherine Dunham's (1909–2006) most enduring informal title is probably as the venerable "Matriarch of Black Dance"[88]—the woman who established the first major modern black company in the United States, combining Afro-Caribbean, ballet, and modern dance techniques.[89] Yet when Dunham was at her peak of celebrity, especially given her international stardom (because like Fuller and Baker, Dunham found more financially lucrative stages to perform in Europe[90]), was called "an ambassador with hips."[91] And if Baker is rumored to have conquered Paris with her derriere, Dunham is said to have forged a dance-based Pan-Africanist community by "forging ties among peoples of the African diaspora"[92] through the eloquent use of her hips and legs. A photograph, snapped by F. S. Schiffer, of Katherine Dunham's famous legs (insured by Lloyds of London for $25,000[93]) reads in the back that Jean Cocteau claimed that "If we writers could say with our pens what Katherine Dunham says with her legs, our writings would be forbidden."[94]

Dunham's rise to celebrity coincided with Baker's decline[95] as the embodiment of the erotic and primal "savage" and Martha Graham's (among other white women) deployment of a then-principally sexless model of modern dancing (i.e., prior to her involvement with Erick Hawkins). In the face of these preexisting and often stereotyped and racialized templates, Dunham was unusual in her determination to include "African dance traditions that featured more forthright acceptance of sexual elements in dance."[96]

And indeed, Dunham's choreography and dance technique not only incorporated the "whitened" (and established) elements of ballet and modern dance, but also a vocabulary of movement that had clear "non-whitened" elements, derived from her fieldwork as an anthropologist in the West Indies (Jamaica, Trinidad, Cuba, Haiti, Martinique).[97] "What Dunham gave modern dance was a coherent lexicon of African and Caribbean styles of movement—a flexible torso and spine, articulated pelvis and isolation of the limbs, a polyrhythmic strategy of moving—which she integrated with techniques of ballet and modern dance."[98] Dunham's dance technique comes closest to the theoretical model, built on Cohen Bull's characterization of Ghanaian dance, of a nonwhite aesthetic I schematized in chapter 2. The technique she developed "emphasized the torso movements of the primitive ritual of Caribbean-African dance and jazz rhythms."[99]

Though Dunham self-identified herself as black and stated, as one of her goals, the aspiration "to [present] dark-skinned people in a manner delightful and acceptable to people who have never considered them as persons,"[100] Dunham was clearly of a mixed racial heritage. Dunham was born in Chicago, Illinois in 1909, the second child in Albert Millard Dunham's marriage to Fanny June Gillaume; according to Dunham's memoir, "her mother possessed Indian, French Canadian, English and probably African ancestry; her father descended from a union of a Malagasy (Madagascan) man and a West African woman."[101] Although Dunham and her brother, Albert Jr., grew up in relatively socially and racially integrated surroundings, where lower middle class families were more or less subject to the same kinds of pressures, Dunham did experience racism, both from within her extended family (as her mother's side was "nearly white"[102] and tended to treat her part-Indian grandmother and retarded half-brother, and her father's side of the family in general, with condescension[103]) and from the white neighborhoods her father sought to move his family into[104] because of his business as a tailor (though her father is painted also as an oppressor especially in relation to her brother[105]).

Dunham's dance background resembles Martha Graham's in that she started taking formal dance lessons comparatively late (probably her early 20s, according to one of her teachers, Mark Turbyfill). As he recalls: "It was in 1929 or 1930 when Mary introduced me to Katherine, but I recall feeling that there was perhaps something a little eccentric in my nature . . . that caused me to accept Mary Hunter's urgent request, namely that I undertake the training of an ambitious Negro girl, who had never had a lesson in her life on the art, but who wanted to become a ballet dancer."[106] In addition to Turbyfill, Dunham began to study ballet with Ludmilla Speranzeva, who had arrived in the United States via a Franco-Russian vaudeville performing group, the Chauve-Souris.[107] Speranzeva was one of the few ballet teachers (but also with some modern dance training) to agree to train black students as dancers,[108] and she ultimately encouraged Dunham to focus on modern dance rather than ballet.[109] Ruth Page, whom Mark Turbyfill invited to watch Dunham, during one of his private lessons with her, remarked that she would "never be a classical dancer" because she "had started too late."[110] But later, Page did recruit Dunham initially for a small part, and then later (in 1933),[111] because of a scheduling conflict requiring that she give up dancing the lead, Page recommended that "this very intelligent and attractive dancer named Katherine Dunham"[112] take the lead, in her stead, in *La Guiablesse*, a ballet whose origins lie in a Martinique legend, of a she-devil who lures a hapless young man from his true love.[113] *La Guiablesse* was a resounding hit, and to some extent, forged the template for Dunham's emerging artistic persona. "Participating in [*La Guiablesse*] was Katherine Dunham's first experience with ritual dance and certainly stimulated her to become involved in the African-based culture of the West Indies."[114]

The reasons for why Page did not think Dunham could become a classical ballerina are varied. On one hand, as mentioned above, Dunham had started too late. Yet on the other, the same questions, discussed in chapter 2, concerning whether a black body could depict a whitened art form authentically and credibly seemed to hover over Page's doubts. Page also maintained a very different reason: that the "time was not yet ripe" for black ballerinas.[115] Particularly within the context of the times, neither the ballet dance establishment nor the public thought ballet to be "appropriate" for black bodies. As Aschenbrenner recounts:

> John Martin, a dance critic for the *New York Times,* wrote as late as 1963 that an Afro-American should not be drawn into ballet since it is "alien" to him culturally, temperamentally and anatomically. He pointed out the differences between fluidity and "erectness" of the spine and contrasted the pelvic movement in Negro dancers to that of the European: "When the Negro takes on the style of the European, he succeeds only in being affected, just as the European dancer who attempts to dance like the Negro seems only gauche."[116]

None of these statements were startling within the context of the cultural attitudes that then prevailed. Yet Dunham, like Graham, in some ways, refused to be defined by the parameters of the classical tradition. She vehemently resisted the stereotype that blacks were spontaneous and "natural" (sensual) dancers—a stereotype Baker had exploited as shown in chapter 3—and pointed out that blacks' own assimilation of this "white" myth led to their own detriment. Young black dancers, thinking the ability to dance their natural birthright, did not have the humility and fortitude to withstand the rigors of classical dance training, ironically resulting in the further reinforcement of stereotypes. Dunham herself exclaimed, with some frustration:

> Girls were constantly dropping out, and in each succeeding class there were new faces. It was disturbing, to say the least, for I had to re-teach them a dozen times a year! And the reason for this was simply that the Negro believes in a certain fallacy the white person had bequeathed him—namely, that the Negro is a natural-born performer and needs no training. I am sure that any Negro will agree with me, if, of course, he has reached any status in the artistic field, that the one thing we face most often is a double standard of judgment, and the result is an appraisal of good for the Negro that is far below the expected good of any other artist. We are too quickly complimented and unless we are exceedingly strong and discerning our work is apt to be aborted in its very beginning. This ready acclamation retarded our progress.[117]

Furthermore, using her anthropological training, Dunham refused to believe blacks were born as pure, savage, primal body, devoid of (and even incapable of) technique. Instead, Dunham stressed the sociological nature of dance. Using a more "scientific" lens, she claimed:

> "The African Negro is habituated to a certain kind of musical technique in which rhythm is basic... But this appreciation is not based on any physical difference, nor is it psychological; we are sociologically conditioned by our constant contact with it... In the West Indies, women dance to the drums almost until the hour the child is born—and they nurse it, still dancing. But that does not mean there is no technique. There is. And it is every bit as essential that we train as vigorously as any other group, even in presenting ordinary folk material."[118]

Certainly, Dunham's combination of academic credentials of the highest caliber, her practical fieldwork experience, and her showy reinterpretation of ethnographic experience into choreographic staging yielded refractory responses from the dance world, critics, and the public. She was called everything from a "hip swinging anthropologist," to a "scholar and serious lecturer of note," "the hottest thing to hit Chicago since Mrs. O'Leary's cow kicked the bucket," and "an authoritative interpreter of primitive dance rhythm."[119] Foulkes illustrates how white critics constantly referenced what must have been viewed a monstrous conjunction between hyperwhitened scholarly credentials and nonwhite sensual movement, performed on public stages that partook of Hollywood glamour. Much like the responses to Baker, Dunham's critics revealed an ambivalent attraction to Dunham's sex appeal—drawn to her as an embodiment of the "hypersexualized primitive." Yet unlike Baker, where the colonial spirit could patronizingly claim rational superiority, some white critics in the United States in particular seemed repulsed by the fact that someone who seemed "pure sensual (feminine/female) body" on stage was also the same person who could also effectively take on rational scholarly pursuit and withstand the difficulties masculine anthropological fieldwork requires.

> "As an anthropologist the gist of Miss Dunham's report seems to be that sex in the Caribbean is doing all right," was how Mr. John Martin, the influential *New York Times* critic put it. "Did you ever see a Degree in Anthropology dancing?" another critic asked. Reviewers slighted the seriousness of Dunham's academic study by continually using it to justify the sexy movements, while at the same time anthropology legitimated these so-called primitive movements in the sanctified realm of the theater for white critics. In either case, as an anthropologist uncovering primitive dances or as a black woman rotating her hips, Dunham decidedly affirmed white critics' conceptions of all black peoples as inherently more sexual.[120]

But Dunham's academic credentials were undoubtedly impeccable, especially given the times in which she, as a young black woman from low middle class origins, gained access to them, while experimenting with dance. The list of Dunham's teachers and mentors reads like a Who's Who among anthropological circles, and includes Robert Redfield, Melville Herkovits, Edward Sapir, A.R. Radcliffe-Brown, Bronislaw Malinowski, and Lloyd Warner, among others.[121] And it is among such anthropologists, especially Redfield, that Dunham found a "haven from racial discrimination."[122] Aschenbrenner describes the kernel of the fundamental values that underlay the critical methodological tools deployed by the University of Chicago's Anthropology Department, which Dunham both assimilated and from which she benefitted.

> The position against racial discrimination for American anthropologists was established by Boas, a German Jew and trained scientist who was appalled by European racism. He argued that race and culture are independent of each other, the one being genetically inherited, the other learned. Consequently, to argue innate inferiority of one group over another on the basis of learned behavior was unscientific; furthermore, since all races had developed civilizations with the highest expressions of art and learning, all had equal inherent potential.[123]

Some sources, such as the *Encyclopedia of World Biography*, wrongly claim that Dunham "earned a doctorate in anthropology,"[124] but it is clear that the highest scholarly degree Dunham finished was a master's degree, produced from field research done in the West Indies (Jamaica, Trinidad, Cuba, Haiti, Martinique) funded by the Rosenwald Travel Fellowship in 1936. Her master's thesis, "The Dances of Haiti,"[125] was eventually published (Northwestern University, 1947),[126] but far beyond academic degrees, Dunham achieved fame as a prolific author and much sought-after lecturer on anthropology and dance. Her numerous articles, as well as the three books she wrote, *Journey to Accampong* (about the Maroon Society of the Jamaican Blue Mountains, published in1946), *The Dances of Haiti* (her master's thesis published initially in Spanish and then in English in 1947[127]), and *Island Possessed* (about her fascination with Haiti and her eventual initiation into the Voudou religion, published in 1969) had a consistent thematic: they emphasized how "African religions and rituals adapted to the New World."[128]

Yet the very same scholarly credentials some white (male) critics attempted to cast doubt on were the very same rhetorical weapons other critics used to defend her and legitimize her work. For example, when Sol Hurok, a savvy business oriented impresario, convinced Dunham to restage *Tropical Revue* for its showing in Boston (and its more puritanical geographical neighbors) without *L'Ag'ya*, which was deemed "too heavy" and to substitute the more lively *Rites of Passage*, Boston critics flew to her defense. To rebut the city censor, Elinor Hughes of the *Boston Herald*, for example, carefully front-loaded her defense of Dunham's ethno-choreography (and Dunham) by itemizing the fieldwork Dunham had done towards her master's thesis, Dunham's being awarded several fellowships to continue her research, and her brother Albert Jr.'s status as a faculty member of Howard University.[129] Yet as Foulke perceptively observes: "Still, Dunham provoked censure while [Ted] Shawn [Graham's former teacher and Ruth St. Denis' husband] and His Men Dancers, performing as nearly nude as possible on Boston stages, did not. The sexual allure of black women caused more consternation than that of white men."[130]

Yet like Baker, Dunham's uniqueness made her celebrity even more unimpeachable in Europe. And like Baker, Dunham was an expert at creating an image, rhetorically manipulating the numerous interviews she gave, capitalizing on both her image as a legitimate scholar and as a glamourized star: a sexy woman with the brain of an academic. For example, in an interview with *Der Spiegel*, one of the most influential postwar German weekly newspapers, she began with expressing dismay over the popular tendency to sexualize her programs, but then switched flippantly to the claim: "I simply portrayed myself as an intellectual, you know." And having gotten her audience to admit the strength of her academic credentials, expertly raised the rhetorical question: "Today I can afford to say: What's wrong with sex?"[131] In that same *Spiegel* feature, Dunham rhetorically positioned herself as a "catalyst who wants to bring together contrasting cultures," rendering herself a "floating island of negritude" that aimed to "return to [African Americans] some of that unadulterated race consciousness, to return the strongly rhythmic impulses, which they consciously or unconsciously deny because of their inferiority complex regarding industrially advanced Americans."[132]

But unlike Baker, Dunham was portrayed as someone with both sophistication and eloquence, as well as the exotic primitivism Baker had come to symbolize. The result was an ecstatic embrace of this "impressive example of the intellectual and artistic potential of the colored race!"[133] A 1954 clipping Fischer-Hornung translates practically hyperbolically gushes over Dunham.

> For four weeks Katherine Dunham has been touring Germany and word has gotten around that this dark-skinned, elegant American, the daughter of a Negro and a Franco-Canadian, is a phenomenal dancer, director, choreographer, impresario all wrapped up in one—very attractive—person. To top

> it off, she holds a Ph.D., is a professor at Yale University, a writer, a renowned ethnologist, honorary member of the Royal Society of Anthropology and a painter.[134]

The fact that Dunham's second husband, John Pratt, was also the Technical Advisor of the Dunham Company and the Consulting Director of the Katherine Dunham School of Arts and Research[135]—the man who costumed her—who was also white, probably helped to further "whiten" Dunham, which worked to her unambiguous advantage in Europe, but proved more refractory in the United States, as we shall later see. So powerful was Dunham's image in Europe that when word got out that Katherine Dunham and John Pratt were looking to adopt a boy, as a companion to their first adopted child, Marie Christine, a German single mother, Elizabeth Willer, who had had a liaison with an African American soldier, wrote to Dunham, pleading with her to give her any kind of work, in order to support her two mixed race sons.[136] That Dunham was perceived as someone who had both the power and compassion to respond to this kind of plea reflects how reverentially she was regarded in Germany at that time.

Choreographically, Dunham is notable for incorporating not only "folkloric" material derived from a broad variety of "exotic" sources, but also the familiar street-derived US social dance steps characteristic of African American entertainers that Baker surreptitiously drew from and exaggerated, either comedically or sensually. Thus, in 1940, she choreographed and presented *Tropics* and *"Le Jazz Hot": From Haiti to Harlem*, adapting "dances from the West Indies, Cuba, and Mexico, as well as early black American social dances such as the juba, cakewalk, ballin' the jack, and strut."[137] But despite Dunham's eclecticism, Dunham did privilege the Caribbean as the ethnographic cradle from which she sought to discover and rearticulate a basic vocabulary that seemed, to her, to be common to African-derived dances in the United States. Dunham drew from the philosophy of one of her mentors, Melville Herkovits of Northwestern University, who believed that even black Americans, despite the trauma of slavery, retained memory of many "Africanisms," and argued for a reforging of links, along lines of similar values, across the Atlantic and the United States[138] Dunham herself explained her motives in choosing to focus on the dances of the Caribbean. "Realizing that the amalgamation of the Negro into white America has in a large measure brought about a complete lack of contact with those things which were racially [culturally] his. I have recently begun an intensive study of the Negro under other less absorbing cultural contacts; in the West Indies, the French, Spanish, and English influence have been of far less importance than that of the American in preserving the dance forms which are truly Negro."[139]

For example, to Dunham's anthropologically trained eye, the Haitian drums appeared to resemble those brought by African slaves than present-day drums in contemporary urban Africa.[140] And drummers played a key role, both in the initiation rites Dunham initially observed and later participated as an initiate, which she eventually reconstructed through performance; Dunham acquired two sets of the three drums used in the *voudun*—one at her own initiation as well as an older set—one apparently kept hidden to protect them from the eyes of the uninitiated during the US Marine occupation.[141] As Dunham observed, it was the drums and the drummers who set the atmosphere and helped induce the mental state necessary to ritual; for example, the "zepaules movement," which involved a "spasmodic hunching forward and release of the shoulders," according to Dunham, was "driven by the piercing beat of the kata, enriched by the broken rhythms of the seconde, and eroticized by the deep, insistent tones of the mama drums."[142] This movement induced a repetitive, deep breathing, which, combined with the overwhelming beat of the drums and the rhythmic movement, induced something similar to possession, which the drummers kept under a tight leash by creating breaks, just as the dancers achieved a critical point of intensity. "The drummers take complete control of these feints once the dancer has indicated, consciously or not, that he is ready for them, breaking the rhythm, sucking air in and hissing it out, ejaculating glottal sounds which are supposed to beat the 'broken' or out-of-rhythm dancer of group of dancers back in line and to show that it is they, the drummers, who dominate the rhythms."[143] This anthropological insight proved crucial to the eventual evolution of Dunham's choreography.

Dunham meticulously studied how form and function are intimately intertwined in dance, as rooted in culture; the primary social functions of dance in the *voudun* are religious, and Aschenbrenner catalogues some of Dunham's findings:

> The zepaules, with its rapid pumping movement of the shoulders, served to clear the air and bring about a semi-hypnotic state. It was usually directed to Legba, the intermediary for the mystéres, and prepared the participants for their reception. The yonvalou, involving a flowing motion along the spinal column, induced a state of complete relaxation and ecstacy associated with prayer. It caused the worshiper to be completely open to the mystéres, especially, Damballa, Erzulie, and Aida Ouedo, although others also might appear. The maison, involving grinding of the hips, was deliberately sexual in effect, acting as an emotional cathartic to someone who was possessed.[144]

Yet not all dances were for religious purposes; some were very secular social dances, such as the "couple dances," like the meringue, rumba, and bolero, all pou' plaisi'—"for pleasure."[145] Others were for large crowds, such the Mardi Gras, where Dunham observed that despite the overt sexuality of these social dances, culturally, they were not supposed to represent literal physical sex. Rather, they were symbolic, anthropologically rooted in agricultural and fertility rites.[146] They also functioned as a culturally sanctioned, specially delimited occasion in which class boundaries became loosened and where classifications based on skin tones became irrelevant, replaced by groupings by age and sex.[147] These, too, became essential animating elements of eventual choreography, but these were largely misunderstood particularly by many (white) American and European audiences, for whom the movements seemed lewd and to whom her choreography reinforced stereotypes.

Dunham's Liminalities

Dunham cemented her career and reputation through what she called "revues"—staging her re-memory of her anthropological experiences and Caribbean dance and music together with the lush settings, plush costumes, orchestral reinterpretations of the Caribbean rhythms and folk music, and the polished look of American showbiz. "Dancers moved through fantastical tropical paradises or artistically designed juke-joints, while a loose storyline held together a succession of diverse dances."[148] Like Balanchine, Dunham was prolific: she choreographed over 90 individual dances and produced 5 revues, 4 of which were successful both on Broadway and on worldwide tours.[149] Given her stature, therefore, it is of vital importance to study what happened when circumstances brought Balanchine and her together to collaborate.

It was after she was already established that Dunham "collaborated" with Balanchine on *Cabin in the Sky* (1940), the Broadway "musical fantasy" whose story revolved around "a kindhearted but morally ambivalent Everyman who dies from being cut up in a craps game and is bound for Hell but is saved by his wife's prayers and given extra time to qualify for Heaven."[150] The cast consisted of: Ethel Waters as Petunia the virtuous wife; Dooley Wilson as her wandering husband; Rex Ingram as Lucifer Jr., and Katherine Dunham as Georgia Brown, the temptress.[151] Bernard Taper, one of Balanchine's celebrated biographers, claimed that not only did Balanchine use his own savings to produce and stage the show, but also did the entire choreography.[152] Yet in an interview cited by Taper himself, Balanchine sounded evasive about who deserved credit for the choreography. "What is the use of inventing a series of movements which are a white man's idea of a Negro's walk or stance or slouch?

I only needed to indicate a disposition of dancers on the stage. The rest almost improvised itself."[153] Balanchine's remarks reflected a common view and a common practice at that time: that any kind of movement, especially of the "primitive" or "exotic" kind, was considered "natural" to (unreflective) black bodies; thus, any choreographic work done by a black choreographer in "collaboration" with a white choreographer, especially one of Balanchine's stature, would be rendered invisible.[154] According to Aschenbrenner, this was a fairly common occurrence: "black dancers choreographed numbers for which either white choreographers were credited or else no one was listed as a choreographer."[155] And indeed, the 1940 Broadway production of *Cabin in the Sky* did not give Dunham any credit as a choreographer.[156]

In Dunham's extended interview with Constance Valis Hall conducted on November 1999 and January 2000, Dunham herself initially appeared to try to duck the question of how much the "co-choreography,"[157] as it has been popularly characterized, was genuinely collaborative. Dunham's initial responses sounded just as evasive as Balanchine's; she repeatedly stressed that she "did not want to take anything away from Balanchine" but at the same time hinted that things attributed to Balanchine's influence were actually her own creations.

> *CVH*: Do you see this picture of Balanchine holding you up by the leg and stretching it?...And look, in this picture, at the way the girls are perched high on the shoulders of the men. That kind of lifting—does that look like something you would do on your company at that time?
>
> *KD*: I think so. *I don't want to take anything away from Balanchine* [italics mine], but I would imagine that that was part of our training.[158]
>
> ...
>
> *CVH*: You added music to *Cabin in the Sky*, didn't you, with your musicians? Two drummers [J. Emanuel Vanderhans and Cándido Vicenty] from your company were also working on *Cabin in the Sky*. Did they influence Dukelsky's musical score?
>
> *KD*: I think so. *Not to take anything away from* [Dukelsky] [italics mine], but I think that our musicians were all root-core musicians. They knew what they were talking about...and they realized also that the achiever [Dukelsky] was the person who could create upon these fundamental beliefs, and they respected Vernon for that reason.[159]

It is only later in the interview, after repeated questioning, that Dunham finally admitted that Balanchine, for the most part, left choreography to her. But in the usual rhetorical pattern, reflecting Dunham's savviness about survival in the dance world, Dunham frontloaded her remarks with praise for his cleverness and European sophistication and then expressed gratitude to the Russian ballet master for giving her as much freedom and responsibility as he did. She thus skillfully avoided politically "taking away anything from Balanchine" while owning her own work as hers. I quote a significant amount of the interview below to show Dunham's hesitations in claiming ownership of her work while not upsetting the established pecking order of "choreographic genius."

> *CVH*: How would you do it? Would he say, "Katherine, I see it this way?"
> *KD*: Well, he would say what had to be done next, and when he had an idea, like the Egyptian scene, maybe I'd add a few things... In the Egyptian scene, I can't tell which one of us did my entrance. There were clothes hanging on a clothesline drying... I would imagine that could have been Balanchine's [idea] because it was a very clever idea, and sort of European. And that's the way we set up things. You know, he said, "I think you should come through these clothes that have been hung up to dry."
> *CVH*: But *no steps* [italics mine].
> *KD*: In *some* [italics mine] of them [Balanchine] would have the idea. I think in most of them he would go through the whole scenario and say *where the dance was* [italics mine]. That was the first musical I had ever done. And I was quite willing to have him give me as much as he could. He never bothered me about the exact step of the choreography. And unless it interfered with the story, he wouldn't stop me in any theme in the way I would want to do it.
>
> As I think about it, and what I want to say about it, I'd say that *he deserves a great deal of credit for what I did* [italics mine]. [He] put me in a position that I wasn't in before, I guess, that I was able to engage the company, to pay them by union [scale].[160]

The interview also reveals that Dunham not only choreographed most, if not all, of the numbers, but also, as Aschenbrenner remarks, that "she staged most of the show, although she was not given credit for it."[161] And indeed, other accounts corroborate Dunham's claims. For example, Sol Hurok described Dunham's "enormous success as actress, singer, dancer and *dance director* [italics mine] in *Cabin*."[162]

But if Dunham carefully chose her words in relation to Balanchine, she did not hide her irritation with Agnes De Mille, (white) choreographer of *Oklahoma!* for her claims that she was the "first" to fuse American vernacular dance, ballet, and Broadway show dancing,[163] when Dunham's plantation dances, which had experimented with such choreographic fusions, preceded De Mille's. She remarked: "I wasn't happy about that... It has happened to me several times: people taking some of the songs I have researched—you know, popular songs—and translating them. I guess it's bound to happen. I was really annoyed with... [De Mille] because I think her idea came from something called the plantation dances, not in *Cabin in the Sky*, but in our concerts."[164]

Similarly, she expressed a clear annoyance with a critic, whose name was omitted from the interview transcript, who condescendingly remarked that Dunham seemed too eager to show that she could "point her foot" [indicating her classical ballet training] in *L'Ag'ya*.[165] She scoffed: "Ridiculous. It was a love scene for me, and for the part I was doing I could get out, wiggle around, take my clothes off, of course. But when it came to this particular love scene, I used the movements of ballet. I think there are times when it *just simply fit, if you know it well* [italics mine]."[166] Rhetorically, Dunham thus again stressed the validity of her credentials as a ballerina, which she repeatedly attributed to Speranzeva's training, as well as Speranzava's "Russian-ness," much like Balanchine.[167] In the same interview, Dunham recalled with sardonic humor that Martha Graham has given her the title of "High Priestess of the Pelvic Girdle,"[168] revealing, once again, that despite her many credentials and innovative work as a choreographer and dancer, Dunham was not immune from racism or racist stereotypes.

Nevertheless, it is clear that Dunham's credentials as an academic, her glamourized image, and the very manner in which she staged her ethnographic research as performances, did privilege her to some extent, especially compared with Baker. Despite Dunham's and John Pratt's misgivings concerning the negative stereotypic depictions of African American life, it is clear that the success of her "collaboration" with Balanchine (and her respectful acquiescence to the raced, sexed, and gendered hierarchy of the dance world) is what launched her into stardom and an eventual successful career. It was after this period that she was able to launch her own dance company as an independent and commercially viable entity in the United States, and it was also at this time that she chose the path of performance, rather than academia. Aschenbrenner recounts that Al Smart of *Esquire*, Dunham and Pratt's friend and colleague, posed the rhetorical question, regarding their misgivings about the negative stereotypes embedded in *Cabin in the Sky*: "Who are we to criticize success?"[169] Compliance with the order of things was the price to be paid for admittance into the world of full celebrity. "Although the company had previously experienced artistic success, now, for the first time, it was beginning to enter into the business of commercial entertainment, and Dunham had to become an entrepreneur so it could survive."[170] It was only after her collaboration with Balanchine that Dunham had the financial independence to attempt some of her more daring choreographic productions. For example, one of her more provocative signature pieces, *Barrelhouse*, which "draws on vernacular dance to explore a woman's loneliness and pursuit of pleasure and connection at a juke joint,"[171] was presented to audiences in 1950.[172] *Southland*, one of her more politically radical pieces, was first staged in 1951 at the Teatro Municipal in Santiago, Chile and was removed from the program because of the pressure the US Embassy applied because of its concern over the nonsalutary image of America it presented abroad.[173]

Thus, Dunham occupied a liminal position, as both a black woman earnestly interested in political activism, as reflected in several of her works, especially *Southland*, which is about the lynching of an innocent black man wrongly accused by a white woman of attacking her,[174] but also as a black woman whitened by her successful integration of a "whitened" aesthetic in her translation of ethnographic research into dance performances. Reynolds and McCormick summarize Dunham's contributions to American dance history in this way:

> The means by which Dunham knit the various elements of her vignettes together included a manifestly theatrical vocabulary of leaps, turns, and leg extensions with sinuous pelvic accents—a blend of modern dance, Latin ballroom, and generalized black vernacular movement from the Islands. In spite of her anthropological credentials and her adaptation of Creole and Latin American myths and ceremonies such as voodoo, she never presented herself as a concert artist in a didactic vein. Instead, Dunham went to great lengths to create an engaging theatrical context for the material she used, along with a glamorous stage persona for herself, both greatly enhanced by the modish costumes and settings of her husband, John Pratt. Her manner was *too innately refined* [italics mine] to do justice to the "primitive" material she occasionally attempted.[175]

Reynolds' and McCormick's remarks reveal an anxiety that repeatedly surfaces in relation to both white and black critics' reception of Dunham's work: the question of "authenticity," as her work, her image, and even her looks, seemed whitened, compared to, for example, Pearl Primus, who pursued similar goals and scholarly interests as Dunham in the 1940's, but who did not have Dunham's numerous liminalities. "Having almost no formal training, Primus began studying modern dance with Graham and Weidman…while pursuing scholarly anthropological research related to dance in Africa and the Africanisms in southern black religious ceremonies."[176] Foulkes points out how the difference in treatment, in relation to the question of "authenticity," could in some ways, be traced to the difference in looks between the two women. Practically all accounts describe Dunham as "beautiful"—but beautiful according to a whitened standard of beauty. On the other hand, Pearl Primus, who physically conformed to stereotypic depictions of the "Negroid" race, with a "broad nose, large expressive eyes, dark pigmentation, and muscular thighs and buttocks,"[177] could be, unlike Dunham, "sensual" without being distracting in terms of sex appeal, and thus credible as a "'strong, rhythmical, wild creature,' a 'young filly' romping over the pasture, showing all the signs of being a 'thorough-bred,' and looking out from 'jungle distances' as, in Martha Graham's words, a 'panther.'"[178] Thus, Foulkes succinctly outlines the significant differences in image between Dunham and Primus in this manner:

> With her lighter color, taller and leaner build, and narrower facial features, Dunham more closely fit white ideals of dancers and beauty and may have triggered a more hidden and festering reason for the derisive comments: she reminded Americans of the truth of their racial heritage—miscegenation... In contrast, Primus—of "unmixed African descent" and with a stockier build that helped her "outjump any man"—generated less criticism.[179]

In relation to this question of "authenticity," Dunham's choreographic interpretation of her ethnographic research has also undergone some critique. For example, her much acclaimed *Shango*, performed by the Alvin Ailey Dance Theater in 1987, has been criticized as lacking scholarly nuance, reifying stereotypes, and even of cultural appropriation. Halifu Osumare clearly distills the essence of these charges against Dunham's reinterpretation of her ethnographic research into glossy revues.

> [*Shango*] is actually an amalgam of rituals from several islands Haiti, Cuba, and Trinidad. The term "Shango" is not only the ubiquitous name for the Warrior Thunder deity of the Yoruba of West Africa, but also the term associated with the Shango Baptist religion of Trinidad. The use of yanvalu movements and the earthly dance of Damballa are obvious Haitian allusions, while the general ceremony could be Haitian Voudou or Cuban Santeria... The pastiche effect of Dunham's *oeuvre* has offended some people from the islands, causing accusations of her work not being true to any one tradition. Inappropriate cultural appropriation is a potential criticism of any artist's work involved in research-to-performance methodology.[180]

Of course, in the hands of someone like Martha Graham or George Balanchine, even if devoid of the intense ethnographic field work Dunham had accomplished, such "inappropriate cultural appropriation" would probably have been interpreted as "artistic innovation," passing copyright's "modicum of originality" test.[181] Additionally, given that Dunham's ethnographic work drew principally from "folklore" might have made any kind of possible copyright claim invalid. But that she wisely used the established kinesthetic techniques and body vocabularies of ballet and modern dance would probably have made any claim she might have raised, especially given the circumstances of *Cabin in the Sky*, perhaps more like a claim to choreographic creation more likely to survive. But given the raced and gendered nature of the politics of the dance world, Dunham wisely refrained. Like Baker, Dunham instead relied on her ability to "curate" her image through the numerous interviews she gave the media. But unlike Baker, Dunham did have some access—even if not full access—to whiteness as status property, and as such, was able to achieve some acclaim as a choreographer in her own right—but only after dutiful service to the ballet master and genius, Balanchine.

Graham and Dunham: A Brief Sketch of Comparisons and Cross-Currents

Clearly, both Graham and Dunham saw their choreographic works as rebellions against ballet's conventions. Some of this was a strategic adaptation: both women started ballet training too late to be able to acquire the idealized body habits required to become prima ballerinas; furthermore, their physical appearances—Martha with her severe "exotic" looks (while recognizably white) and Dunham with her sensual "exotic" look (while recognizably black) also militated against their effective assimilation into the conventional dance hierarchy, which preferred willowy, fragile and lyrical bodies as the conventional canvasses upon which ballet masters' choreographic creations could be metaphorically painted. But both were clearly driven by a desire to innovate—to strip dance of what she considered "extraneous" movement, in Graham's case; and to cultivate an appreciation for "Negro" dance, in Dunham's case.

Crucial to their innovation was the development of new dance vocabularies and new techniques. For Graham, this involved the development of contraction and release—"[a] forceful exhalation of breath produced a percussive flexion of the torso and that this 'contraction' could initiate a sequence of wavelike impulses flowing from the center of the body outwards. The opposite action—the intake of air . . . —she called 'release.'"[182] This method of breathing naturally affected how the dancer's weight could be shifted and broke the seamless lyricism of ballet, allowing her to emphasize the angularity and stiffness of bodily opposition, as expressive outlets. Traditional ballet needed a narrative to make the movement coherent; for Graham, the movement was the (emotional) narrative. Graham's iconic look was forged during her earlier work, characterized by an utter rebellion against ballet, with its forceful energy and desire to strip itself of the ultrafemininity required of ballerinas. "Whereas the ballet dancer stretched her feet to continue the line of the ankle, Graham forcefully flexed the foot to create a right angle. Her arms were not rounded in balletic port de bras, and her hands were used sparingly, almost as if to deny their traditional expressiveness. Graham's technique projected enormous nervous vitality based on her own wiry, sinewy, electric strength."[183]

Unlike ballet, which demanded that all ballerinas become the embodiments of ethereal beauty, Graham's early signature look was one of tangible severe austerity—some called it "purity;" others called it "ugliness." Graham's dancers "were easily recognizable in their drab clothing reminiscent of studio garb; their taut spines, blanched complexions, and hair pulled severely back gave them an air of anointment."[184] The cultural sources she seemed to draw from, and acknowledged as such, were from Latin American, Native American, Egyptian, and Asian, as in one of her enduring master works, *Primitive Mysteries* (1931), in which she choreographed a "striking ritual about a ritual—a Hispanic-Indian ceremony in honor of the Virgin."[185] As Deborah Jowitt observed:

> [In] "Primitive Mysteries," she created a "primitive" style based in part on the straight, narrow look of American Indian dancing. This early Graham style had the purity of an earth-sky rite, with its rooted look, pounding feet, stiffly vertical posture, arms that branched occasionally into angular gestures. Austere, hopeful, unambiguous dancing that reflected her ruthless asceticism and her desire to purge dance of all trivialities of movement.
>
> Graham also utilized... features of the so-called "archaic" style derived from Egyptian friezes... feet walking in one direction while the upper body twists open against the base—[became] an ardent ambivalence. She kept the twist, increased it, bent the body in several places, tipped it slightly off center until in one of her famous fall sequences, she arrived at a position in which the arms opened in one direction, while the knees remained pressed together, hips averted from the focus of the reaching arms.

Elements of various Far Eastern styles have also enriched Graham's vocabulary, but these, too, she restructured. Frantic, beating arm gestures or a bowed head made decorative Cambodian knee-walks look anything but decorative. She added a twist to a flex-footed attitude (also Cambodian or Siamese), so that her head could look backward—away from where her feet were going.[186]

And while modern dancers in general adopted, arguably, from black dancers, a looseness of the spine and the isolation of body parts, the movement of the hips and the pelvis (culturally charged with sexualized and erotic connotations) remained taboo, associated with low class burlesque acts and racist stereotypes. "Sexual movements signified lower art, and modern dancers' attempt at sexlessness revealed the gender, class and racial prejudices that codified a cultural hierarchy of high and low within modernism."[187] Graham justified this choice of "sexlessness" (in which, arguably, female bodies acquired more "masculine" characteristics, rather than being stripped of gender) by employing a paradoxical rhetorical reconstruction to turn conventional aesthetics upside down; she argued: "[U]gliness may be beautiful if it cries out with the voice of power."[188] In so doing, Graham, and other white modern dancers, reinforced the dichotomy between "high" art versus popular culture—a dichotomy that easily mirrored the white–black divide, and reinforced the association between whiteness and status property.

Thus, Dunham's anthropologically based insertion of the pelvis into her choreography as not necessarily rooted in sex and eroticism, but in rituals of fertility, was met with ambivalence, given the prevailing cultural preconceptions. Dunham, like Graham, sought freedom from the strictures of classical ballet, although she did use balletic techniques to enhance and authorize her own technique and lexicon of bodily movements. And she was certainly not averse, like Baker, to exploiting the "exotic" image the press forged for her, as an "anthropologist with hips"—a serious academic capable of staging glitzy stage and Hollywood productions, and like Graham, performing in the central role. Nevertheless, like Graham, Dunham drew from a variety of sources, ranging from "dances from the West Indies, Cuba, and Mexico, as well as early black American social dances such as the juba, cakewalk, ballin' the jack, and strut."[189] Thus, whereas Graham sought to insulate herself from anything that resembled vaudeville, popular culture and social dancing—and from anything that could be called a "Negro" aesthetic (though she was not averse to using black dancers in her ensembles, to frame her)—Dunham embraced these as legitimate sources of choreographic innovation. For her, the *terra incognita* that required exploration lay not in "classic Greek" or "Oriental" landscapes, which to her had already been plumbed by (white) women like Martha Graham and Mary Wigman, but in those dance forms heretofore ignored. Dunham observed:

> I would say that the dance of the primitive has been scarcely touched, and this, perhaps, unlike the classic Greek and Oriental, it is the work of a student of ethnology, as well as a student of dance, to observe and record that which can be transferred to the field of art and which will serve as a stimulus for creation. Additional work in ethnology, particularly research work among the Indians and Negroes of America, island peoples, and primitive Africa, would contribute to science a comparative analysis of dance which has, I believe, not received adequate attention from scientists.[190]

But knowing the hierarchy within the dance world, Dunham forged a series of techniques that hybridized ballet, modern dance, popular social modes of dance, and dance elements derived from her anthropological fieldwork. For example, Albirda Rose's description of the Dunham Technique begins with traditional barre work, as well as what she calls "Dunham presentation," in which the focus is on the raising of the arms dramatically, but in which ballet's focus on the centering of the spine is kept.[191] From there, body rolls follow, which seem, to some extent, especially given the language used to describe the training, a specialized application of Graham's contraction and release to the pelvic area.

- In the pelvic area, contract and release should be repeated approximately four times working each specific area
- Using the gluteus, contract and release and repeat four times
- Move into the lower back area, contract and release four times (The student is still in the flat back position.)
- Move up into the middle area, contract and release four times
- Upper back area, contract and release, repeat four times
- Head area
- Then all of these body parts are put together in continuous motion to complete the full body roll.[192]

There are other elements of Dunham's choreography: progressions, which include the "Dunham Walk," traveling isolations, and progressions in cultural context, which most heavily show the imprint of Dunham's Haitian-derived ethnographic work. These progressions in cultural context include Damballa, in which "the upper torso is moving in continuous fluid motions that move throughout the entire spine;"[193] Yanvalou, in which the undulating movement of the torso that is characteristic of Damballa is moved to any part of the body, whether, arms, hands, hips or torso... where the "even within the traditional ceremony itself, the level of improvisation is unlimited;"[194] Zépaules, which uses rapid, staccato shoulder isolation but with the shoulders moving forward in unison in a downward motion;[195] and Mahi (my-ee), which emphasizes a fast rhythm and percussive movement for the feet, juxtaposed with the upper torso moving at a different tempo and quality of movement.[196]

Dunham also readily admitted to a Cuban influence. The Cuban anthropologist, Fernando Ortiz, introduced Dunham to the renowned drummers, La Rosa Estrada and Julio Mendez.[197] And indeed, the Cuban rhumba and nanigo, which depicts cowboys or gauchos, became favorite numbers of the Dunham Company.[198] According to Marta Moreno Vega, director of the Caribbean Cultural Center in New York, Dunham was the first to feature the bata, or the Cuban double-headed drum, in New York performances. In addition, the East Indian influence persisted in Dunham's stress on the seven chakras (especially the nonrepression of the groin chakra, the source of sexual energy in African and Latin movements) in her master classes.[199] Later on, in 1966, when she had become a well-established artistic celebrity with a fully developed body vocabulary and choreographic style, she was hired by Senegalese President Léopold Senghor to help train the Senegalese National Ballet.[200] But by then, it was less a matter of Senegalese traditions influencing her art, than the Senegalese National Ballet being educated into her techniques.

But precisely because Dunham's very statements seemed to tie her choreographic creations with "unearthing" some kind of "fundamental" body vocabulary unique to Negro or black dances, many critics seemed to expect her choreographic creations to display a certain "authentic" or documentary connection to its roots. Yet much as Dunham composed her published memoirs well after her field work was over, Dunham created her choreographic reconstructions of what she recalled of her ethnographic field work, not as strictly documentary material but as artistic and hybridized transformations, glamourized with all the staging effects of Hollywood sophistication, inclusive of fashionable costumes and trend-setting hats. It is important to note that whereas she was burdened by the requirement of proving authenticity, Martha Graham was not. As Vévé A. Clark astutely observes:

> Many [critics] expected Dunham to represent Caribbean regional dances in documentary form. When she did not do so, she was chided for stylizing authentic dance forms. Criticism of this kind is irrelevant, because it fails to understand that Caribbean dance has been stylized and transformed throughout history. More important, stylization has been a tradition in American modern dance since its inception. Note, however, that other moderns were not criticized when they visualized milieu de mémoire that no longer existed (e.g., Martha Graham's *Primitive Mysteries*) or that never possessed a dance tradition (e.g., Helen Tamiris's *Negro Spiritual*).[201]

There is one final anecdote that reveals Dunham's savviness, either eerily prescient of the legal skirmishes over ownership of intellectual property rights over choreographic works that resulted from Graham's death, which extended from 2000 and ended in 2006 (the same year Dunham passed away), or her awareness of the undercurrents in the dance world with respect to the competitive relationship between the Martha Graham School/Foundation and the Martha Graham Center. Concerned about the future of Dunham's legacy, Dunham's own advocates, Marta Vega, the founder of the Caribbean Cultural Center in New York; Vévé Clark, an art historian; and Richard Long, a dance historian, collaborated on initiating a series of meetings about trying to set up an endowment and attract private funding; they proposed setting up an organizational barrier separating Dunham's personal welfare and artistic agenda from the more institutional, programmatic elements, such as the operation of Dunham programs.[202] In Fall, 1999, the Caribbean Cultural Center spearheaded a set of meetings designed to identify and render more accessible information on the Dunham Technique, either from existing film footage, photographs, music, reviews, designs, stage directions and notes, and even projected documentation through interviews with living Dunham company members.[203]

Despite the overwhelming support and the successful search for foundation funding to preserve Dunham's legacy, to be administered through the Library of Congress, Dunham "refused to sign away her rights to all her choreography, writings and other materials,"[204] resulting in the award "remaining in limbo."[205] Nevertheless, despite Dunham's initial reservations, in 2000, after the Dance Heritage Foundation named Dunham one of "America's Irreplaceable Dance Treasures," the Library of Congress received $1 million from the Doris Duke Charitable Foundation to undertake the Katherine Dunham Legacy Project and in 2002, the Library of Congress began the process of creating a comprehensive record of the Dunham Technique.[206] Thankfully, no similar legal skirmishes between Dunham's estate and the Library of Congress erupted over ownership of her choreographic works or associated intellectual property, such as set design or costumes, as had occurred between the Graham School/Foundation and the Graham Center. Again, this may be attributable to Dunham's savviness in navigating the intricacies of a system that simultaneously allowed her some access to whiteness as status property, but denying her full access, unlike Graham, who had presumed full and eternal access.

Chapter 6

Moving into New Directions: Cunningham and Ailey

Introduction

It may seem strange to review Merce Cunningham's choreographic heritage within the context of this project. The standard narrative regarding this master of avant-garde rebellion is usually devoid of any analysis of race. And unlike Fuller, Balanchine, or Graham, for example, there is no scandalous court case regarding copyright infringement to mar his legacy. Similarly, though the issue of race is certainly crucial to Alvin Ailey's biography as a dancer and eventual choreographer, the multiracial nature of his company, as well as the successful establishment of Alvin Ailey Dance Company and institutionalization of Ailey's choreography, seems to run counter to the central rationale of this project.

Nevertheless, as this chapter will show, the issue of whiteness is still crucial to the analysis of these more recent developments in the history of American dance. And perhaps, in this case, different forms of the same questions can be adopted: why did Cunningham and Ailey succeed in establishing unambiguous and uncontested copyright protection of choreographic works, where Fuller and even Graham, failed?

Cunningham: Navigating Cross-Currents of Avant-garde and Conservative Forces

The standard and now iconic narrative regarding Merce Cunningham (1919–2009) is that he broke away from the hegemony of Martha Graham's interpretation of modern dance and purged dance choreography of the need to reference a story, symbolism, emotional expression, or even musical interpretation. As Jonas remarks, among the many trappings characteristic of the later Graham productions that Cunningham abandoned, when he left Graham's company in 1945, were "story-telling, character development, emotional expression, musical cues, and what might be called the 'tyranny' of the choreographer."[1] Certainly there is some basis to this interpretation. Deborah Jowitt, while reviewing a 1973 Cunningham performance for the *Village Voice*, recalled a conversation between an unnamed little girl and Cunningham; to the little girl, looking at his dancing was like "'looking at the inside of a watch,' where everything was moving at the same time, but at different speeds, and 'some things affected other things.'"[2] That image, simple as it is, perhaps is one of the most perceptive and accurate descriptions of Cunningham's choreographic creations. Cunningham's choreographic experiments seem designed to strip dance of anything extraneous to pure movement, whether rooted in everyday acts (such as that of shaving or playing cards) or more theatrically rooted (such as balletic basic movements). Furthermore, in keeping with his attraction to Zen Buddhism, Cunningham, in one of the few written pieces he authored about choreography (using a form that defied the usual grammatical rules of prose and the conventional formatting rules of poetry), observed:

> joy, love, fear, anger, humor, all can be "made clear" by
> images familiar to our eyes. and all are grand or meager
> depending on the eye of the beholder.
> what to some is splendid entertainment,
> to others merely tedium and fidgets;
> what to others seems barren, to others
> is the very essence of the heroic.
> And the art is not the better nor the worse.[3]

More explicitly, in a printed interview, Cunningham explained the essence of his choreographic process this way:

> The ideas of dance come both from the movement, and are in movement. It has no reference outside of that. It has no reference outside of that. A given dance does not have its origin in some thought I might have about a story, a mood, or an expression; rather than proportions of the dance come from the activity itself. Any idea as to mood, story, or expression entertained by the spectator is a product of his mind, of his feelings; and he is free to act with it.[4]

The essential facts of Cunningham's biography, in relation to his evolution as a dancer and choreographer, are well known. Cunningham was born in Centralia, Washington, to a family of lawyers and judges,[5] and began studying dance at the age of 12;[6] his first exposure to dance was not classical ballet, but folk, tap, and exhibition dancing.[7] He also served as an altar boy for the Roman Catholic church—an experience, he claimed with humor, that served as an invaluable preparation for his apprenticeship with Martha Graham because he ended up spending a considerable amount of time on his knees.[8] After high school, Cunningham was a student for two years at the Cornish School of Fine and Applied Arts in Seattle, Washington,[9] where he took lessons from Bonnie Bird, who performed with Graham, and met John Cage,[10] who eventually became his lover. In 1938, after a brief vaudeville and nightclub tour in Oregon and California,[11] he studied at Mills College under the tutelage of dancer-choreographer, Lester Horton,[12] the man who was also a mentor to Alvin Ailey, as we shall later see. Martha Graham also saw him dance in her classes at Mills College and based on that, invited him to join her group;[13] he became the second male to join Graham's company after Erick Hawkins.

Cunningham accepted Graham's invitation to join his group, expecting to become one of her disciples, but it turned out that Graham had first of all not expected him to actually show up, and that she found herself uncomfortable choreographing for men in general. He recalled: "I'm sure it was just by accident that I became part of her company, simply because I appeared. But she didn't really know very much about dancing for men. I began to study in her school and to see other things."[14] It was Graham herself who suggested that Cunningham takes ballet classes from Lincoln Kerstein[15] at Balanchine's School of American Ballet.[16]

In the interview with Lesschaeve, Cunningham politely conjectured that Graham "thought it would be good for me to go to another place where there was a technique which would push my body in a different way than her particular work did."[17] According to Carolyn Brown, who recounted her version of the story and its effects on her teacher, Graham told Cunningham: "'I can't train you fully in terms of speed and jumping,' and she sent him off to study ballet... I think Merce knew that the vocabulary needed to be extended into the legs and feet. So much of the Graham repertory in those years... was centered on contraction and release and so much work on the floor (it is very difficult for many men to do all that work on the floor: their pelvises aren't constructed to do that). So Graham is the one who sent [Cunningham] off to study ballet."[18]

Despite all the logical reasons stated above, Bertram Ross, who joined Graham's company in 1954 after Graham's unhappy split with Hawkins, claimed that when Graham choreographed parts for men, she preferred giving verbal instructions rather than demonstrating them because "she did not have a man's body."[19] Tim Wengerd, who joined the Martha Graham company in 1970, was also interviewed in the same *Dance Magazine* article and confirmed Ross' claim. Wengerd conjectured that both Hawkins and Cunningham probably had a great deal of independence (compared to Graham's female dancers) to shape or provide the basic material and that Graham simply fashioned what she could from this raw material to suit her purposes.[20]

As one of only two males in the troupe, Cunningham immediately found himself cast in soloist roles, opposite Graham and Hawkins—an immediately privileged role in a profession overpopulated by women. And it is to Cunningham that Graham gave her more complex masculine (and one could even say androgynous) choreographies—the counterpoint to Hawkins' unidimensional and more conventionally masculine roles. As Deborah Jowitt observes, Graham often cast herself in roles that were caught between the two types of masculinities that Hawkins and Cunningham embodied.

> Hawkins was called "The Dark Beloved" in the somber, seething Deaths and Entrances, and he played this role—sexually alluring, masterful, potentially dangerous—in more than one dance. Cunningham was 'The Poetic Beloved,' a slightly mystical, even androgynous figure: he was the blithe acrobat to Hawkins's whip-wielding ringmaster (*Every Soul is a Circus*), the winged Pegasus to [Hawkins's] swaggering husband (Punch and Judy), the gentle Christ figure in *El Penitente*, the fanatic Revivalist in *Appalachian Spring*. After Merce Cunningham left the company. Graham made no more dances that expressed this double image of man.[21]

Despite his relatively privileged spot on Graham's troupe and his personal admiration for her, Cunningham disagreed with Graham's emphasis on the cultivation of style as well as her insistence that every movement should "mean" something. Ironically, it was precisely those ballet lessons at Balanchine's School, the bastion of the New York City Ballet, that drove Cunningham to become curious about the mechanics of movement, as an end in itself, rather than as tied to expressing emotion, and he increasingly became drawn to the "'facts of moving' rather than the expression of personal feeling."[22] Cunningham was also doubtful that Louis Horst's (Graham's accompanist and former lover-mentor) use of music from the past, to enhance what increasingly seemed a histrionic display of the emotions, was a sufficiently revolutionary break from classicism.[23]

Thus, approximately four or five years after Graham recruited Cunningham to join her company, Cage, his eventual lover-mentor-financier, convinced Cunningham to break away from Graham and do his own work. Thus, in 1942, Cunningham cochoreographed three works with Jean Erdman and created two solo works, both based on music by Cage.[24] What is curious about the initial positive response by critics to his dancing is that he is simultaneously praised as a "classicist" for his purity of line and rhythmic movement, while being praised, implicitly, as "modern" for insisting, like Cage, on the independence of dance from music but debunked for his "lack" of expressivity and theatricality.

> The reviewer for Horst's *Dance Observer* praised [Cunningham] for putting everything he had to say into "clear, beautifully timed and executed movement which was a joy to watch. He is a classicist." The critic... commended the young artist for obviously believing that dance is an independent medium, but chided him for a lack of warmth and variety into his work[;] he will have the same attraction for a less specialized audience.[25]

Despite the critics' general agreement on Cunningham's "elegant" lines, the way in which his body is described, to some extent, resembles the way nonwhite women, such as, in particular, Josephine Baker, have been described. For example, Edwin Denby of the *New York Herald Tribune* remarked: "[Cunningham] is a virtuoso, relaxed, lyrical, elastic *like a playing animal* [italics mine]. He has an *instinct* [italics mine] for form that makes its point by repetition, each repetition being a little different and the phrasing of each difference exceptionally limpid."[26]

Stripped of some of the conventionally masculine trappings of ballet, the protective buffer of narrative, or the theatrical accoutrements of music as accompaniment and lush costumes as distractions from movement, Cunningham's body, and his choreographic positioning of it, grows dangerously close to the position occupied by nonwhite others, such as Josephine Baker. And indeed, Cunningham's choreography, like Graham's, articulates and isolates body parts but does not emphasize the pelvic area. Simone Forti, a dancer who attempted to train with Cunningham, but whose inclinations were much more organic and holistic, wrote, with some exasperation: "An important element of the movement seemed to be the arbitrary isolation of the different parts of the body. I recall a statement I made in exasperation one day in the studio. I said Merce Cunningham was a matter of adult, isolated articulation. And the thing I had to offer was still very close to the holistic and generalized response of infants."[27]

But like Katherine Dunham, what ultimately elevates Cunningham's choreography from the realm of "pure, unreflective body" is the clear intellectualism with which his choreography is infused. Much of that intellectualism is due to Cunningham's interactions with John Cage, with whom Cunningham forged a lifelong partnership, both personal and professional, of open-ended collaboration. Cunningham's dance aspirations would probably not have been realized without Cage's unflagging support.

In many ways, Cage's innovations in music composition defy succinct description. John Cage (1912–1992), a student of Henry Cowell and Arthur Schoenberg, was obsessed by the project of rethinking and creating his own musical language from first principles.[28] Cage posited that anything auditory—even noise or silence—could be the subject matter of music; hence, Cage experimented with electronic sounds and employed various objects as musical instruments.[29] Perhaps one of his most notorious experiments was the "prepared piano"—a piano into which he inserted pieces of wood, cardboard, rubber, and metal between the piano strings, so as to deform its conventional sound, making it resemble a percussion instrument.[30] Instead of written musical scores, Cage gave instructions to his musicians verbally, altering the notion of what constituted musical notation,[31] much as sitting in silence at the piano for fifteen minutes at a concert altered expectations and conventions regarding music, theatricality and the acts of performing and listening to music.

Much of Cage's music is infused with the dadaesque irreverence for convention mingled with a sense of humor. Cage eschewed self-expression in favor of "events"—experiments in collective improvization that "gave the 'opportunity for experience,' free from the composer's individual taste and imagery as well as of the traditions of musical literature."[32] Cage believed that art and life should be treated as inseparable, and that is why he did what seemed like outrageous things, such as the "water gong," which replicated the sound vibrations perceived by dancers in a swimming pool;[33] regardless of whether or not critics approved of his work, critics and many other avant-garde communities paid attention to his work and took his work seriously.[34] All these elements helped shape the development of Cunningham's career as a dancer and choreographer. They helped cement a common base in terms of principles and practices, as well as audiences. "Both [Cage and Cunningham] shared the belief that neither dance nor music need function as a dependent of the other, that the two have nothing arbitrarily in common but custom, that their combination is less necessity than reflex, and that they can be advantageously freed of another's syntax."[35]

Influenced by both Zen Buddhism and Nietzsche's philosophy, Cage and Cunningham studied the ancient Chinese text, the I Ching (the Book of Changes) and its notion that one could randomly toss sticks or coins to divine meaning in the present or even give guidance for the future[36]—something completely antithetical to the then-reigning conventions of musical and choreographic composition. Thus, the idea of "chance organization" or "noncontrol" as a principle of composition emerged in both of their works and their collaborations; this idea surpassed "the modern concept of open form in art and introduced elements of ambiguity and paradox in their work."[37]

Initially, when Cage and Cunningham collaborated, the manner in which they composed resembled the typical method, though it was Cage who wrote music notated to choreography already composed, rather than the other way around.[38] The two men agreed on the external framework of a specified length of time, identifying specific points at which music and dance would converge.[39] However, as they developed as artists, the usual symbiotic connections between music and dance grew less and less.[40]

For example, in *Solo Suite in Space and Time* (1953), Cunningham numbered the blemishes visible on ordinary sheets of white paper when these sheets of paper were illuminated by a bright light, treating the resulting numbered arrangements as "found arrangements."[41] What resulted seemed a rigorous threefold process of ensuring randomization. These "found arrangements" became the basis for the lengths of the five sections, as well as the sequence of the performance of the movements, after they had been selected by tossing coins.[42]

In 1955, Cunningham used the same technique to generate the choreography for *Suite for Five* by "assigning numbers to particular dancers to determine where in space their movement occurred, and superimposing several sheets of paper so that some blemishes coincided, to establish when people would dance together."[43] Although the Cunningham dancers knew the sequence of acoustic effects in Cage's compositions, the time-lengths of each effect would vary from performance to performance (though the length of the collective sections was always consistent); thus, the Cunningham dancers were given far more interpretative room: they could perform movements with a very loose connection to the music or occasionally, "surrounded by silence."[44]

Cunningham's insistence on the independence of dance from music, lighting, and set design, leading to no one knowing how the whole is to come together—something completely antithetical to conventional notions of the aesthetics of staging dance productions—led many, both critical and popular, audiences to dismiss Cunningham's work as devoid of any design, structure, or rigor. Unlike Wagner's Romantic vision of the *Gesamtkuntswerk*, where all the elements of opera work strictly in tandem, orchestrated to produce a unified larger whole meant to express and evoke emotions, Cunningham's choreography took a radical, almost postmodern turn. Until the night of the performance, no one, not even Cunningham himself, knew how the whole would come together, and the emphasis was less on making sure each movement expressed meaning and conveyed or evoked emotion than on uncovering motion and rhythm as ends in themselves, enfleshed in physical bodies in space-time, interacting with others, and with the various elements of staging productions, such as lighting, music, set design, among others.

Yet the sources of rigor and structure in Cunningham's choreography were twofold: 1) in the discipline of timed segments; 2) the rigor of muscular rhythms, which often appeared effortless and simple, but actually required extreme precision and control, demanding endless hours of rehearsal. Cunningham relied on a stopwatch to mark specific segments, a process that initially shocked his audience at Connecticut College during the first summer the company performed there and led, according to Carolyn Brown, the woman Cunningham most often partnered with, the misimpression that Cunningham's choreography was "cold, inhuman, impassive, expressionless."[45] Indeed, Cunningham himself stressed the centrality of time to his choreography.

> It is erroneous to think that my work is not structured. It's clearly structured, but in a different way. The structure is in time, rather than themes or through an idea. It's not dissimilar to the continuity in television acts. Television shows fit the time between the commercials.[46]

The analogy to television is telling, making it clear that Cunningham was not afraid to explore things normally kept outside the boundaries of what is considered "dance." One of the things that seemed to contribute to the success of Cunningham's use of intellectual property law to protect his choreographic works was his enthusiastic embrace of, and experimentation with, new technologies to generate choreography. For example, after the Second World War, Cage returned from a European tour with "musique-concrete" by Pierre Schaffer[47] (i.e., the use of the magnetic tape to capture sound). Cunningham innovated by being the first to design choreography using original music on magnetic tape.[48] This integration of technology into his choreographic creations probably helped make his work more protectable as it incorporated cutting edge science (which unambiguously met the "innovation" standard of patents—a standard more rigorous than the mere "originality" required for copyright protection) into what became perceived as cutting edge evolving art.

The more extended story of this groundbreaking event—of using timed segments on magnetic tape, rather than to notes of music annotated on a page—is recounted by Mazo:

> [Cunningham] point[ed] out that music changed after World War II when the tape recorder "brought the idea of space into music—it put it into inches." The first piece of tape Cunningham used was *Symphonie pour un home seul* by Pierre Schaffer and Pierre Henry, to which he was

> commissioned to make a dance in 1952. He could find no way to relate to that music in any conventional way "because you'd always be late. It would be like a spook moving. There was no way to count it in any metered sense." So he tried another approach. He knew that the music lasted seven and one-half minutes, so he made a dance lasting seven and one-half minutes, put with together with the score and went from there. He is quite comfortable working this way, because time for him is not metered time "but a length of time you can divide any way you like."[49]

Yet the sense of "time" that is at the heart of Cunningham's choreography, at least as phenomenologically described by Carolyn Brown, one of his principal dancers and the person he chose to partner with, seemed to come less from an external source than from the dancer's internal sense of rhythm. She wrote, eloquently:

> Merce requires of his dancers that the rhythm come from within: from the nature of the step, from the nature of the phrase, and from the dancer's own musculature; not from without, from a music that imposes its own particular rhythms and phrases and structure, or from a narrative or "mood." For Merce, I believe, a "musical dancer" phrases from the muscles, the sinews, the gut, and the soul. Each movement is given *its* full value, *its* own unique meaning—the movement is expressive of itself.[50]

Cunningham was celebrated as a great "collaborator," but if so, his notion of "collaboration" was unusual. Other than giving the barest of information (e.g., the length of time of the piece and the number of people dancing), Cunningham allowed those with whom he collaborated, such as musicians, lighting technicians, set designers, among others, the greatest of latitude—which is hardly "collaboration" in the conventional sense of the word. Yet in relation to his dancers (much like Balanchine and Graham), there was no such *laissez faire* attitude and there was no democracy. This set of conditions of "collaboration" placed extremely high demands on his dancers because even if the movements had an improvisational quality to them, they were still unconditionally exact, even in unpredictable and even dangerous conditions; sometimes the stages were too darkly lit, the music too loudly played and the stages filled with potential perils. Regardless of these contingencies, when a dancer overstayed her time onstage, Cunningham simply and unceremoniously carried her offstage because it interfered with the overall rhythm of the piece.[51]

Steve Paxton, another Cunningham dancer, recalled one of Cunningham's helpful pointers: "In my era, one of the things [Cunningham] said...was 'If you want to get the time right, make every detail clearer,' and that seemed to work. We would be able to shave 15 seconds off [a] two-or-three-minute phrase that we had been slagging a little just by sharpening up very small units inside the phrase—a tenth of a second here, a tenth of a second there—and finally getting it right."[52] Viola Farber, however, recalled a darker version of that story: "I remember that sometimes rehearsals were very unnerving. Merce would sit and look at his stopwatch, and the only thing he would say when we had finished a dance was 'You're a minute too slow.'"[53] Finally, Carolyn Brown summed up a general overview of Cunningham's choreography, differentiating between dances based on "chance choreography" and dances with "indeterminate" structure.

> There is a big difference between the works that were choreographed by using chance procedures and the very few that were indeterminate in actual performance. The chance works were made precisely, with exact time, exact space, exact steps, and we were expected to do them precisely. There were very few indeterminate works.[54]

The remarks made by Cunningham's dancers emphasized the discipline and rigor Cunningham's choreography demanded, much like Balanchine's and Graham's. "In addition to the legs and the feet of a ballet dancer, Cunningham valued a flexible spine, an active torso, and an emphasis on the body's ability to make quick changes of direction."[55] If one were to choose between Graham and Balanchine as influencing Cunningham's choreography, Cunningham was probably closer to Balanchine than Graham because the root of his choreography still partook of the balletic aesthetic—especially in the spine and the legs, which is what enabled some dance critics to appreciate his work; that connection to the realm of the whitened ballet aesthetic, in terms of its movement vocabulary, was what rendered his work, to some, intelligible, and accessible as still legitimate "dancing," despite its avant-garde elements. Steve Paxton, one of Cunningham's dancers, explained his view:

> [M]odern dance was the style for him, more or less, into which he would incorporate balletic arms and balletic legs—use them inventively, change the ballet, incorporating other things he had picked up, other ways he saw movement going and later, doing it from his *own* work...I think if he had been working with movement as radical as his compositional movement were, it would have been completely undecipherable.[56]

However, given the liminal and revolutionary nature of Cunningham's choreographic *oeuvre*, there was considerable disagreement among even his dancers. While Paxton described Cunningham's movements using a whitened, ballet-derived vocabulary, Gus Solomons vehemently denied any affiliation with the ballet and instead emphasized the nonwhitened elements of Cunningham's choreography, emphasizing the articulation of the spine, rather than its balletic uprightness, and the sharp, abrupt movements, rather than flowing and lyrical movements. "[Cunningham] use[d] the spine as another *limb*, with equal articulation in all the joints of that spine, and reduces the center from the whole torso to just the pelvis so that the spine becomes as free as a limb."[57]

And indeed, in many ways, Cunningham, like Graham, exploded so many aspects of the whitened aesthetic of the ballet. In addition to reconfiguring the relationship between dance, music, and other theatrical elements, Cunningham refused the traditional configuration of the balletic stage, meant to privilege the vantage point of the rich patron of the ballet, who was historically the sovereign. Much like the vanishing point in painting, there was a crucial spot in the theatre, usually reserved for the richest and most powerful of ballet's patrons, from which the spectacle of the ballet could be best observed. And unlike the ballet corps, relegated to uniform movements meant to serve as a backdrop to the principal dancers, each Cunningham dancer was essentially a soloist, capable of individually commanding the gaze of any part of the audience. James Klosty observed:

> By choice Cunningham decentralized stage space through chance, transforming central focus into field perspective. There is no best spot on a Cunningham stage. In dances that permit the dancers to choose where they will move, there is no crush of bodies at stage center... [T]he most characteristic quality of the use of the stage in Cunningham is that no matter how few dancers are on stage the space always appears to be full. When they are in two-, three-, or four-sided arenas, some dancers are assigned different "stage-fronts" than others, and these directions alternate throughout the evening. Thus, the stage is not merely decentralized, it is demagnetized.[58]

If sight is the sense privileged by ballet, characteristic of a "whitened" aesthetic, and sound is the sense privileged by a nonwhite aesthetic, glimpsed in, for example, traditional Ghanaian dance as described by Cohen Bull in the second chapter, then the kinesthetic sense of rhythm and movement, which is felt, rather than seen or heard, is what predominates Cunningham's choreography. Unlike the conventional ballet instruction, in which mirrors are crucial to the dancer's feedback loop regarding lines and the nature of the partnering, Cunningham's dancers worked in unison, less by seeing each other and knowing in advance what was to come, than by somehow kinesthetically sensing and responding to the other's movements—a clear precursor to contact improvisation,[59] where that kinesthetic sense is heightened through touch.

Without the external rubric of music to hang on to in order to produce unison, Cunningham's dancers relied on an internal sense of rhythm that they collectively sensed emanating from each other. Perhaps it is in this sense that Cunningham "is concerned with Einsteinian, not Newtonian, physics."[60] Valda Setterfield, a Cunningham dancer, remarked: "The rhythms were always so incredibly strong. The audience may not have heard anything, but the rhythms were pounding in our blood."[61] Numerous stories abound among his dancers to support this view. I shall cite simply one, recounted by Viola Farber.

> About unison: in *Rune*...there was a section where the whole company had to take a cue from someone (who shall be nameless!) who was behind us, and who danced very lively [sic] and lightly, so there was no pounding of feet. And we learned to do it. *Somehow we learned to feel what was going on behind us* [italics added]. So I think we developed sensibilities that were quite nice to have. They were maddening, sometimes, to try to develop.[62]

In many ways, Cunningham's choreography constituted a rebellion against Graham's revolt against classicism. Graham, as I noted in a prior chapter, tended to appropriate nonwhite elements into her choreography, while still maintaining her status as a white woman; one of these elements was the flirtation with the notions of the "primitive" and "ecstatic."[63] Yet a rebellion against a rebellion tends to reinscribe, or at least reference, the first point of negation. And that explains, to some extent, Cunningham's choreography becoming perceived as more rational—more Apollinian/more predominantly "white" rather than "nonwhite"—and thus, more "high art" than "mainstream" than some of its more postmodern successors. In a radical reversal of the way ballet is usually thought of, in relation to modern dance, Klosty observed:

> Far from Bacchic abandon, the rule for Cunningham's dancers is absolute definition. Traditional ballet is a far more Dionysian enterprise, for the dancer can ride the musical impulse, using it as a kind of surrogate heartbeat on which bodily functions play without consciousness. Absence of metrical accompaniment only intensifies the mental effort needed to establish the strict order that supports each dancer's part. Cunningham's dancing is a *rigorously Apollonian activity* [italics added]: it is the dancer, not the music, who recreates the spatial and temporal structure that is each dance.[64]

Carroll and Banes found an eloquent way of describing the quality of movement in Cunningham's choreography as displaying a form of "bodily intelligence," more akin to Balanchine's ballets than Graham's hyperdramatized modern dances. They remark:

> In opposition to the technique of the Graham style (from which he emerged). Cunningham's movement is rapier-fast, covering space both quickly and hyperarticulately...It has an air of exactitude and precision. In turn, these formal bodily properties—lightness, elasticity, speed and precision—suggest a particular description of the mind as an agile, cool, lucid, analytic intelligence of the sort once referred to as Gallic or Cartesian, but also appropriate as an ideal of post-World War II America. Whereas Graham was heavy, organic, brooding, and altogether nineteenth century, in Cunningham it is permutational, correlational, strategic, rarefied, and airy.[65]

In addition, as I mentioned earlier, Cunningham infused and integrated his choreographic processes and products with new technology, inclusive of film, video, and computer programs, as well as avant-garde art. For example, *Variations V* (1965) was a multimedia fantasy in which "dancers' movements activated slides, films, and the sounds of an electronic score by means of radio antennas mounted about the stage."[66] *Signals* (1970), employed laser projections in its lighting effects.[67] In *TV Re-run* (1972), composer Gordon Mumma equipped the dancers with belts that had sensors and transmitters, which translated their movements into audible pitches, which were transmitted in the pit, amplified and conveyed to the audience via loudspeakers. In all these productions, even just the selection and arrangement of these incorporated elements into his choreography increased the perception of the originality of his works, according to copyright standards.[68]

As Cunningham aged, the types of movements his choreography drew from became more clearly identifiable as balletic, but stripped of anything extraneous. Clarity and efficiency seemed to be the main motivations for his choices, but once again, Cunningham's choreography, in terms of its body vocabulary seemed to draw closer to its whitened precursors, rather than its nonwhitened forebears. As Reynolds and McCormick observe:

> In later years, the vocabulary [Cunningham] used to introduce new ideas tended to rely more and more heavily on abbreviated balletic forms—the basic port de bras, foot positions with a modicum of turn-out, tendu, plié, relevé, retire, and related leg gestures. [Cunningham] showed little interest in épaulement or the presentational stylizations of the ballet, however, and never combined steps in a way that suggested an enchaînement. Cunningham's reliance on a simplified balletic vocabulary seemed mainly a matter of legibility and convenience.[69]

Yet like Balanchine and Graham, who remained active, as choreographers and dancers, well into their senior years, Cunningham had an unusual longevity enhanced by his ability to draw inspiration from, as well as utilize, emergent technologies. For example, in *Trackers* (1991), Cunningham used the computer as a source for exploring movement, producing arm formations that were awkwardly placed behind the torso, with increasing isolated torsions of various body parts.[70] In the hour-long *Enter* (1993), which was titled after the computer key, "a sense of overarching design receded as the sensation of cerebral intensity increased."[71] Cunningham himself sometimes directly attributed the genesis of some of his later choreographic works to his experiments with software. For instance, Cunningham's sole statement about *Ground Overlay* (1995) was: "This dance was begun by processing phrases of movement into LifeForms, the dance computer (software) I utilize. It continues my interest in dancers dealing with movement complexities."[72] Vaughn catalogues some of the later Cunningham pieces that were particularly inspired by, and dependent upon, interactions with computers—all of which enhanced the "rational," more "scientific," or "fact-centered" rather than "artistic" or "emotional" look of Cunningham's later choreographies.

> Like all of Cunningham's dances since 1991, Windows was made in part with the use of Life-Forms. The titles of many of these works (Enter, Trackers, CRWDSPCR) derive from computer language, in this case the "windows" that divide up the space of the computer screen and can be moved around on that space.[73]

Finally, Cunningham's love of experimentation with new technology resulted in a collaboration with Paul Keiser and Shelley Eskar, on a multimedia film, installation, and computer project titled *Hand-drawn Spaces*.[74] In April 1997, during the early stages of the project, Cunningham, in collaboration with two dancers, Jeannie Steele and Jared Phillips, choreographed approximately 70 dance "phrases," which were conveyed to a computer screen via a program called Biped, through reflective spheres attached to the dancers' bodies.[75] This constituted a reversal of the choreographic process Cunningham used when he employed LifeForms, where the computer, and not the dancers, was the source of the motion recorded. Finally, Cunningham, Kaiser, and Eshkar collaborated with Aaron Copp, the company's lighting designer, to create a way of using the installation as part of the set design for the new dance to be performed alongside a composition by British composer Gavin Bryars.[76]

Pragmatically, as well, the use of these new technologies, including film, enabled new forms of fixation that recorded Cunningham's choreographies in ways other than the conventional format of Labanotation. Terry Teachout, a *Wall Street Journal* critic, remarked that Cunningham's earlier use of film seemed unsophisticated and bare, probably due to budgetary limits, compared to his later staging of dances that were recorded on film.

> *Beach Birds for Camera* [(1992)] is the first film in which Cunningham and his current director-collaborator Elliot Caplan have completely solved the vexing problem of "where" a dance film takes place. Most of Cunningham's films are shot in his New York studio, and no attempt is made to conceal the fact that we are watching dancers in a studio, or to create the illusion of stage space. Looking at earlier films, one felt that Cunningham took this line because he didn't have the money to do anything else; the results usually seem cheesy and, occasionally, coy. But *Beach Birds for Camera* was filmed in two different locations, a dance studio and a sound stage. We are carefully distanced from the former by the subtle use of soft focus, translucent light, and handsomely grainy black-and-white cinematography. Then, just as Alan Good begins to dance with Victoria Finlayson, the film abruptly changes locales—and switches to color.[77]

Regardless of the degree of sophistication (or lack thereof) in Cunningham's use of film, the active exploitation of film as a medium for recording the dance enhanced the copyrightability of Cunningham's work by making the fixation requirement integrated into the (re)production of the choreography itself. Vaughn notes that in Cunningham's later collaborations, which included work on film and video, Cunningham actually choreographed to the space the camera saw, rather than the stage; he realized that the sense of space visible on film and on video differed from theater space. Nevertheless, since the choreography was first fixed on film or video and then adapted to stage, the usual hurdles in relation to the fixation requirement were actually already integrated into the very process of choreographing. Vaughn reports:

> In the last fifteen years Cunningham has extended his collaboration to film and video, working first with Charles Atlas and then with Elliot Caplan, resident filmmakers with the Cunningham Dance Foundation. Nearly all of Cunningham's work in these media has been in the form of dances choreographed for the camera, rather than of previous pieces "reconceived." Contrary to the usual practice, he has in most cases later reworked them for stage presentation. He recognized in his first tentative experiments that the space seen by the camera differs from that seen by the spectator in a theater: a triangle that widens from the camera aperture as opposed to a rectangle that narrows. His decentralization of the space in his theater choreography has enabled him to deal with this situation, just as working in precise time-lengths has enabled him to deal with the necessity for such limitations in television.[78]

Nevertheless, even Cunningham's earlier experimentations, such as his treatment of dance as "coexisting"[79] with music, as a separate musical entity, already tended to privilege his choreography. Separate from the demand that dance must correspond to music, Cunningham rode the wave towards abstraction that began with Balanchine, radicalizing dance to emphasize its independence as a separate art form not requiring rootedness in narrative to be considered as a sufficient "advancement" of the arts in order to acquire copyright protection.

In terms of the gendered representations, Cunningham is typically given credit for having pioneered "unisex" choreography—that is, theatre dance in which, "superficially at least, differences between male and female dancers are not especially important to an appreciation of the aesthetic possibilities within abstract dance movement."[80] Along with that impression of gender neutrality is also the impression of meaning neutrality—that is, that the "meaning" of a piece is left purely to the audience's subjective impressions. For example, as Gerald Jonas recounts:

> In a piece called *Story* (... 1963), an indeterminate number of dancers may perform all or any of eighteen choreographed sections on any given night; sets, costumes, even the choice of instruments is left up to the performers. But the "story" of the title, according to Cunningham, belongs to the audience: "The title does not refer to any implicit or explicit narrative, but to the fact that each spectator may interpret the events in his own way."[81]

Yet one wonders how much of this androgyny was necessitated, to some extent, by the pragmatic considerations of staging abstract pieces, especially given the rate of attrition of dancers lured to other venues by higher pay scales and more established institutional reputations? Carolyn Brown, the most enduring member of Cunningham's company reflected on the interchangeability of bodies that resulted in, for example, *TV Re-run* (1972). She thought that the interchangeability of bodies resulted, ironically, in the effacement of individuality, not its celebration—something that Cunningham had always proclaimed as essential to his choreography.

> After a particularly devastating year of losing male dancers, Merce made *TV Re-run* (1972), a dance in which everyone learns the same material but is free to choose spontaneously in performance what parts of it she or he wishes to perform. It is a dance which can be done by any number of dancers, and the whole is never jeopardized by the departure of any one dancer... *TV Re-run* presents the curious situation in which each dancer knows that he or she is completely dispensable... instead of revealing the uniqueness of each person, we seemed to become anonymous.[82]

Of course, one could always save the paradigm by claiming that because every dancer is an individual and has different ways of executing the same text, therefore technically, there is no such effacement of individuality. But that would be effectively making any activity, no matter how collectively uniform, an expression of individuality. Nevertheless, there is evidence that Cunningham did not, in general, produce works that effaced all differences between "masculine" and "feminine" lines.

And indeed, an interview with Catherine Kerr, one of the women Cunningham partnered with after Carolyn Brown had left the company—who was probably the equivalent of Suzanne Farrell to Balanchine—reveals that Cunningham's choreography is not completely devoid of gender distinctions, and the traditional model of pairing male and female bodies. The relationship between Cunningham and Kerr, as danced, had hints of the usual hallmarks of (heterosexual) gender and power in the dance world: teacher–student; older gentleman–younger woman; "prowler"—"prey."

Kerr, reminiscing about her relationship with Cunningham remarked:

> Of course, I was extremely flattered. I mean, I was always aware that, of course, I wasn't Carolyn [Brown] or Viola [Farber], because I wasn't his peer. I always thought that every duet played on the master-student relationship, whether it was *Squaregame* [1976] or in *Rebus* [1974] or *Roadrunners* [1979]... When Merce taught his part [in *Duets*] to Robert, "You're *prowling* [italics added]," as he promenades the woman in attitude. Then Merce looked at me and smiled. Well, I had always sensed that. So there must have been some kind of frisson that I suspect was part of his creative imagination.[83]

As Earle Brown outlines the typology of Cunningham's choreographic works, there were three kinds: 1) the "very strange, seemingly psychologically oriented solos, usually to the music of Christian Wolff, such as *Lavish Escapade*;"[84] 2) the "rather severe and 'abstract' works such as Solo Suite in *Space and Time*;"[85] and 3) the "'romantic-classic' kind of piece which always seemed to be about something, but one could never quite grasp what it was actually about. *Springweather* was distinctly the latter type."[86] It is in this third type that many critics have found (more conventionally) aesthetically appealing, in contrast to his more severe, abstract, and androgynous pieces. For example, in Terry Teachout's description of *Beach Birds for Camera* (1992), when Cunningham had already developed a flair for using the camera as an artistic medium to stage dance movement, the dance critic writes:

> This jolting transition [from black and white to color] is obviously intended to mark off the main structural event of the dance. But it also reinforces

> the romantic atmosphere of the pas de deux. It is as if Good, entering into a sexless Edenic community of bird-dancers, carries with him the charge of sexuality that brings Finlayson to life (i.e., full color). The climatic phrase of their mating dance, so memorable on stage, becomes almost unbearably intense on film.[87]

Indeed, some revisionist critics, noting the more traditional gendered elements of this kind of choreographic work, have taken Cunningham to task for not sufficiently breaking away from the traditional heterosexual performance paradigm characteristic of the dance world. Jill Johnston did a review of Cunningham's *Roaratorio* (1983), and, generally summarized, found unrevolutionary Cunningham's conventional use of ballet partnering.[88] Susan Foster has argued that Cunningham's emphasis on formal issues allowed him to hide and deflect any questions regarding his sexuality;[89] both Foster and Yutian Wong have decried Cunningham's failure to recognize the persistence of racial inequalities in modern dance.[90]

There is indeed evidence that these accusations, or negative assessments, have some accuracy. For example, in the remake of *Points in Space* (1987) as stage work, in the sequence in which Kerr formerly danced with Cunningham, and now danced with Alan Good, the balletic elements, and the resemblance to Balanchine's style, are clearly etched:

> In one sequence, twice repeated, Kerr is held under her armpits by Good so that her seat is near the floor (it's like Leto's two handmaidens in the Prologue of Balanchine's Apollo...); then she sweeps one leg out and around, pins down the foot to the floor, and pulls herself and Good in that direction. The passage has a drama reminiscent not of Apollo but of some great duets from other Balanchine ballets. So does the backbend she does in his arms, in which she walks forward, unseeing, advancing one leg through high forward developpé before planting it and moving on.[91]

Carolyn Brown noted that Merce retained a deliberate reticence about what his pieces "meant," save for some vague allusive hint, perhaps similar to a Joyceian clue. "Perhaps Merce [felt] that his dances need have no meaning for anyone but himself; certainly he [took] precautions to see that little of it is intelligible to an outsider, or for that matter to an insider. But he [did] leave clues."[92] Even more radically, Cunningham, according to Brown, stopped giving information regarding any personal information his work might have in 1953; he insisted that any reference to anything explaining his private intentions or the personal meaning of a work be redacted from an article being written by Remy Charlip, a Cunningham dancer, for the January 1954 edition of *Dance Magazine*.[93] Ramsay Burt, following the lead of queer historian Jonathan Katz,[94] points out that this period in the United States—the 1950s, the period of the Cold War and the McCarthy witch hunts—was a particularly repressive period for homosexuals; thus, for Burt, Cunningham's immersion in formal and abstract issues in order to destabilize conventional notions of order was actually a subterranean way of revolting against heteronormativity.[95] In taking this interpretation, Burt distances himself from art historian Moira Roth's interpretation of Cage's and Cunningham's artistic styles as "characterized by tones of neutrality, passivity, irony, and often, negation."[96] For Roth, Cage, and Cunningham, among others, "consciously espoused indifference as a virtue, as the correct way to deal with an uncertain world."[97] Despite acknowledging the "newspaper like" (i.e., fragmented and discontinuous) quality of Cunnningham's works, Burt argues that this seeming detachment did not necessarily mean a-political withdrawal but rather, strategic masking. He thus aligns himself with Katz and states:

> [Katz]...argues that [Cage and Cunningham, et. al.]'s shared aesthetic stance constituted a strategic way of resisting complicity with inimical social and political pressures. Being openly gay, [Katz] points out, was not a realistic option in the 1950s for Cage, Cunningham, Johns, or Rauschenberg. By troubling and undermining the normative, heterosexual way masculinity was represented within abstract expressionist painting and within expressive ideologies of dance and music, Katz suggests, Cage and fellow artists were far from being complicit with hegemonic norms.[98]

An example of such a deconstructive moment occurred in *Septet*, where Cunningham danced a solo that featured extremely demanding ballet-derived movements that somehow managed to both make themselves identifiable as "balletic" while at the same time, conveyed oddity, unsettling conventional expectations. Marcia Siegel observed that Cunningham's solo was "punctuated with very odd gestures—shoulder shakes, contractions of the upper back, a sudden fall back towards his heels and an equally quick recovery."[99] Burt interprets this as either displaying a wounded kind of masculinity or at the very least, as problematizing one of Graham's dogmas: that there is an immediate conjunction between emotional expression in dance and subterranean psychological pressures.[100] There is one more way in which Cunningham's choreography could be seen as destabilizing heteronormativity and the conventional gendered expectations regarding how male and female bodies should interact through dance. This is through the use of a subtle sense of humor. Even though Cunningham himself, when he was able, often danced duets and played the traditional supporting role, often allowing his partner to achieve extreme shapes, he never assumed the adoring stance required of balletic danseurs. Instead, like his dancers, he kept a cool, impassive, "mask like"[101] face, and often looked straight at the audience, rather than at his partner, as these muscular exploits were performed. Such a disruption of conventional expectation was unsettling to many audiences; but it could also be interpreted as a humorous and playful poke at the traditional roles assigned to ballerina and danseur.

Nevertheless, despite Cunningham's iconoclasm as a choreographer, he did maintain some conventional boundaries. First, in terms of gendering, he actually never treated male and female bodies as interchangeable, asexual units; although female dancers were given more latitude in terms of the range of movements they were allowed, male performers still had to stay within the realm of the clearly "masculine," relative to the women. As Burt notes:

> Despite this neutral stance towards gender, a real blurring of masculinity and femininity rarely if ever occurs in his work. Male dancers rarely take on movement qualities and conventions that are in the range associated with feminine behavior. Female dancers, however, get to dance material or movement qualities conventionally associated with masculinity, so that they get to be "normal" rather than mysterious, problematic, and feminine.[102]

There was another way in which Cunningham hewed to traditional boundaries in the world of dance: he strictly adhered to the distinction between a "professional" dance company and, for lack of words, amateurs—members of the larger public who could have a serious interest in dance but did not have the extensive dance training, with reputable dance professionals that he had. Thus, to the Judson Church Group, which had further radicalized and democratized his ideas to include the larger public, he had "sold out to the establishment."[103] In this area, regarding the professional status of the true dancer, Cunningham aligned himself with Balanchine and Graham: arduous training, with professionals, for him, was necessary to produce the kind of movement he sought to choreograph, even if he gave dancers relatively more latitude than either Balanchine or Graham ever had. Reynolds and MacCormick summarize the essential points in this way:

> [Cunningham] had often incorporated pedestrian movements in his pieces as one option among many, but he would not broaden his concept to sanction performers with no dance training at all, as the Judsonites did...Although Cunningham acknowledged that his notion of dance was difficult to define, he insisted it had to do with "enlargement" –an amplification of energy—something that *can be achieved only through disciplined dance technique* [italics added].[104]

In an interview, Cunningham was asked to differentiate between his work and Ann Halprin's. Halprin had founded the groundbreaking San Francisco Dancer's Workshop and whose students included, among others, Meredith Monk, Trisha Brown, Yvonne Rainer, Simone Forti, Dohee Lee, Dana Iova-Koga, Shinichi Momo Iova-Koga, Isak Immanuel, G Hoffman Soto—some of who became key figures in the even more controversial and experimental Judson Church Group.[105] Cunningham's answer was emphatic and unambiguous:

> One of the major differences between Ann Halprin and myself is that *I work with a formally trained dance company* [italics added]... From what I know of her work, she has dealt with both trained and untrained dancers in different kinds of environmental situations... She is often concerned with a particular environment and the individual's reaction to it. Well, I do that in a certain way too, but it is different because *we are a troupe of dancers. We are a repertory company* [italics added], and we tour and do pieces over and over in changing situations, so that we have to keep adjusting ourselves in a given dance anew.[106]

At the heart of this setting of boundary lines seems the anxiety that haunts the attempt to render porous the relationship between professional performer and audience: the anxiety that the resultant dance form will not be taken seriously; that it will be dismissed as simply "popular" and "pedestrian;" that it will slip from the whitened category of "high art" to the nonwhitened category of the "amateurish" and "tawdry." Nevertheless, I argue that it is precisely the maintenance of these outposts of conventional boundaries that rendered Cunningham's choreography, at least to the dance world, as both "legible" (i.e., recognizable as "dance," as opposed to gesture or movement) and legitimate. And despite the democratization of the credits of Cunningham dance concerts (a "democratization" similar to the mass of names at the end of a movie, affirming the dominance of the director or producer), Cunningham definitely emerged, like Graham or Balanchine, as the key figure who towered above his dancers, even as he expressly gave them credit for giving expression to, and thus cochoreographing, his works. The effect of having a key figure to attribute "authorship" to, eliminated any possible doubts, if any emerged, regarding whose intellectual property the choreography was.

The rest of the story of why and how Cunningham succeeded in establishing unquestioned copyright authorship of his choreographic works is more of an institutional story and its outlines are well sketched.

Despite audiences walking out on many of his performances, Cunningham, through his association with Cage, gained a loyal following and eventually, a critical audience appreciative of his work. Among his numerous awards were the National Medal of Arts (1990) and the MacArthur Fellowship (1985);[107] in addition, he was also showered with other awards, some of which were international: Jacob's Pillow Dance Award (2009), Japan's Praemium Imperiale (2005), and the British Laurence Olivier Award (1985).[108] He was also named Officier of the Legion d'Honneur in France (2004).[109]

But more importantly, perhaps learning from the success of Balanchine's estate, the Merce Cunningham Trust was established in 2000 to represent and administer the intellectual property rights to Merce Cunningham's oeuvre, which includes more than 150 dances and over 800 "Events."[110] In 2002, the IRS recognized the Trust as a 501(c)3 nonprofit corporation, "with the mission to preserve, enhance and maintain the integrity of the choreographic and artistic works of Merce Cunningham, and make such works available for the benefit of the public."[111] In 2001, the Jerome Robbins Dance Division of the New York Public Library for the Performing Arts acquired the Merce Cunningham archive.[112]

Prior to the establishment of the Trust, Cunningham (unlike Balanchine), revealing both ambition and foresight, envisaged the Legacy Plan that the Cunningham Dance Foundation announced in June 2009. The Legacy Plan included a comprehensive documentation and preservation program that ensured that pieces from Cunningham's repertory could be studied, performed, and enjoyed by future generations of dancers with knowledge of the dances' genesis.[113] In addition, the Plan provided the Merce Cunningham Trust with control over all of Cunningham's dances for licensing purposes. Cunningham also left detailed and extensive records of the dances so they could be registered with the US Copyright Office and licensed, keeping with standards of authenticity set up by Cunningham.[114] Finally, to safeguard, as much as possible, the authenticity of the presentation of Cunningham's body of work, the Legacy Plan also included an international tour for the Company, and ultimately, to close all legal loopholes (and probably prevent the kinds of legal squabbles characteristic of Graham's legacy), the closure of the Cunningham Dance Foundation, and Merce Cunningham Dance Company. It also included the transfer of all intellectual property rights and other assets to the Merce Cunningham Trust. The final stages of the plan came into full fruition on March 15, 2012.[115] Today, the Merce Cunningham Trust, like Balanchine's estate, commands a self-sufficient dance empire; perhaps having learned lessons from Balanchine's and Graham's examples, Cunningham astutely set into place an airtight way of ensuring control over his intellectual property. Despite his iconoclasm, Cunningham's choreography stayed safely within the whitened realm of "high art," which explains, to a large extent, his success at achieving, essentially, dance immortality.

Alvin Ailey: Recapturing Emotional Expression and the Theatrical

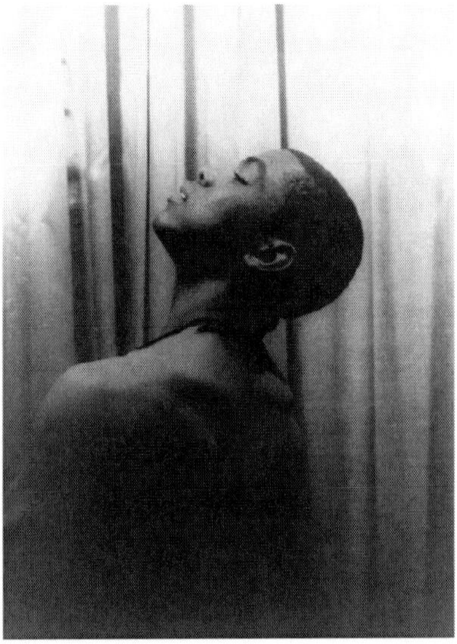

Figure 6.1 Public Domain Image of Alvin Ailey. From the Library of Congress. http://www.loc.gov/pictures/collection/van/item/2004662475/.

I end with a brief review of Alvin Ailey's choreographic and performance heritage, mainly because of the issue of race and because demonstrating that nonwhite dancers can dance (especially the ballet) as excellently as white dancers was front and center to this project. Furthermore, Alley's ownership of his choreographic works, the continuing performance of his works, as well as some of the performance practices he instituted, continue to the present. The Alvin Ailey American Dance Theater remains a commercially and artistically successful venture to this day, under the current leadership of Robert Battles who is the third person to take over the helm since the company was founded in 1958.[116] I thus wrestle with the same questions I have been struggling with throughout this project—do the categorizations of whiteness and nonwhiteness still operate with his successful establishment of a black or multiracial dance company? Why did he succeed more than not only Katherine Dunham, but also, in some quarters, more than even Merce Cunningham himself in seeking sponsorship money?

Alvin Ailey (1931–1989) was born in racially segregated Rogers, Texas during the Great Depression. His mother, Lula, was 18 years old at the time of his birth; three months later, his father, Alvin Ailey Sr., abandoned his young family.[117] Ailey's childhood was thus characterized by fatherlessness, poverty, and racism. Ku Klux Klansmen actively struck terror in the area where Ailey grew up, and the Texas newspapers featured headlines like: "Lots Drawn for Souvenirs of Lynched Negro's Anatomy," "Triple Lynching Follows Thrilling Texas Man Hunt," and "Heart and Genitals Carved from Negro's Corpse."[118] Even more horrifying for the five-year-old Alvin, he saw his mother come home late at night, crying and bruised; the young boy inferred, despite his mother's attempts at secrecy, that she had been raped—probably by white men. In his autobiography, coauthored with Peter Bailey, Alvin Ailey recalls:

> When I was about five years old, my mother was raped by four white men. She never admitted to me that it happened. She only recently found out that I knew about it. One night she didn't come home until ten P.M.... She probably had been working in some white people's kitchen. That was the other kind of work, along with picking cotton, available to black people. It was very clear to me that my mother was crying. She had bruises all over her body. I don't think she ever told anyone about it except maybe her sisters or friends from church. I kept quiet and pretended I was asleep the whole time.[119]

These experiences were formative and cemented a fear or suspicion of whites in the young Alvin. Nevertheless, his childhood also spawned the germinal elements of some of his seminal works, such as the centrality (and theatrical power) of the church to the black community and the power of emotional vulnerability and expressiveness. Thus, again, in his autobiography, Ailey remarked:

> The church was always very important, very theatrical, very intense. The life that went on there and the music made a great impression on me. At a church in Cameron, when I was about nine, I watched a procession of people, all in white, going down to a lake. The minister was baptizing everyone as the choir sang "Wade in the Water." After baptism we went into church where the minister's wife was singing a soulful version of "I've been 'Buked, I've been Scorned.' The ladies had fans they fluttered while talking and singing. All this is in my ballet *Revelations*."[120]

Revelations is undeniably one of Ailey's most enduring, classic pieces and arguably his masterpiece and the signature piece of the company. The piece is choreographed to spirituals, performed by soloists and a choir. The scene Ailey describes above is recreated, artistically, in the second part of the trilogy after a now-iconic solo, "I Want to be Ready," which involves a male dancer, seated on the floor, performing a series of contractions and releases, to rise, and execute an equally strenuous series of balancing moves.[121] Joseph Mazo provides a vivid, spellbinding description of this section of the dance as it moves into its climax:

> [B]lue and white gauzes, a white pole decked with streamers, and huge white imbrella turn the stage into a riverbank on a hot afternoon. A baptism is in progress. The dancers' undulating arms and hips flow like the stream. Short, skipping steps, pelvises forward, provide an image of freedom; arms reaching out and heads tossed back speak of religious ecstasy. When the baptized girl is carried off, protected from the sun and from evil by the white umbrella, cleansing has been accomplished.
>
> After a flashing male trio ("Sinner Man") the piece moves toward its climax. Women in bright dresses, carrying huge fans, seat themselves on stools to gossip. They are joined by the men, neatly attired, and the dance scolds, flirts and prances its way through "Rocka My Soul" as the audience claps along with the beat.[122]

Although the subject matter and temperament of *Revelations* is clearly rooted in Ailey's personal and communal black experiences, *Revelations* is one of those productions that tend to transcend racial representations, enabling audiences, regardless of race, to appreciate the artistry of dance. Not only did Ailey successfully illustrate that black dancers could perform, using ballet and modern dance technique, as beautifully as white dancers, but also that white audiences could appreciate an art form depicting black experiences without necessarily threatening or appropriating the black experience. It is fascinating that the aesthetic and theme of *Revelations*, in some ways, still parallels the whitened aesthetic of Balanchine's ballets in the overwhelming use of white in the costumes and mise en scene, as well as the thematic: breaking away from the "sinfulness" of the flesh towards a less enfleshed mode. Admittedly, Ailey's dancers do not exude ethereality, but they do have balletic arms and legs, much like Cunningham's dancers. Although some sources trace Ailey's theatrical flourishes to Martha Graham's influence[123] (and it is possible that training under her enhanced his aptitude for theatrical effects), Ailey's own remarks reinforce the notion that it was Lester Horton who most dramatically nurtured, developed, and ultimately helped shape his choreography. But before Horton, it was the glamour and charisma of Katherine Dunham's dance company's performances that created a lasting impression on the young teenager who had never seen black performers on a stage, dancing the way Dunham's company did (as opposed to vaudeville productions). Jennifer Dunning recounts how entranced the young and impressionable Ailey must have been:

> [Dunham] liked to dress in exquisite clothes or silk dressing gowns in intense blues and other vivid colors as she signed autographs and greeted friends... Backstage was satisfyingly mysterious and full of a tumultuous, different kind of life. The dancers he observed were exotic creatures, their bodies dressed and faces painted in bright and glowing colors. And Dunham herself, light skinned and speaking in a slow, soft voice, exuded not just the gaiety and power so visible onstage but the bruisable and perfumed beauty of a gardenia.
>
> He asked for [Dunham's] autograph. He would return, he knew—and he did, several times a week during the three-week engagement, recognized eventually by a kindly Dunham dancer who passed him through the stage door and into the theater without a ticket. He got more glimpses of backstage life, but it was what happened onstage that gripped his imagination. For there was theater that was both new and yet familiar, as hot and irresistible as the preachers and singers and moaners of Texas church Sundays. The women who danced were beautiful. The men were big and virile and unlike any other male dancers he had ever seen. And they were black. They were all black.[124]

Yet unlike Graham, who knew, after watching Ruth St. Denise dance, that she wanted to become a professional dancer, Ailey, probably because of the insecurity that comes with being born poor and black in a racist society, did not initially conceive of himself as a dancer. Despite his adoration of Dunham, the young Ailey aspired to be either a teacher of foreign languages or a preacher.

> I loved preachers. I thought it was the height of power and meaning to get up in front of a congregation in a wonderful costume and talk about fire and brimstone, making everyone sweat. Standing in front of the choir, I thought, was very theatrical, very exciting. But I never thought of myself as a theatrical person—not, that is, until I got to know Carmen de Lavallade.[125]

Interestingly, though there are clear indications that Ailey's sexuality was amorphous (e.g., a near-drowning episode and the frantic efforts of Chancey, an older boy, to pump the swallowed water out led to a sexual awakening),[126] Ailey declared himself very much attracted to, and "in love with" Carmen de Lavallade from the moment he set eyes on her.[127]

Although he fantasized about dancing with her, conventional norms regarding masculinity were not conducive to his attempting to explore that possibility.

> One day a young choreographer in the school picked Carmen to dance the ballet *Scheherazade* for a school assembly. She blew the whole student body away with the combination of her looks and extraordinary dancing...I remember fantasizing about dancing onstage with her, but that was impossible. No boy who put any value on his reputation dared dance the way she did and move to that kind of music. He would immediately be branded a sissy. Even those who were clearly sissies didn't have the nerve to try it.[128]

So, although Ailey admired Gene Kelly (1912–1996) and Fred Astaire (1899–1987) and took tap lessons[129] (dance lessons that did not endanger his masculinity as a man, and considered culturally appropriate for a black teenager), he did not dare to explore dancing any further. It was Carmen, after watching Alvin doing gymnastics (and probably realized, in addition to the natural grace he had, that he would be perfect for doing lifts), who actively invited him to join her in taking classes from Lester Horton.[130] De Lavallade later explained: "He was doing free exercise, and that always looked like dancing to me."[131] Like Dunham, Ailey got his break mainly because a white choreographer-teacher took him under his wing and became the father figure Ailey never had. And it was his partnering with de Lavallade, a woman like Katherine Dunham, who had "exotic" good looks, a fair complexion, and charisma and grace onstage[132] that paved the way to his becoming a serious and widely acclaimed modern concert dancer.

Lester Horton, like Martha Graham, was inspired by a performance by Denishawn to become a professional dancer; he dropped out of high school and pursued his ambitions with passion.[133] He was lucky enough to become the choreographer, dramature, and star of *The Song of Hiawatha*, an Indiana community- or little-theater production and was spotted by arts patron Clara Bates who installed him in her carriage house, paid for lessons, and sent him to Chicago where Horton was exposed to more spectacular and avant-garde trends in dancing and to Santa Fe, where Horton learned about native American dance and music.[134] Bates was also Horton's ticket to California, where, to her chagrin, he decided to stay behind in Los Angeles where he toured with Michio Ito, an innovative Japanese dancer and choreographer from whom Horton learned many things that influenced his later style.[135] "Horton learned to move large groups of dancers around the stage in formal patterns. And props, he discovered, need not be simply an element in a set or a device to further a narrative; used organically, as a part of choreography, props could extend and color movement."[136] In addition, by the time Ailey started taking lessons from Horton, Horton had replaced his earlier fascination with native American themes with political critique—a fact that threatened to endanger him during the communist witchhunts of the 1940s and 1950s.[137] All these qualities were eventually to find their way into Ailey's own style of choreographing. Ailey admitted, when he had to unexpectedly take over Horton's position after Horton died of a heart attack in 1953,[138] that initially, all he could conceive of was to imitate what he thought Horton would probably have done had he remained in charge. Ailey remarked:

> I did everything I thought Lester would do. I designed the costumes, I did Noguchi-type sets, I went to the shops for fabrics. And I began to choreograph dances. I didn't know anything about form and such. *I only knew how to imitate Lester* [italics added].[139]

There were other aspects of the Horton aesthetic that had attracted Ailey to him, even while Ailey continued to study college-level courses in Romance languages (at various times, with UCLA, Los Angeles City College and Berkeley); Ailey enjoyed, in particular, the works of James Baldwin, Langston Hughes, Carson McCullers, Tennessee Williams, while taking dance lessons from Horton.[140] Among Horton's many pieces, Ailey found the following particularly appealing: "dance theatre pieces based on pictures by Paul Klee, poems by Garcia Lorca, music by Ellington and Stravinsky, and even Mexican themes."[141] Another Hortonesque influence on Ailey was the firm conviction in building a multiracial dance company. Horton defended this conviction fiercely, which was very much against the temper of the times.

> Horton's company was the first established multiracial troupe in the country, and he resisted all suggestions that he split his dancers into segregated units, even though that lost him much-needed nightclub jobs. A champion of all his dancers, he campaigned, tirelessly, angrily and successfully, to get charges dropped against a gentle young black student—one he knew to be incapable of violence—who had been wrongly accused of raping a white woman.[142]

Ailey wrote candidly of the pervasive racism in the dance world in his cowritten autobiography, citing only Horton and Graham as the exceptions to the general norm. Ailey recalled that during the 1940s and 1950s, racism was standard practice in the American dance world. Racism was justified in various ways: black feet weren't "shaped right," black derriers were deemed "too big," black legs "wouldn't turn out correctly" and so on.[143] Both major and minor ballet and modern dance companies shut their doors to aspiring black dancers. The only exceptions were Martha Graham and Lester Horton. "Lester—a happy exception—opened his arms to talent when and where he saw it." [144]

Ailey inherited Horton's multiracial dance company, temporarily, when Horton unexpectedly died.[145] Ailey threw himself into his new post with enthusiasm. Within one year, Ailey had created three original dances for Horton's company: *Creation of the World*, choreographed to the music of Darius Milhaud; *According to St. Francis*, set to the music of Gershon Kingsley; and *Mourning Morning*, influenced by Tennessee Williams and choreographed to the music of Gertrude Rivers Robinson.[146] Unfortunately, reviews of the young Ailey's choreography were mixed, and even worse, these same works were greeted by even harsher reviews when they were presented at Jacob's Pillow, the dance Mecca headed by Ted Shawn.[147] One particularly scathing review, penned by David Bongard of the *Herald*, bore hints of racism. Dunning summarized the essence of his review this way:

> "The frustrated world of Tennessee Williams is conceived in the most abstract terms in 'Morning Mourning' [sic] so that if program notes weren't available for proper advice, the net effect would easily have been 'According to St. Francis,' which was the second Ailey premiere for the same evening," Bongard wrote. He went on to add, in rather thoughtless language, given the race of the choreographer, that the second piece was "tarred with the same brush."[148]

Nevertheless, at least Ailey did receive full credit as choreographer—at the young age of approximately 22;[149] this was inconceivable for women like Fuller and Baker, and even Graham, who was known, initially, more as a performer than a choreographer. Nevertheless, shortly thereafter, de Lavallade and Ailey decided to accept the invitation to join, as featured dancers, the cast of the Broadway show, *House of Flowers*, adapted by Truman Capote from one of his short stories; the show was to be staged in New York under the direction of Herbert Ross.[150] Although Ailey promised to return (and probably intended to), he never did; the Horton Dance Company limped on for six more years before it ceased to exist.[151]

It is a fascinating footnote to the story that Balanchine was originally hired to choreograph *House of Flowers* but he was fired because "according to Ailey, Balanchine's choreography was both too good and not showy enough for the Broadway stage."[152] The statement is telling because it reveals both Ailey's and Broadway's preference for spectacle that audiences can relate to, rather than the muscular discipline that both Balanchine and to a more abstract extreme, Cunningham valued. It reveals, to some extent, a relativity in dance aesthetic: what is considered the paramount standard in ballet is not necessarily appropriate on a different kind of stage. Unfortunately, it also reveals that Ailey's natural propensities and talent for theatrical staging were double-edged swords—they were the means through which dance could potentially reach broader public audiences, but they were also the means through which Ailey's work could be dismissed as "mere entertainment" or "mere spectacle" for the masses, a criticism that sounds strangely like the N.Y. District Court's dismissal of Fuller's copyright claims discussed in chapter 3. This is a criticism that would continue to haunt Ailey, despite or even because of, his popular success, as we shall later see.

He remarked that Balanchine's choreography for the show was "very, very good" as a "kind of neoclassical mambo" with "wonderful staging."[153] However, the problem with Balanchine's choreography, for Ailey, was that "it didn't have enough commercial bump and grind."[154] That lack of commercial appeal led to Balanchine's being replaced by Ailey. Ailey's reflections are again insightful, revealing that even if Balanchine was interested in popularizing dance as well, there were limits, usually concerning the overt representation of sexuality that he would not breach, unlike Ailey. Balanchine's choreography, in other words, remained safely insulated within the realm of "high art," despite its popularity precisely because it would not breach whitened kinesthetic conventions of choreography. Ailey, on the other hand, reached even broader audiences through Broadway than Balanchine, but his choreography, despite its use of whitened elements, would never rise to becoming Balanchine's rival, especially in the highly esteemed world of ballet. Ailey's key virtue, compared to Balanchine, therefore amounted to commercial savviness rather than choreographic brilliance. This, too, is a critique that persists, even today, as we shall see later.

Nevertheless, while Ailey was at New York, he made sure to take lessons from the "greats" in the New York arts scene; these included Martha Graham, Hanya Holm, Charles Weidman, and Katherine Dunham as well as her protégée, Syvilla Fort.[155] He also further credentialized himself by studying ballet with Karel Shook, composition with Doris Humphrey, and acting with Stella Adler.[156] These credentials, he probably realized, as did Dunham, allowed him more access into the whitened world of dance on the East Coast, which did not have someone like Lester Horton, whose color blindness seemed without peer.

New York Broadway stages tended to be closed to blacks, save for the usual token blacks who usually visually resembled white aesthetic preferences, but even those were also relegated to the background as actors, even if they could dance. Blacks could be cast as "islands" in *South Pacific*, but even these bit parts were usually given to whites, who then changed their skin color through make-up.[157] The same questions and the same justifications discussed earlier in chapter 2 regarding whether or not blacks could dance as well as whites were very much a part of the atmosphere. A common rationale was that there were literally no shows about blacks, or that blacks self-excluded themselves by not auditioning.[158] But when blacks did show up, no matter how well they auditioned, the "token blacks" were usually already in place or they were blatantly rebuffed despite an open admiration for their abilities.[159] Ballet stages were even worse because critics tended to be reluctant to accept blacks in "nontraditional" (i.e., "ethnic") roles; in 1932, *New York Times* critic John Martin warned black artists against both "copying the white man's art" as well as generating the more conventional work that whites "choose to believe is Negro art"[160]—advice that revealed the double-bind in which blacks found themselves. Again, the usual justifications for excluding blacks were rampant on both ballet and modern dance stages: blacks did not have the "right" physique; they therefore always looked "out of place" or "miscast," sometimes even when they were fairly complected.[161] White critics like Martin worried incessantly about the "authenticity" of performances if black dancers were allowed on to balletic, modern and Broadway stages,[162] but Martin did not question the authenticity of a white woman's (like Helen Tamiris' or Martha Graham's) ability to surround themselves with nonwhite dancers in order to stage their version of what blackness or nonwhite cultures signified according to their imagined reconstructions.

Nevertheless, as his reputation grew, Ailey did find work. He danced with the companies of Sophie Maslow, Anna Sokolow, and Donald McKayle.[163] In 1955, he was featured in the off-Broadway play, *The Carefree Tree*. In 1956, he toured the country featured in two shows: 1) Harry Bellefonte's *Sing Man Sing*, choreographed by Walter Nicks, in which he partnered with Mary Hinkson; and 2) Geoffrey Holder's *Caribbean Calypso Carnival*, along with a cast that included Donald McKayle and Maya Angelou.[164] However, Ailey did not take either too seriously; they were simply jobs to pay the bills for him and they were generally considered "popular" rather than anything resembling "serious" dancing. Unfortunately, Ailey did share one trait with Josephine Baker, which sometimes made it difficult to work with him and may have helped reinforce stereotypes—because he did not have formal training, he had a habit of not keeping track of set patterns and tended to improvise—much to the chagrin of those who collaborated with him. Dunning recounts:

> In *Sing, Man, Sing*, [Ailey] exasperated Mary Hinkson, his partner, and, like him, a featured dancer, with his lack of formal dance training and the unpredictability of his onstage behavior. In part, the problem was his old one of forgetting choreography. Sometimes he was so distant that he seemed to be in another world. And he would occasionally seize on an idea for ornamenting his performance but neglect to tell Hinkson, who once found her grip slipping in one moment of partnering because Alvin had experimented with oiling his body a little to give it an extra gleam onstage.[165]

In addition, Ailey's unusual looks, especially for someone who attempted balletic movements, probably added to his "exotic" appeal, much as Dunham's unusual looks, combined with academic degrees, allowed her some passage into the whitened realms of privilege. Christine Lawson, another beautiful dancer who was five years younger than Ailey, and with whom Ailey cochoreographed and performed a duet and became hired as lead dancers for the cast of *Jamaica*, reminisced: "I remember Jack Cole [the director and choreographer] telling Alvin there wasn't a stage in the world big enough for him to dance on because he was all over the place. Alvin had that incredible look! He looked like a truck driver but he was a lyrical mover, which was a terrific dichotomy to behold."[166] Lawson's remarks reveal that though male danseurs are typically expected to look masculine and exude power, Ailey's gymnastically sculpted black male body somehow seemed, in comparison, hypermasculinized and much more muscular/fleshy in appearance. But he could move as lyrically as any typical looking danseur, which was both a shock and a source of fascination for the white dance world.

It is important to note that Ailey was cast for a Broadway show, *Jamaica* (1957), which featured "exotic" looking actors and dancers. The stars were Lena Horne and Ricardo Montalban, along with Ossie Davis and Josephine Premice.[167] Among the dancers were Billy Wilson, Audrey Mason, Pearl Reynolds, Barbara Wright, and Claude Thompson.[168] But Ailey learned to appreciate Horne for more than being a pretty face with a sultry voice.

> Beneath her radiance and honeyed reserve was a woman who had sidestepped racial stereotyping by playing femme fatales instead of mammies. Her film career languished and her friendship with the outspokenly leftist Paul Robeson put Horne in further jeopardy. But she had continued to push for integration in the world in which she worked. "I fought for a black stage manager, for mixing minority musicians from the union and for a multiracial show, with Asians, blacks, whites, Mexicans, Puerto Ricans," Horne said of *Jamaica*. "You broke down the wall and opened another door."[169]

The choice between femme fatale and mammie roles clearly outlined the choices black actresses faced in the whitened realm of Hollywood. Nevertheless, Horne had successfully achieved stardom, despite her slippage from the "A" list; and it is precisely because of the glamour of that stardom that she was able to open doors for others. And it is through one of those doors that Ailey, whom she affectionately called "Earth Man," and constantly complimented on his dancing,[170] that Ailey was fortunate enough to step through.

However, 1958 was the year that the Alvin Ailey American Dance Theater, as the entity, was formed.[171] The group had 12 performers, including Ailey; the concert, held on March 30 at Ninety-second Street YM-YWHA,[172] featured two premieres, one of which was the trend-setting *Blues Suite*, which has been described as a "visual equivalent of blues."[173] The subject matter of the piece is the lifestyle of the men and women who inhabit the "honky-tonks of the Brazos Valley;" it implies that there is no real escape from the conflicts that characterize such neighborhoods, save for brief, temporary respites—the cycles of socioeconomic stasis, imprisonment in poverty and sexual dueling will go on, despite a temporary break, even for social misfits. Interestingly, the mise en scene and narrative resemble those traditionally enacted in Argentine tangos, which are usually set in bordellos or the street and have a similar "ethnicized" look of sensuality, passion, and poverty, and a similar narrative of the unremitting cyclicality of such economically dire and emotionally perilous conditions.

But the choreography of *Blues Suite* clearly introduced what became a hallmark of Ailey's choreography—"the gliding step, the pelvis thrust forward, the head pushed up, the long body line. The strong torso that provides a center for the limbs comes from Horton, but the rest comes from Ailey and the Brazos Valley."[174] Although Ailey clearly incorporated balletic elements, it has been hailed principally as "a major step forward in the development of black American dance."[175] In retrospect, *Blues Suite* has generally not been interpreted as an expressionist political tract, but simply "an honest response to honest music."[176] That is, Ailey's work has been read, by critics, not as a "black" dance but as an art form that expresses universal sentiments—an interpretation denied to, for example, Josephine Baker and Katherine Dunham, despite the persistence of similar choreographic elements (and subject matter, such as the "naturalness" of sexual relations between men and women), especially in the case of Dunham, such as the persistence of "high heads, free pelvic thrusts, curved, reaching bodies."[177] One can only surmise that again, in Ailey's case it was masculinity or the social valuation of maleness, rather than blackness, that enabled the possibility of entering into the realm of representing universal emotions, regardless of race.

Nevertheless, despite the success of the staging of *Blues Suite*, again, the usual analogies to "animal" qualities and "innate" abilities that haunted both Josephine Baker's and Katherine Dunham's reviews, still persisted alongside what rhetorically seemed very carefully measured praise. John Martin of the *New York Times* remarked that *Blues Suite* was "overflowing with variety, beautifully staged with excellent décor and costumes by Geoffrey Holder and *on this occasion* [italics added] was superbly danced." He described [Ailey] as having a "*rich animal quality of movement* [italics added] and an *innate sense* [italics added] of theatrical projection."[178] *Dance Magazine* chimed in, using similar rhetorical flourishes: "[Ailey] reminds one of a *caged lion full of lashing power* [italics added] that he can contain or release at will. And perhaps because he is so unusual, he knows *instinctively how to compose* [italics added] for other unusual dancers, notably Charles Moore and Clive Thompson."[179]

But despite, or even because of, the resounding success of *Revelations*, Ailey continued to be haunted by doubts about his talents. What if it would be misrepresented by later generations of dancers? What if it would be misunderstood by later audiences? How could he maintain artistic and legal control of it? How could he introduce just enough novelty, each time it would be performed, so it would not turn stale and caricaturesque? What if he could not produce another such masterpiece? These, of course, are the thoughts of someone who engages with what he knows is a precariously fickle and racist system, whose demands of "genius" seem impossible to bear to someone who has always been taught that even his physique was not the "right type," let alone his movements. Dunning remarked:

> The success of *Revelations* dogged Alvin all his life. He knew the worth of the dance and cherished it in spite of himself, allowing only one other company to dance it, and that for a limited time. But he worried that impressionable young dancers, hearing the wild applause that invariably greets the piece, would assume that their performances were perfect. He worried that they could not understand its soul, coming as they did from worlds so different from the dancers for whom it was created. And, always, the singular and unrepeatable-seeming success of *Revelations* underscored Alvin's doubts about his gifts, driving him to compete uneasily with himself for his entire career.[180]

Perhaps as a response to the pressure of producing new work, after the resounding success of *Revelations*, Ailey shrewdly added, as part of his vision of the dance company, the dimension of being a repertory dance theater—one that would showcase major works of American modern dance. In 1959, after *Blues Suite*, his company performed *Phoebe Snow*, choreographed by Talley Beatty; *Phoebe Snow* depicted the "violence and desolation of life in the black ghetto of a Midwestern city, and is charged with the jagged flashes afforded by jazz technique."[181] Ailey also chose, many times, to showcase the work of lesser known choreographers, perhaps choosing strategically to make allies of his potential rivals. Paul Szilard, who became the company's international booking agent, used to complain: "Why not a Robbins, a Balanchine, a Graham? No one has ever heard of these Jimmy Smiths and Larry Browns."[182] Perhaps it was Ailey's determination to showcase choreographers, regardless of race, who created things that in his view, were interesting, that prompted him to make these decisions. But Ailey also made strategic choices regarding better known works and successfully made his dance company the stage upon which the "history of modern dance"[183] could be reenacted. In 1972, he produced May O'Donnell's *Suspension*; in 1973, he continued this retrospective staging by producing Donald McKayle's *Rainbow 'Round My Shoulder*, Katherine Dunham's *Choros* and Ted Shawn's *Kinetic Molpai,* in addition to works choreographed by Paul Primus and José Limón, among others.[184] But even more telling was Ailey's rhetoric. Regarding how the repertory should be viewed against the challenges of memory and posterity, he remarked:

> "[M]odern dancers should do repertory as classical companies do. We've lost too many works over the years. The idea of presenting important pieces still needs to be dealt with in a serious way in American dance, and it's important to keep the ballets alive. *They are part of our cultural heritage as Americans* [italics added]."[185]

In taking this position, Ailey aspired to not only enshrine modern dance as worthy of such memorialization alongside ballet, but also of himself as its historian, with his tastes and instincts regarding what constitutes "good dancing" as the guide as to what would constitute the canon. Even more dramatically, Ailey used the word "ballet" to mean "any serious work, not only one made in the classical style;"[186] such a radical revision of dance vocabulary would have been inconceivable to both Baker and Dunham, for example. Finally, Ailey strove to represent, not only the black community, but also "America" in general—a goal that had been impossible to achieve, even for someone as talented, beautiful, and educated as Katherine Dunham.

But the time was ripe for such ambition as the Civil Rights Movement was gaining momentum, and grants and other forms of support were being set aside for minority artists. Interestingly, Naima Prevots' research has shown that when rivaling applications for funding were submitted by both Cunningham's and Ailey's groups, the dance panel of the American National Theater and Academy (ANTA), the grant-giving body of the State Department that funded foreign tours, decided against two applications by Cunningham and approved funding for Ailey's Pacific Asian tour in 1962.[187] Prevots shows that the dance panel then dismissed Cunningham's work as simply sensationalist and publicity seeking,[188] while ANTA remained interested in sponsoring Ailey's work as an ambassador of American dance since 1958.[189]

Although Ailey was suspicious of the government's motives, fully aware that the company was being used as a pawn propagandistically, "seeking to advertise a false tolerance by showcasing a modern Negro dance group,"[190] Ailey accepted the funding, which boosted his dance company's reputation to becoming, like Dunham's, a "cultural ambassador to the world."[191] Like Dunham's company, international success became the crucial pathway to national renown; in its earliest years, the company seemed to spend most of its time touring and performing internationally.

> The AAADT [Alvin Ailey American Dance Theater] established its vast international reputation through a series of tours begun in 1962 by a five-month engagement in Southeast Asia and Australia. Sponsored by the International Exchange Program under the Kennedy administration, this tour established a pattern of performance in foreign countries that continued with a trip to Rio de Janeiro (1963); a European tour including London, Hamburg, and Paris (1964); an engagement at the World Festival of Negro Arts in Dakar, Senegal (1966); a 16-week European tour, including the Holland Festival in Amsterdam (1967); a visit to Israel (August 1967); a U.S. State Department-sponsored nine-nation tour of Africa (1967); and a performance at the Edinburgh Festival in Scotland (1968). In 1970 the AAADT became the first American modern dance company to perform in the postwar Soviet Union. The company has retained peerless stature as a touring ambassador of goodwill since the 1970s.[192]

Internationally, it was very clear that Alvin Ailey's work represented the best and most cutting edge of American modern dance choreography. Nationally, however, how far, how consistently, and how effectively, he represented "the best in American modern dance" was still up for some debate—a trend that continues today. Ailey is acknowledged for his theatricality and his ability to draw in large, heterogenous audiences; but he is not, to traditionalists, truly groundbreaking as a choreographer, the way Balanchine and Cunningham were. He is perceived as a popularizer—something that is a positive trait, in relation to Balanchine, but less an unambiguous compliment, in relation to Ailey. Mazo, who is often complimentary of Ailey, wrote, synthesizing the "conventional" wisdom regarding what constitutes "greatness" in choreography:

> Ailey is definitely not a member of the avant garde. In some ways, he goes back to the simple, direct style of Denishawn. His dance celebrates athleticism, his presentations celebrate theatricality, his theater celebrates excitement. He has brought black audiences into the theater and shown white audiences something of the tradition of black dance. He has made his stage a place where various styles of dance can be presented in proximity to one another, and he has brought about a fusion of balletic, jazz, and modern techniques. *His faults and virtues are those of American show business* [italics added]. He can slip into banality, even into crassness one evening, and rise to excitement, to a keen

> sense of theatrical presentation, and to emotional power the next. He has made life a little easier for black dancers and choreographers, and he has sent a lot of people away happy and willing to come back.[193]

Perhaps that assessment is attributable to the fact that unlike Graham or Cunningham, for example, who had clear kinesthetic techniques associated with their choreographies, Ailey had no such program in place. Instead, Ailey simply built on whatever training they had prior to joining the company; and instead of specializing, he instead required his dancers to learn the choreographic works and dance techniques of different choreographers, whether they be balletic, modern, Broadway, or "ethnic." Interestingly, this is certainly the philosophy behind such contemporary popular reality TV shows such as *So You Think You Can Dance*, but it is clear that such TV shows occupy a less "serious" stature in the dance world. It is also clear that Ailey's dance company did not have the same uniform look and homogenous, cohesive movement characteristic of other, more specialized dance companies, whether in ballet or modern dance. Mazo remarked:

> There is a question as to whether the Ailey dancers can take on a variety of techniques and mannerisms without diluting their own immediately recognizable style. The troupe moves with energy, muscularity, and wit, with big driving gestures and clearly defined rhythms. Individual personalities define themselves so clearly that *ensemble passages look less like the drill formations of a regular army corps than the exercises of a dedicated band of guerillas* [italics added]. One reason for this is that the battalion has not been recruited from the same kinetic population.[194]

However, one of Ailey's dancers attempted a description of what she called the "technique" Ailey used, although admittedly, it was Lester Horton who had designed it, not Ailey. Marjorie (Berman) Perces explained that Lester was especially talented at analyzing movement. For Perces, Lester was very concerned with each individual dancer's body; thus, Lester's technique focused on "developing weaker parts of the body," such as the feet, back, and abdominal muscles.[195] Using simple lines, Lester choreographed new movements that dancers could easily execute. In addition, Lester's technique also focused on "motion designed to extend joint mobility" and on constant experimentation on ways to descend to and ascend from the floor into horizontal positions.[196] Designed in this way, Horton's choreography possessed the potential to "evoke a rich variety of expressive emotions."[197]

Unfortunately, Ailey himself, probably because he was not classically trained, talked about qualities, rather than specific mechanisms of training the body, when he described what he looked for, and tried to inculcate, in his dancers. In one statement, he remarked that he sought "the total dancer, who has an early ballet background and an overlay of modern dance training and some knowledge of jazz or ethnic styles;"[198] and to explain the attributes that embody this ideal, he pointed to "speed, line, placement, technique, and physical beauty."[199] And even more poetically, he wrote:

> "I look for dancers who have something unusual about them physically—a special turn of the leg, a special stretch of the back. I look for dancers who have rubato in their bodies...I look for dancers who have an oozy quality in their movement. I like dancers who are temperamental, who are expressive, who show their feelings, who are open and out, not hidden, who want to show themselves to the audience. I like personalities, not cookie-cutter dancers—a row of this, a row of that. That's what I accuse Balanchine of: making everyone who dances for him blank-faced."[200]

The contrast, therefore, between Ailey's aesthetic and Balanchine's (and Cunningham's) focus on technique could not be more apparent. Unfortunately, however, Balanchine's and Cunningham's focus on technique and a more "scientific" (i.e. fixable and replicable) approach to choreography have a tendency, given both current attitudes in the dance establishment and contemporary copyright laws, to privilege their choreographies and methods more than Ailey's more emotional, intuitive, improvisational approach. Thus, we come full circle—although it is clear that Ailey's ownership of his choreographic works are uncontested, perhaps it is in the realm of public appeal that he, like Loíe Fuller, achieved unambiguous immortality. Much as Fuller dismissed the mechanical quality of her legions of imitators, Ailey dismissed the cookie-cutter production of dance technicians: "Today's kids are very technical. They can do eighteen pirouettes on a dime and get their leg way over their head and hold it there. But the insight is not the same: It's not the same as giving, not as warm. They need to give themselves to the dance, to project themselves from the inside out."[201] And this is where we see, clearly, both Horton's and Graham's influences on Ailey, and the contrast with Balanchine and Cunningham, whose choreographies, in comparison, stay much more in keeping with a rational, whitened aesthetic.

At the time Ailey first built his dance company, even if Ailey aspired towards the same multiracial composition as Horton had, all of the members of his company were black, much as Cunningham's core of committed dancers remained white; nevertheless, like Dunham, Ailey encouraged his dancers to share the stage with instrumentalists and singers. After the first six years of being an exclusively black dance company, Ailey's reputation was sufficiently entrenched, and he was able to enlarge the group's composition to include "a more diverse repertory [and] he hired Hispanics, Asians, and whites as well."[202] Nevertheless, in his coauthored biography, Ailey acknowledged that attempting to keep this vision of a genuinely multiracial dance company is an ever-shifting target, constantly endangered by underlying tension and disagreement.

Thus, despite Ailey's desire to integrate a mixed race company, he acknowledged the more commercially lucrative works of either television or film, which tended to siphon off most white dancers who could dance at the same level as his dance company. He admitted that "superb" white artists, such as Maxine Sherman, tended to leave his company "because [Sherman] said she would never get to do *Cry*, and she was right... Other [white or nonblack] dancers in the company feel the same way. They're convinced I favor the black dancers and that I'm never going to put an Asian or a Caucasian above the black women in my company."[203] His ultimate response to this critique of racial partiality was that whites and dancers of other races had performed other leading parts, except for *Cry*, which Ailey set aside for black female dancers as the piece "dedicated to my mother and black women everywhere."[204]

Cry (1971) is a solo Ailey choreographed to Alice Coltrane's "Something about John Coltrane," Laura Nyro's "Been on a Train," and The Voices of East Harlem's "Right On, Be Free."[205] Like *Revelations*, it is about the journey from pride to degradation, and back up to a new sense of self-worth, but it is meant to be danced by a particularly powerful and expressive female soloist; it was designed for Judith Jamison, one of Ailey's star dances.

> At first, an exile, she unwinds the headband she wears and uses it as a rag with which to scrub the floors of other peoples' homes. Her hands reach high and flutter like captive birds. She contracts in anguish, doubles over, swings wildly from the waist, stretches toward freedom in arabesque.
>
> She sinks to the ground, but pulls herself up, writhing and fighting, until at last she stands erect, rises to half-toe and moves toward the wings of the stage in short, rhythmic, ecstatic steps.[206]

The movements are derived from the body vocabularies of African dance, modern technique, jazz styles, and ballet, but the movements are simple, pared down to their expressive core. It is hardly surprising that Ailey meant this to be a piece dedicated to "all black women everywhere—especially our mothers,"[207] and for that reason, he reserved it purely for black female dancers, despite his remarks that he "could not forgive Agnes de Mille"[208] for her thinly veiled justification that it was "historically inaccurate" to allow black dancers into a Texas musical, *Ninety Degrees in the Shade*.[209] The difference between Ailey and de Mille was that whereas Ailey allowed other solo parts to be danced by white and nonblack dancers, de Mille refused to hire any black dancers for her productions.

Ailey did not flinch from stating that "the question of dance and race is an ever-present one." But to him, the question was more complex than whether he was in collusion with "white" or "black" communities. Thus, in 1970, when he was commissioned to choreograph Duke Ellington's *The River* for the American Ballet Theater, he found himself ambivalent when the lead role was given to the only black man on the company, regardless of his dance abilities.[210] Similarly, when he started using both white and Japanese dancers in *Blues Suite* and *Revelations*, he "got flack from black groups who resented it" and received many letters in protest against that decision."[211] Still, Ailey defended his position by saying:

> What we are talking about here is dance. We're talking about fantasy, not reality. We're in the theater, not in a history seminar. It's the same as saying that Japanese dancers can't dance the blues—well, they do in *my* company. Japanese dancers understand the blues as well as, anybody.[212]

Nevertheless, Ailey did create some pieces that got behind the façade, fantasy, and glamour of stardom. *Flowers* (1971), set to Janis Joplin's music, *The Mooche* (1975), choreographed to one of Duke Ellington's compositions, and *To Bird—With Love* (1984), set to a medley of the music of various jazz greats, including Charlie Parker, all contrasted public adulation with private alienation and sadness. While not specifically a "black theme," these can be interpreted as having a more intense resonance for black communities, for whom the star system simply magnifies these conflicts.

In terms of sexuality, although there are hints of other possibilities, such as in Ailey's choreographic depictions of the misfits in *Revelations*, Ailey's choreography generally stayed safely within the expected boundaries of conventional heteronormativity. The men in his choreography, in general, were still essentially studs, exuding all the expected masculine traits, set by the template of Ted Shawn—powerful, fast, muscular. As Burt notes, "[m]ost of the choreography Ailey created for male dancers fits the sorts of representation of masculinity [characteristic of Ted Shawn's and Martha Graham's choreography]. Like Shawn [and Graham], Ailey choreographed rugged hypermasculine roles that deflected any suggestion that he or any of his male dancers might be gay."[213]

Despite Ailey's studied eclecticism and his hybridizing of a "balletic bottom" with a "modern top," among other body vocabularies,[214] the specter of his commercialism haunts his work—a charge that when applied to Balanchine, becomes a compliment, rather than an inadequacy. To this charge of commercialism, Marcia Siegel attempted to defend him by writing that his commercialism did not "vulgarize or cheapen the modern idiom."[215] Laying a clear contrast between Ailey and Cunningham, Siegel further argued:

> [Ailey] picks out features that are most distinctive and appealing about modern dance and heightens them—its concern with the dancer's relationship to space, for example, or the adaptation of movement to dancers' individual styles, rather than the subordination of the individual to the demands of movement. He avoids the strangeness and choreographic idiosyncrasy that made people think modern dance was "difficult" and presents a very clear, unambiguous event.[216]

And to the charge of commercialism (and its implied darker twin, trivialization), Ailey himself shrugged and remarked: "It doesn't bother me to be called popular, in the good sense of the word, or commercial, in the good sense of the word... First, get the people in the theater; then you can show them anything you want. But you can't show them anything at all if they're still outside."[217] Nevertheless, it is clear that unlike his most credentialed female equivalent, Katherine Dunham, Ailey had achieved much more in terms of establishing choreographic ownership of his works and of creating at least some pieces that even white critics described as "works of genius."

By the time Ailey passed away on December 1, 1989, allegedly due to a "blood disorder," but actually due to AIDS (which he hid, to spare his mother the public embarrassment),[218] his stature as a choreographer was firmly in place, in spite of his persistent financial troubles, drug abuse, and the emotional crisis caused by the death of one of his close friends, Joyce Trisler,[219] eventually culminating in a much-publicized breakdown.[220] He had choreographed about 79 ballets, many of which were performed by a host of major dance companies, including the American Ballet Theatre, The Joffrey Ballet, Dance Theatre of Harlem, Paris Opera Ballet, and La Scala Ballet.[221] Among the many awards he was showered with were: the Dance Magazine Award (1975); the Springarn Medal (1979), given to him by the National Association for the Advancement of Colored People (NAACP); the Capezio Award (1979);[222] the Samuel H. Scripps American Dance Festival Award (1987); and the Kennedy Center Honors Prize (1988).[223] Ailey also received honorary doctorates from Princeton University, Bard College, and Adelphi University.[224]

Yet unlike Cunningham's "Legacy Project," the AAADT does not seem to have an imposing legal and institutional mooring. Ailey stopped performing in 1965, and in the 1970s, slowed his choreographic efforts down to attend the mundane tasks of administration and fundraising[225]—tasks both Balanchine and Graham tried their hardest to avoid and in spite of which, the company's financial difficulties persisted. After Ailey's death, Judith Jamison became the artistic director of the company, working closely with rehearsal director and veteran company member, Masazumi Chaya.[226] But it was only in 1992 that *Dance Magazine* proclaimed the AAADT "recession-proof" due to the concerted efforts of the Dance Foundation Incorporated's board of directors.[227] In some ways, this is not surprising, as Ailey himself acknowledged that in the funding community there are "two dance worlds and two very different ways of thinking."[228] First and foremost is the ballet world, which "gets the lion's share of the money."[229] Ballet budgets are "naturally" bigger because they need expensive pointe shoes and require pianists. As a counterpoint to the balletic dance world, Ailey gestured to the modern dance world, which he characterized as "barefoot and not elitist."[230] And hardly surprisingly, Ailey pointed to a long history of economic sponsorship and cultural privileging that elevated the ballet world as more "worthy" of being regarded as "high art" and thus, of funding, compared with modern dance. "Automatically, because of its elite position in everyone's mind, having come, as it did, from the royal courts over the centuries, classical ballet is the funding world's pet project."[231] Despite Cunningham's and Ailey's common revolt against ballet and classicism, Cunningham remained closer to the whitened world of "high art," while Ailey strove to make dance as accessible as possible to all popular audiences, relinquishing the status of "high art" for "popularity." And that, to some extent, perhaps explains why their funding mechanisms and choreographic legacies are perceived very different. Nevertheless, both achieved something denied to Fuller, Baker, Dunham and to some extent, Graham—unambiguous ownership of their choreographic works.

Conclusion

In many ways, Cunningham and Ailey intersected in their revolt against classicism and the dominance of ballet, and their creation of hybrid forms of dance, combining both white and nonwhite elements of choreography. However, whereas Cunningham subtly problematized conventional depictions of heteronormative masculinity, the aesthetic he developed remained safely within the whitened realm of "high art" with its emphasis on technique. In contrast, though Ailey achieved the distinction of being more than a "black performer" to become an internationally recognized "American choreographer," his predominant depictions of gender relations remained safely within the heterosexual realm (one attribute of whiteness as Richard Dyer argued and which I have explained in chapter 2), despite Ailey's private life. While Cunningham experimented with integrating avant-garde art and cutting edge technologies into his predominantly abstract works, Ailey preferred to return to the basics of theatrical staging, focusing on simpler lines, emotional expressiveness, costuming and lighting, and connection with popular audiences. Cunningham's inclusion of new technologies, such as magnetic tape, film and video into his choreography probably strengthened his claim to choreographic ownership thus helping him to overcome the usual copyright hurdle of fixation, and probably increased the perceived originality of his work. In contrast, Ailey's preference for more conventional means of staging, devoid of, or at least without the deliberate inclusion of new technologies or new methods of fixing choreography, probably helped bolster the impression, at least among traditional dance aficionados rather than the public, that in general, Ailey's work was "less original" than Cunningham's. Nevertheless, in both men's cases, masculinity trumped race or sexuality.

Chapter 7

Conclusions: Quo Vadis?*

Summary of Findings

This project has illustrated how the effort to win copyright protection for modern dance in the United States, during the turn of the nineteenth century to about 2006, just as choreography was becoming a federally copyrightable category, was a simultaneously racialized and gendered contest. Copyright and choreography, particularly as tied with whiteness, have a complex history, and not one reducible to simple binaries.

I began with an introductory chapter where I reviewed relevant literature and differentiated this study from parallel studies, dealing with similar issues. I closed that introductory chapter with a review of different reasons why choreography has been difficult to copyright and with a quick sketch of the parameters of this study. In chapter 2, I began with a simple binary, opposing an aesthetic of "whiteness" and "nonwhiteness" only because it is analytically useful to start this way; it is not meant as a totalizing schema but as a simple heuristic, meant to be problematized and even exploded by more detailed and nuanced analyses, some of which I did in the succeeding chapters. To understand how "whiteness" is a "property" as much as an "aesthetic," one must plot, to the extent one can, how systems function to produce these differences, in operation. Briefly summarizing the findings of chapter 2, ballet, as the paradigm template of a "white" aesthetic in American dance, displays many of the characteristics Richard Dyer observed in film. For example, hierarchy, virtue, rationality, linearity, heterosexuality, and noncorporeality are crucial components of ballet, as a "whitened" dance form. In Balanchine's work, one can find traces of the same kind of whitened aesthetic that seems to authorize him as America's premier guardian of these traditions in dance.

To understand what a "nonwhite" aesthetic is in American dance, I think one must return to the most fundamental distinctions in American culture, which, in dance as an art form, still remains at the culturally imagined binary between "black" (Africanist) versus "white" (European) culture. Legally, of course, within the United States, this dichotomy finds moorings in the "one-drop" rule: that one drop of black blood, no matter how light (or close to white) one's complexion is, is sufficient to classify a miscegenated child as black—that is, given the history of slavery, initially as property, or as someone "different" to enough to treat as essentially a separate species. Choreographically, especially in modern dance, this white—black dichotomy has meant appropriating key characteristics of nonwhite aesthetics, or even venerating these alleged mythic "primal" or "primitive" qualities, while still denigrating or treating with patronizing condescension the real people and cultures that generated these aesthetics.

I adopted Cynthia Jean Cohen Bull's[1] description of traditional Ghanaian dance as ballet's counterpoint, not because as I see it as literally exhausting the pluripotential modes of representation possible in trying to imagine ballet's "other(s)" but rather because I see a pragmatic, heuristic value in attempting to sketch a radical opposition to ballet: one (even if theoretically) imaginatively unfettered from the trauma and history of slavery, attempting to reach back into deep African roots—a project that resembles, to some extent, Katherine Dunham's project of fusing ethnographic field practice with choreographed and costumed staging as we saw in chapter 4. I chose Cohen Bull's description of Ghanaian dance (even if one can quarrel with specific details) largely because contrasts, using Cohen Bull's schema, can readily be drawn between it and ballet, opening up new body vocabularies, new ways of configuring the relationship between performer and audience, new ways of thinking about bodies in relation to dance movement.

Thus, briefly summarizing some key points in chapter 2, ballet, embodying a whitened aesthetic, is European in its origins; emphasizes the primacy of the visual sense especially through cultivating vertical lines kinesthetically expressed through an elevated torso and upright spine; subordinates movement to music; has strict ideals concerning the dimensions of physical bodies related in a strict heterosexual economy of roles; and reflects the class consciousness of its origins through its use of the turn-out of the hips, legs, and toes to maximize specularity for those in the audience privileged enough to occupy the position formerly occupied by the monarch—now the theatre box. In contrast, Ghanaian dance, as described by Cohen Bull, is Africanist; emphasizes the primacy of hearing through the polyrhythmic movement that isolates the upper body from the lower body; does not necessarily limit the ideal of bodies to literally young and nubile bodies or designate a strict heterosexual distribution of lines (while distinguishing between "masculine" and "feminine" movement); and in her view, allows a porousness in interaction between performer and audience through the use of a circular spatial configuration, centered around the drummers.

Having established a rough schema of what I mean by a "white aesthetic" versus a "nonwhite aesthetic," I sustain a brief genealogy of a white aesthetic in American Dance in relation to Loïe Fuller's (chapter 3), George Balanchine's (chapter 4) and Martha Graham's (chapter 5) portraits as pioneers of American dance. I focus on major figures in American dance history because this is the way copyright history, through case law, creates an implicit history concerning choreography as a federally copyrightable category—and it is no accident that in all these landmark cases, whiteness is a factor, both as status property and as an aesthetic. In focusing on how landmark cases are rooted in the cultural and artistic frameworks of their specific time frames, I sketch the outlines of how whiteness as property has evolved in the complex relationships binding copyright and choreography.

For example, in the case of Loíe Fuller, she initially struggled to create an identity for herself as the creator of the skirt dance and to gain adequate financial compensation through the suit she raised against one of her competitors and imitators, Bemis.[2] Simultaneously, Fuller also had to fill a variety of roles, in addition to choreographer and dancer; she created her own costumes, designed and patented the lights, planned the staging of the movements onstage, did her own self-promotions.[3] Fuller attempted to gain copyright protection, only to have her work dismissed as "mere spectacle," devoid of any moral purpose that could further science or the arts.[4] Even if the interplay between sex, gender, and class trumped whiteness in her case, she did partake in the advantages of whiteness as status property, especially in stark contrast to Josephine Baker, who was her successor, as the "Black Venus," (as opposed to Fuller being the "Goddess of Light") in Europe. I will return to an analysis of Josephine Baker's significance to this project in relation to my discussion of two different types of nonwhite aesthetics that contemporaneously existed during the time periods in which Fuller, Balanchine, and Graham were actively forging their own choreographic forms a little later in this discussion.

Continuing with the thread of a white aesthetic enshrined in the paradigm cases of American copyright law in relation to choreography, compared with Fuller, Balanchine, with his classical Russian training, had the financial support of Kerstein,[5] and as such, skipped over many of the steps Fuller struggled through, to gain reputability and comparative financial stability.[6] From the start of his move to America in 1933, Balanchine had a school of pliant young dancers whose flesh and spirits he could shape to his choreographic designs without fear of them becoming his competitors,[7] and a support staff who could take care of the other production-related tasks, such as lighting, costuming, and publicity.[8] In addition, ballet, unlike skirt dancing, had a long-established tradition of being a dance form of the higher classes, regarded as a "classic" art form.[9] Ballet, unlike skirt dancing, also had a long-established tradition of having a dominant, tyrannical male ballet master, which further cemented Balanchine's authoritative position.[10] Thus, it hardly surprising that buttressed by his unquestioned possession of status property of white (male) privilege, evidenced in the very rhetorical patterns used by the court to buttress its findings in *Horgan II*, that Balanchine's estate maintained effective control of all intellectual property rights—even those in a different media—in relation to his choreographic works.

In comparison to Balanchine, Martha Graham, partly because of the force of her personality, probably exercised as much control over her dancers, both male and female, as Balanchine did.[11] And even as she surrounded herself with the antithesis of Balanchine's hyperwhitened hyperfeminized ideal (i.e., nonprofessional ballerinas,[12] and nonwhite dancers),[13] her dances were designed to showcase her stardom as a white woman choreographer—a "woman who could do her own work."[14] And even as she costumed herself in the look of the "exotic," her dances were always premised on her recognizability as "the" Martha Graham—a white woman masking herself as "exotic."[15] Graham appears to have turned to the exotic because she could never be the hyperwhitened beauty her idol, Ruth St. Denis, was;[16] unable to compete for stardom on those terms, Graham turned to its opposite, to forge her own artistic identity.[17] At the heart of her choreography thus still lies a frustrated longing to be what she cannot be, which is essentially still Balanchine's ideal, even if costumed in the "exotic" trappings of St. Denis' dances.[18] Nevertheless, for all Graham's (popularly acclaimed) "genius," when it came down to deciding who maintained control over her choreographic pieces, in contrast with Balanchine, the Court (in specific, the Second Circuit) decided that because of the work for hire doctrine, that Graham was simply an "employee" and her choreographic pieces were mere works for hire, whose ownership she had contracted away in exchange for funding and financial stability.[19] Even if the interplay between sex and gender again appeared to have trumped whiteness in her case (as the court, in *Martha Graham School v. Martha Graham Center* (2d Cir. 2004)) never rose to the rhetorical honorifics as it did in *Horgan v. Macmillan*), the fact that she was able to initially pass on her choreographic works to her estate, taking advantage of the same provision in the 1976 Copyright amendments as Balanchine did, attests to her possession of whiteness as status property, even if refractorily so.

This is not to say Balanchine did not undergo difficulty; his life appears to have been composed of successive seasons of feast and famine, with ballet companies ephemerally rising and expiring around him.[20] Balanchine, unlike Fuller and Graham, lived for the present and was not bothered by the thought of his ballets passing into obscurity, much like beautiful butterflies that were spectacular at the height of their glory, but swiftly passed away. In contrast, Fuller's and Graham's every act seemed focused on creating a memorial for themselves that would withstand the test of time. In particular, Fuller's savviness in negotiating legal hurdles (even submitting a detailed description of the skirt dance in her failed infringement claim), ironically, did nothing to ensure her success at acquiring copyright protection.[21] Neither did Graham's hard-earned status as a "genius" (comparable to Picasso and Wagner)[22]—in the media and popular culture, but not in the court's statements (unlike Balanchine), protect Graham from being relegated to the status of an "employee" when it came to deciding who had control of her choreographic works, past her death.[23]

Given these differences in personality, it is ironic that it is Balanchine who succeeded where Fuller failed, in acquiring copyright protection, and where Graham failed, in maintaining control over her choreographic creations. Nevertheless, Fuller, Balanchine, and Graham were "stars," and part of the creation of their celebrity was their integration of a hyperwhitened aesthetic into their choreography. Fuller accomplished this through making her less-than-perfect body invisible, through the use of extended wooden wands, yards and yards of white silk, and the magic of lights.[24] Balanchine accomplished the same task through hyperdisciplining his dancers' bodies, whom he carefully chose, to become the vessels of his artistic ideal: the embodiments of the all too Romantic vision of the feminine-as-eternally-fleeing; young women chiseled down to such thinness so as to become virtually evanescent; marble princesses, with skins like "peeled apples," devoid of aging and infirmity. Graham accomplished this through appropriating unto herself various forms of the "exotic" (ancient Greek, Egyptian, native American) and surrounding herself with "nonstandard" bodies, including black and Asian dancers,[25] while maintaining her status as a white woman choreographer. While Fuller produced no heir and until recently, was not recognized as a pioneer of modern dance, Balanchine's and Graham's cultural legacies are now very well entrenched. However, where Graham's estate lost control of most of her ballets, Balanchine's estate not only commands the royalties to choreographic productions licensed to 150 ballet companies worldwide,[26] but now also possesses the trademarks of Balanchine's style and technique and even his name.[27] To be able to perform a ballet, a company representative has to have a consultation with the particular ballet's legatee concerning consent, terms, who should be recommended to do the staging, and any other special conditions; if the recommended stager does not think the company can do the work justice, the company will not acquire the license to perform it.[28] Finally, so uncontested is Balanchine's estate's control over his choreography and even name that it now can also compel companies who perform Balanchine's ballets to include a trademark and licensing notice in their programs.[29] Crucial to that establishment of absolute control over his choreographic creations were Balanchine's aesthetic pursuit of an ideal of hyperfeminized whiteness and his confident possession of (masculine and male) whiteness as status property. Although both Fuller and Graham had some access to whiteness as status property, their stories, as women choreographers, are more complex.

My task for the remainder of this summary of findings focuses on comparing concrete examples of two distinct historically grounded nonwhite aesthetic possibilities glimpsed through the examples of Josephine Baker and Katherine Dunham. Again, gender imbricates with race in this cultural imagination of a "white" versus a "nonwhite" dance aesthetic, much as postcolonial imaginings of a "primitivist" and "exotic" other (in the case of Baker, and to a more limited extent, Dunham), refracted through the prisms of stardom and image making, form a complex narrative. An additional layer of nuancing appears to be how comparatively darkly complected Baker was (or in Dunham's case, how lightly complected she was), and how closely both embodied (and deconstructed) the colonial fantasy of the "Black Venus." In both cases, as international superstars, both women had some access to whiteness as status property; but both did not have the extent of access as their white female predecessors or counterparts, Fuller and Graham.

Baker stepped into a series of historical convergences that iconized her as the "Ebony Venus," the "Black Venus, the "Jazz Empress," and the very embodiment of Black Womanhood.[30] In compliance with the image projected on her by her promoters and audiences, Baker employed five performative strategies of image and identity construction, which included: exoticizing race and gender; overturning racial and cultural codes and meanings; performing "difference" through nudity, cross-dressing, song, and dance; exploiting these images of difference; and generalizing the outcome to allow the performative messages to reach larger popular audiences.[31]

In order to remain "the same"—as an "exotic" sexualized object of fascination—Baker would have to constantly remake herself. And a key component to Baker's many transformations was her consistent "whitening" as a wild child civilized into Parisienne culture. This process of transformation took place both personally and professionally, as Baker moved from being a body acted upon, to becoming a specular projection of the star system. Choreographically, the roots of the "authentic Africanist" dance style Europe venerated were African American street dances magnified through Baker's hyperbolic and flamboyant exaggerations. More precisely, they lay in Baker's spontaneous improvisational reinterpretations of popular American "street" dance steps.[32]

In some ways, Baker's case parallels Fuller's: both rose from American working class origins, were principally self-taught, and yet managed to capture the European imagination as artistic Goddesses—Fuller as an icon of light and ethereality,[33] Baker as an idol of nonwhiteness and hypersexualized embodiment. But whereas Fuller managed to achieve patents in her name for her inventions for her staged productions,[34] there are no such documents attesting to Baker's "ownership" of her "intellectual property." Although Fuller preceded Baker by several decades, there is no indication that Baker ever attempted to demarcate the artifacts and traces of her artistry as her personal property the way Fuller had done, using the legal system,[35] through both Fuller's successful patent applications and her unsuccessful bid to claim ownership over the "Serpentine Dance" through copyright. But in terms of choreographic legal protection, like Fuller, Baker's claim to ownership of her choreographic improvisations, if she had dared to mount such a claim, would have failed, not simply because it would probably have been dismissed, like Fuller's claim, as pure "spectacle"[36] but also because, given her performances' overt eroticism and closeness to vaudeville traditions and "popular" dance steps, her claim would probably also have been roundly dismissed as "obscene,"[37] lacking originality, and not "promoting the advancement of science and the useful arts," which is the principal objective of patent and copyright protection.[38]

In comparison with Baker, Dunham's rise to celebrity coincided with Baker's decline as the embodiment of the erotic and primal "savage" and Martha Graham's (among other white women) deployment of a then-principally sexless model of modern dancing (i.e., prior to her involvement with Erick Hawkins). In the face of these preexisting and often stereotyped and racialized templates, Dunham was noteworthy in her self-proclaimed project of integrating "African dance traditions that featured more forthright acceptance of sexual elements in dance."[39]

And indeed, Dunham's choreography and dance technique not only incorporated the "whitened" (and established) elements of ballet and modern dance, but also a vocabulary of movement that had clear "nonwhitened" elements, derived from her memory of her fieldwork as an anthropologist in the West Indies (Jamaica, Trinidad, Cuba, Haiti, Martinique).[40] Dunham's dance technique comes closest to the theoretical model, built on Cohen Bull's characterization of Ghanaian dance, of a nonwhite aesthetic I schematized in chapter 2, but hybridizes it with white elements, which, like her academic credentials, served to authorize her work, particularly in Europe. The technique she developed "emphasized the torso movements of the primitive ritual of Caribbean-African dance and jazz rhythms."[41]

Though Dunham self-identified herself as black, and declared a social activist impetus to her work,[42] Dunham was clearly of a mixed racial heritage and her own autobiography emphasized that hybridity. In addition, Dunham's combination of academic credentials of the highest caliber, her practical fieldwork experience, and her visually arresting reinterpretation of ethnographic experience into choreographic staging yielded refractory responses from the dance world, critics, and the public. Nevertheless, unlike Baker, Dunham was portrayed as someone with both sophistication and eloquence, as well as the exotic primitivism Baker had come to symbolize. The fact that Dunham's second husband, John Pratt—the man who costumed her—was also white, probably helped to further "whiten" Dunham, which worked to her unambiguous advantage in Europe but elicited more ambivalent responses in the United States.

Choreographically, Dunham is notable for incorporating not only "folkloric" material derived from a broad variety of "exotic" sources, but also the familiar street-derived US social dance steps characteristic of African American entertainers that Baker surreptitiously drew from and exaggerated, either comedically or sensually. But despite Dunham's eclecticism, Dunham did privilege the Caribbean as the ethnographic source from which she sought to discover and forge a basic vocabulary that seemed, to her, to underlie African-derived dances in the United States.

Dunham cemented her career and reputation through what she called "revues"—staging her re-memory of her anthropological experiences and Caribbean dance and music together with the lush settings, plush costumes, orchestral reinterpretations of the Caribbean rhythms and folk music, and the polished look of American showbiz. But it was only after she was already established that Dunham "collaborated" with Balanchine on *Cabin in the Sky* (1940). Ironically, the 1940 Broadway production of *Cabin in the Sky* did not give Dunham any credit as a choreographer. [43]

Nevertheless, in Dunham's extended interview with Constance Valis Hall conducted on November 1999 and January 2000, Dunham revealed, after much prodding, that Dunham not only choreographed most, if not all, of the numbers, but also, as Aschenbrenner remarks, that "she staged most of the show, although she was not given credit for it."[44] Nevertheless, it is clear that Dunham's credentials as an academic, her glamorized image, and the very manner in which she staged her ethnographic research as performances, did privilege and protect her to some extent.

There appears to be an anxiety that repeatedly surfaces in relation to both white and black American critics' reception of Dunham's work: the question of "authenticity," as her work, her image, and even her looks, seemed whitened, compared to, for example, Pearl Primus, who pursued similar goals and scholarly interests as Dunham in the 1940's, but who did not have Dunham's numerous liminalities, inclusive of her looks, which conformed more to whitened standards of beauty, as opposed to Primus' physical appearance. In relation to this question of "authenticity," Dunham's choreographic interpretation of her ethnographic research has also undergone some critique as being overly reliant on hybridization, losing specificity, and perhaps even stereotyping Caribbean culture in general. Contrastively, in the hands of someone like Martha Graham or George Balanchine, even if devoid of the intense ethnographic field work Dunham had accomplished, such "inappropriate cultural appropriation" would probably have been interpreted as "artistic innovation," passing copyright's "modicum of originality" test easily. Additionally, that Dunham's ethnographic work drew principally from "folklore" (and from non-American sources) would probably have made any kind of possible copyright claim invalid. But that Dunham wisely used the established kinesthetic techniques and body vocabularies of ballet and modern dance would probably have made any claim she might have raised, especially given the circumstances of *Cabin in the Sky*, more likely to survive. But given the raced, sexed, and gendered nature of the politics of the dance world, Dunham wisely refrained; that savviness is what eventually cemented her commercial success and artistic independence. Like Baker, Dunham, instead of banking on copyright protection, relied on her ability to "curate" her image through the numerous interviews she gave the media. But unlike Baker, Dunham did have some access—even if not full access—to whiteness as status property, and as such, was able to achieve some acclaim as a choreographer in her own right—but only after loyal apprenticeship to the ballet master and legally and culturally enshrined genius, Balanchine.

I closed with a comparison and contrast between Merce Cunningham and Alvin Ailey because such an approach is instructive, when trying to understand how race, gender, and in the case especially of Cunningham, sexuality intersect with kinesthetic conventions of choreography; copyright law takes a back seat in this chapter because unlike Fuller, Balanchine, and Graham, there are no law suits, contesting choreographic ownership. That absence of legal squabbling itself deserves some scrutiny, as it illustrates how Cunningham (and his lawyers) probably learned from the examples (and mistakes) of Balanchine's and Graham's estates, and how Ailey, following a similar approach as Dunham, succeeded in establishing unambiguous legal ownership of his choreographic work, even at the young age of 22.[45]

There are many ways in which Cunningham and Ailey intersect, but in a manner similar to the way in which the two legs of a compass intersect—as counterpoints rather than mirror images. Cunningham and Ailey were similar in their rebellion against classicism and the dominance of ballet as well as their development of hybrid forms of choreography, combining whitened and nonwhitened body vocabularies. In Cunningham's case, his iconoclasm extended not only to a reconfiguring of the classical time-space of the balletic stage and its conventional privileged vantage point, but also to reconfiguring the relationship between music and dance as coexisting, rather than having dance choreography dependent on musical expression in a linear manner.[46] Furthermore, Cunningham rebelled as well, against Graham's intense focus on dance to depict emotion or narrative, though he did take from her some nonwhite elements in choreography (such as the ability to arbitrarily contract or release any part of the body);[47] nevertheless, kinesthetically, his choreography remained classically infused with balletic lines.[48] And even as he rebelled against conventions of heteronormative masculinity and femininity,[49] he did not treat male and female bodies interchangeably but still hewed to the conventions of the balletic pas de deux when he decided to use these, even if ironically or humorously.[50]

Ultimately, whereas Cunningham subtly problematized conventional depictions of heteronormative masculinity, the aesthetic he developed remained safely within the whitened realm of "high art" with its emphasis on technique, classical lines, and the discipline of structure, even if that structure were not the conventional time-space.[51] Cunningham also firmly upheld the distinction between a dance "professional" (one trained and mentored through the system) and a mere "amateur"[52]—something some of his dance descendants regarded as conservative and proestablishment. This prudent balancing (and masking) of rebellion with conservatism helps explain why Cunningham has left behind a dance empire very similar to, and arguably surpassing, Balanchine's estate, especially in terms of intellectual property protection.[53]

Cunningham, especially with the mentorship and support of Cage, found a safe enclave among a staunch set of supporters, many of whom were not actually members of the dance world.[54] His integration of not only avant garde art forms but also cutting edge technologies and media, such as film and video, among others,[55] enhanced not only the apparent originality of his work, but also probably successfully overcame a hurdle most choreographers struggled with, to gain effective copyright protection: the requirement of fixation. Finally, the launching and completion of the "Legacy Plan" created what appears to be, legally and institutionally, an airtight structure for achieving both dance immortality and unambiguous control over his choreographic works, under the administration of the legal entity he created to oversee the licensing of his work.[56] Although Cunningham underwent difficulty as a gay man, this did not trump his access to whiteness as status property, especially through his partnership with Cage, whose intellectualism and credentials were unquestioned.[57]

In contrast, Ailey, like Dunham, achieved some access to white privilege largely through the sponsorship and mentorship of a white man—Lester Horton.[58] But unlike Dunham (despite her whitened credentials, hybrid "exotic" looks, and business savviness), who had to go through the system of apprenticing for Balanchine without being given due credit for her work until much later, Ailey was immediately allowed access to the title "choreographer," even if his works were not initially positively received.[59] Furthermore, Ailey achieved the distinction of being far more than a "black performer" and became, despite his suspicion that the government may have been using him and his group as propaganda, a state-sponsored internationally recognized "American choreographer,"[60] unlike Dunham, whose commercial and reputational success initially came from foreign audiences.

If Cunningham's dominant mode of relating to his dance predecessors was one of rebellion, Ailey's principal response to his mentors was one of affirmation. One easily sees the influences of both Horton and Graham in his work, for example.[61] Thus, like Horton, who admired Ted Shawn, Ailey's predominant depictions of gender relations remained safely within the heterosexual realm[62] (heterosexuality, even if only performed, in this case, is an attribute of whiteness as Richard Dyer[63] has shown), despite Ailey's private life. In contrast to Cunningham, who experimented with integrating avant garde art and cutting edge technologies into his predominantly abstract works, Ailey preferred to return to the basics of theatrical staging, focusing on simpler lines, emotional expressiveness, costuming and lighting, and connection with popular audiences.[64] Thus, Ailey's preference for more conventional means of staging, devoid of, or at least without the deliberate inclusion of new technologies or new methods of fixing choreography, probably helped bolster the impression, at least among traditional dance aficionados, rather than the public, that in general, Ailey's work was "less original" than Cunningham's.[65] Nevertheless, in both men's cases, masculinity trumped race or sexuality, even if Ailey's blackness did not grant him as much access to white privilege as Cunningham unambiguously did.

Julia Foulkes presents a vivid summary of the broad historical outlines this project eventually affirms, though it has arrived at this point via a very different set of paths and using different tools.

> Modern dance gathered momentum in the 1930s because a focus on bodies coalesced with the search to find an American way in the arts that favored an experiential approach, attention to the polyglot nature of the country's population, and revivification of the democratic tradition in the midst of

> an economic depression and an impending crisis in Europe. This desperate time promoted fluidity in social roles. White women rejecting stereotypes of femininity and white gay men countering notions of effeminacy molded an American modern dance to allow for new models of gender and sexuality. For African American dancers, culture and nation overlapped but did not necessarily coincide in their dances. While they fought for and pushed Americans to realize ideals of equality of opportunity and open democracy, they embraced the culture of Africa and the Caribbean to which they felt they more truly belonged.
>
> White gay men took over leadership roles and secured increasingly substantial roles in the avant garde.[66]

In brief, while white women, gay white men, and black men were able to use the momentum of modernism to destabilize the dominance of balletic conventions and establish choreographic ownership of their works, black women, for the most part, did not benefit as greatly. Ultimately, masculinity trumped both race and gender, in terms of access to white privilege, as men, such as Cunningham and Ailey, gradually came to occupy leadership positions in a profession heavily populated by women.

Quo Vadis: A Postscript

In retrospect, it is hardly surprising that few choreographers have achieved the degree of legal protection Balanchine (and his heirs) have.[67] The requirements for gaining copyright protection, and especially for the "fixation" requirement, are both time consuming and expensive. Yet the issue of delimiting the copyrightable from the noncopyrightable remains a vexatious question, especially given that the 1976 Copyright Act, section 450.03(a) which *Horgan II* cited, specifically excludes "social dance steps" and "simple routines" from copyright protection.[68] Congress declined to provide a definition, a supplementary explanation, or even any policy consideration justifying the distinction.[69] Thus, one is left to speculate on the policy reasons behind the exclusion. First, perhaps the House Committee was trying to draw a bright line between dancing done in private, for individual enjoyment, and dancing performed for the public, for profit.[70] Second, perhaps the Committee on the Judiciary viewed social dance steps as not meeting the minimum standard of creativity required for copyright protection.[71]

Either way, the distinction between mere "social dance steps" (noncopyrightable) and "original dance" (copyrighted) is problematic given that, for example, many of the steps used by Fred Astaire and Ginger Rogers (and many other musicals) were based on social dance,[72] such as the foxtrot and waltz. To characterize such dances as lacking creativity seems anomalous with the times. The waltz and foxtrot would probably not meet much opposition as "copyrightable" partly because they occupy the same hyperwhitened aesthetic realm as Balanchine's ballets did, when they moved from the public domain into the protected sphere of the copyrightable; one of Balanchine's ballets was specifically choreographed to include the look of the Viennese Waltz. The waltz, having well-established European roots, and the foxtrot, a dance of white, upper-class Americans, combined with glamorous sheen of Fred Astaire and Ginger Rogers' legendary stardom, easily meet the requirements necessary for whiteness as status property, from their very inception.

But it is the nonwhite ballroom dance forms that have resisted the aesthetic of whiteness, whose copyrightability might be problematic. Though this is beyond the scope of this book, some scholarly work has already been done, showing how the Latin dances (such as the rumba, the salsa, and the mambo), in their competitive ballroom forms, have actually been racially stereotyped to be performed as the hypersexualized, orientalized other of their European-based counterparts.[73] The degree of performance of nonwhiteness requires the tanning or chemical burning of white skin in order to make white skin "authentic" enough to pass as nonwhite (while being recognized as white/privileged),[74] as ballroom competitions are still predominantly patronized by, and competed in, especially in the pro-am (professional-amateur) division, by white, upper class elites. In addition, other scholars have done nuanced postcolonial studies of the ethnic roots of the "whitened" Latin ballroom forms, such as the tango. Robert Farris Thompson, for example, persuasively argues, using a historical and choreographic analysis, that the "strongest root" in the original Argentine tango is "Kongo-style dancing, as elaborated in black dancing groups called candombes that also existed in black Uruguay."[75]

Thus far, I have been unable to uncover a suit of copyright infringement involving specifically ballroom choreography. It could be that ballroom choreographers are not as concerned about seeking copyright protection, especially with the explosion of popular modes of entertainment like *Dancing with the Stars* and the possibility of seeking legal protection through other mechanisms, such as trademark law. It may, in fact, be advantageous that ballroom dance choreography remain in the public domain, given the costs and complexities of fixation, the effort it takes to protect choreography from infringement, and the pace of choreographic evolution that becomes possible with material remaining in the public domain. It is also worth noting that in *Dancing with the Stars*, the most commercially successful television format to feature ballroom dance, the celebrity of ballroom champions, in the United States, is still eclipsed by, and parasitic upon, catering to the "stardom" of its amateur clientele. But it could also be that, much as ballroom's transformation from being a social pastime into an Olympic sport has achieved mixed gains, ballroom dance has not sufficiently moved from the modern day equivalent of the burlesque, the merely "entertaining," to become "whitened" enough to become "art," and thus, worthy of copyright protection.

And certainly, there are areas in which this study can be improved and expanded. The initial rough heuristic setting up a white aesthetic versus a nonwhite aesthetic could be expanded to become less a binary, thus better reflecting contemporary choreographic possibilities.[76] Further research can be done to nuance Cohen Bull's characterization of Ghanaian dance. As Kariamu Welsh-Asante points out that there are "literally thousands of African-centered aesthetics that exist in the world," perhaps a more productive avenue of analysis would be the attempt to "describe what the issues and characteristic terms of an Afrocentric aesthetic might be."[77] To limit the paramaters of this book, this study has remained focused on the white—black divide because legally, that is the important criterion to keep in mind, but certainly, the notion of what a "nonwhite" aesthetic is should expand to include, for example, Hispanic, Indian, and Asian and other elements, as these were part of the choreographic palette, culturally, even if they were not acknowledged legally. Certainly, colorism as well as color casting remain very much part of the balletic dance world.[78] Furthermore, further excavations could be done, such as an examination of the legacies of Isadora Duncan and Ruth St. Denis, who chronologically followed Fuller but preceded Graham, drawn against the evolving relationships binding whiteness, choreography, and copyright. Additionally, further studies, this time charting the intersections between masculinities, sexualities, and race, would deepen the analytic potential of this study. Certainly, one could easily analyze in greater depth, and comparatively for example, the choreographic innovations of Ted Shawn, Merce Cunningham, Arthur Miller and Alvin Ailey. Thus, one could perform a parallel genealogy on how gender, race, and sexuality, this time tracked on to masculinities and male bodies, are culturally and legally interpreted in relation to copyright's aims of "promoting the progress of arts." Furthermore, it is noteworthy that all the figures discussed in this book experimented in film in some way, some in more *avante garde* formats (Fuller), some using some initially documentary footage (Dunham) but the majority in more mainstream, Hollywood-related venues. It would be instructive to chart how the aesthetic of whiteness maps on to the copyrightability of these films and the status and power of these figures in relation to the films produced. Far from being the last word on this topic, this book is simply the beginning.

Notes

1 Introduction: Preliminary Remarks

*Adapted with permission from Caroline Joan S. Picart, "A Tango between Copyright and Critical Race Theory: Whiteness as Status Property in Balanchine's Ballets, Fuller's Serpentine Dance and Graham's Modern Dances," *Cardozo Journal of Law and Gender* 18, no. 3 (Spring 2012): 685–725.

1. Donna J. Haraway, "A Cyborg Manifesto: Science, Technology, and Socialist-Feminism in the Late Twentieth Century," in *Simians, Cyborgs and Women: The Reinvention of Nature* (New York: Routledge, 1991), 149. I explore the idea of autoethnography in Caroline Joan S. Picart, *Inside Notes from the Outside* (Lanham, MD: Lexington Press, 2004).
2. "DanceSport" is the athletic, competitive form of ballroom dance; I specialize in "Cabaret," which is a hybrid form mixing ballroom dance, ballet, and gymnastics. The term "DanceSport" was officially used by the IDSF (International DancesSport Federation), formerly the IBDF (International Ballroom Dancing Federation), adopted the use of the term as a potential sport for inclusion in the Olympics. Caroline Joan S. Picart, *From Ballroom to DanceSport: Aesthetics, Athletics and Body Culture* (Albany, NY: State University of New York Press), 70.
3. *Fuller v. Bemis*, 50 F. 926 (C.C.S.D.N.Y. 1892).
4. *Horgan v. MacMillan, Inc.*, 789 F.2d 157 (2d. Cir. 1986).
5. *Martha Graham Sch. & Dance Found., Inc. v. Martha Graham Ctr. of Contemporary Dance, Inc.*, 455 F.3d 125 (2d Cir. 2006).
6. *Martha Graham Sch. & Dance Found., Inc. v. Martha Graham Ctr. of Contemporary Dance, Inc.*, 380 F.3d 624 (2d Cir. 2004).
7. Cheryl Harris, "Whiteness as Property," *Harvard Law Review* 106 (1993): 1731.
8. Kimberle Crenshaw, "Mapping the Margins: Intersectionality, Identity Politics, and Violence Against Women of Color," in *Critical Race Theory: The Key Writings that Formed the Movement*, eds. Kimberle Crenshaw, Neil Gotanda, Gary Peller, and Kendall Thomas (New York: The New Press, 1995), 350.
9. Kenneth B. Nunn, "Law as Eurocentric Enterprise," *Law and Inequality* 15 (1997): 323. See also, Reginald Leamon Robinson, "Race, Myth and

Narrative in the Social Construction of the Black Self," *Howard Law Journal* 40 (1996): 1.

10. Nunn, "Law as Eurocentric Enterprise", 331. In terms of international human rights law, Makau Mutua makes a similar critique. See generally, Makau Mutua, *Kenya's Quest for Democracy: Taming Leviathan* (Boulder, CO: Lynne Rienner Publishers, 2008); Makau Mutua, ed., *Human Rights NGOs in East Africa: Political and Normative Tensions* (Philadelphia, PA: University of Pennsylvania Press, 2008); Makau Mutua, *Human Rights: A Political and Cultural Critique* (Philadelphia, PA: University of Pennsylvania Press, 2008). I thank Berta Hernandez-Truyol for this addition as well as her mentorship on international law in general.
11. Richard Dyer, *White: Essays on Race and Culture* (London and New York: Routledge, 1997).
12. For observations regarding Fuller's cinematographic "fairy tales," see Sally Sommer, "Loïe Fuller," *The Drama Review* 19 (1975): 65.
13. Bernard Taper, *Balanchine: A Biography with a New Epilogue* (Berkeley, CA: University of California Press, 1984).
14. Harris, "Whiteness as Property," 1716.
15. Ibid.
16. Ibid., 1728–31.
17. Ibid., 1730.
18. Ibid., 1731.
19. Ibid., 1734.
20. Ibid., 1750–56.
21. Ibid., 1757.
22. Crenshaw, "Mapping the Margins," 350.
23. Ibid., 358.
24. Ibid., 357.
25. Ibid.
26. Nunn, "Law as Eurocentric Enterprise," 334.
27. Ibid., 335.
28. Ibid., 335–36.
29. Ibid., 336.
30. Ibid.
31. Ibid.
32. Ibid., 337.
33. Ibid., 351.
34. Dyer, *White*, 3.
35. Joane Nagel, *Race, Ethnicity and Sexuality: Intimate Intersections, Forbidden Frontiers* (New York: Oxford University Press, 2003), 16. For an account of how what was a cultural rule became a legal rule, see Shirley Biagi and Marilyn Kern-Foxworth, *Facing Difference: Race, Gender and Mass Media* (Thousand Oaks: Pine Forge Press, 1997), 230.
36. Dyer, *White*, 4.
37. See, for example, Edward W. Said, *Orientalism* (New York: Random House, 1978).

38. Judith Butler, "Performative Acts and Gender Constitution: An Essay in Phenomenology and Feminist Theory," *Theatre Journal* 40, no. 4 (1988): 525.
39. Ann Laura Stoler, "Colonial Archives and Arts of Governance," *Archival Science* 2 (2002): 109.
40. Bennetta Jules-Rosette, *Josephine Baker in Art and Life: The Icon and the Image* (Champaign, IL: University of Illinois Press, 2007), 49.
41. Anthea Kraut, *Choreographing the Folk: The Dance Stagings of Zora Neale Hurston (Indigenous Americas)* (Minneapolis, MN: University of Minnesota Press, 2008).
42. Kevin J. Greene's "Papa's Got a Brand New Bag: James Brown, Innovation, and Copyright Law," in *African American Culture and Legal Discourse*, eds. Lovalerie King and Richard Schur (New York: Palgrave Macmillan, 2009), 177–190.
43. Taper, *Balanchine: A Biography.*
44. Ann Cooper Albright, *Traces of Light: Absence and Presence in the Work of Loïe Fuller* (Middletown, CT: Wesleyan University Press, 2007)
45. Kimberle Crenshaw, Neil Gotanda, Gary Peller, and Kendall Thomas, eds., *Critical Race Theory: The Key Writings that Formed the Movement* (New York: The New Press, 1995).
46. Richard Delgado and Jean Stefancic, eds. *Critical Race Theory: The Cutting Edge*, 2nd ed. (Philadelphia, PA: Temple University Press, 2000).
47. Stuart Greene and Dawn Abt-Perkins, eds., *Making Race Visible: Literacy Research for Cultural Understanding* (New York: Teacher's College Press, 2003).
48. Bruno Latour, *Science in Action: How to Follow Scientists and Engineers through Society* (Cambridge, MA: Harvard University Press, 1987), 4.
49. Dyer, *White*, 82–102, 122–42.
50. US Const. art. I, § 8, cl. 8.
51. See generally, "United States Copyright Law: Copyright Clause and First Copyright Law," History of Copyright: What are Copyrights?, http://www.historyofcopyright.org/pb/wp_fe548a29/wp_fe548a29.html?0.9602877043269001.
52. See Nicholas Arcomano, "Choreography and Copyright, Part One," *Dance Magazine*, April 1980, 58–59.
53. See Gary D. Ordway, "Choreography and Copyright," *Bulletin of the Copyright Society U.S.A.* 13 (1965–1966): 225–240.
54. Melville B. Nimmer and David Nimmer, *Nimmer on Copyright* (New York: Matthew Bender, 1981), § 2.07[B]. 17 U.S.C. § 102 provides for seven copyright subject matter, inclusive of: literary works; musical works; dramatic works; pantomimes and choreographic works; pictorial, graphic, and sculptural works; motion pictures and audiovisual works; and sound recordings. See Melville B. Nimmer, "The Subject Matter of Copyright under the Act of 1976," *UCLA Law Review* 24 (1977): 978–1003. The amendments Congress did to produce the Copyright Code of 1976 seemed to be spurred by both a forward-looking desire to join the Berne Convention, as well as the following

factors: "(1) due to increased life expectancy, the then-term of 56 years was not long enough for an author and his dependents to receive the economic benefits from his work; (2) growth in communications media had greatly lengthened the commercial value of many works; (3) too short a term harms the author without giving any benefit to the public, as the public pay the same for a work in the public domain and publishers might be reluctant to invest in the dissemination of a work without the exclusive rights; (4) a large number of countries had adopted the term of life plus 50 years and with copyrighted works able to move across borders faster, it could have economic ramifications." "United States Copyright Law: Copyright Clause and First Copyright Law," History of Copyright: What are Copyrights?, http://www.historyofcopyright.org/pb/wp_fe548a29/wp_fe548a29.html?0.9602877043269001.

55. See Julie Van Camp, "Copyright of Choreographic Works," in *1994–95 Entertainment, Publishing and the Arts Handbook*, eds., Stephen F. Breimer, Robert Thorne, and John David Viera (New York: Clark, Boardman and Callaghan, 1994), 59–92, http://www.csulb.edu/~jvancamp/copyrigh.html.
56. *Fuller v. Bemis*, 50 F. 926 (C.C.S.D.N.Y. 1892).
57. *Martinetti v. Maguire*, 16 F.Cas. 920 (C.C.D. Cal. 1867).
58. Ibid.
59. Ibid. at 921.
60. Ibid. at 922.
61. Ibid.
62. Ibid.
63. Ibid.
64. Taper, *Balanchine: A Biography*, 400.
65. Ibid.
66. Ibid.
67. Ibid.
68. Ibid., 401.
69. Lee Ann Torrance, "Copyright and Dance," *Explore!* (blog), March 15, 2010, http://leeanntorrans.com/copyright-and-dance (post discontinued).
70. The restrictive effect of the Court's denial of copyright protection to Fuller (and how Fuller's work prefigures modern music and dance) comes into sharp relief when one examines characterizations of modern music and dance stated by artists like John Cage and Merce Cunningham: "We are not, in these dances, saying something… [If] we were saying something we would use words. We are rather doing something… There are no stories and no psychological problems. *There is simply an activity of movement, sound, and light.*" John Percival, *Experimental Dance* (London: Studio Vista, 1971), 20 (emphasis added).
71. US Copyright Office, *Copyright Law of the United States and Related Laws Contained in Title 17 of the United States Code* (Washington, DC: U.S. Copyright Office, 1978): § 102, http://www.copyright.gov/title17/92chap1.html#102.

72. Francis Yeoh, "The Value of Documenting Dance," *Ballet-Dance Magazine*, June 2007, http://www.ballet-dance.com/200706/articles/Yeoh200706.html.
73. Francis Sparshott, *A Measured Pace, toward a Philosophical Understanding of the Arts of Dance* (Toronto: University of Toronto Press, 1995), 420.
74. Leslie Erin Wallis, "The Different Art: Choreography and Copyright," *UCLA Law Review* 33 (1986): 1459.
75. Ibid.
76. Ibid.
77. Cynthia Lyle, *Dancers on Dancing* (New York: Drake, 1977), 115.
78. Martha M. Traylor, "Choreography, Pantomime and the Copyright Revision Act of 1976," *New England Law Review* 16 (1980): 235, 237.
79. Ibid., 235, 238.
80. William Patry, "Choreography and Alternatives to Copyright Law," *The Patry Copyright Blog*, August 18, 2005, http://williampatry.blogspot.com/2005/08/choreography-and-alternatives-to.html.
81. Labanotation is the principal method employed to record choreography with symbols, but there are others as well. See generally Rudolf Benesh and Joan Benesh, *An Introduction to Benesh Movement Notation* (London: A & C Black, 1956); Leonide Massine, *Massine on Choreography: Theory and Exercises in Composition* (London: Faber & Faber, 1971).
82. US Copyright Office, *Compendium II: Compendium of Copyright Office Practices* (Washington, DC: US Copyright Office, 1984), §§ 450.07(b), (c).
83. Margaret Putnam, "Notation Takes Steps to Preserve Dance," *Dallas Morning News*, December 6, 1998, 1C.
84. Joi Michelle Lakes, "A Pas De Deux for Choreography and Copyright," *New York University Law Review* 80 (2005): 1854.
85. Melanie Cook, "Moving to a New Beat: Copyright Protection for Choreographic Works," *UCLA Law Review* 24 (1976–1977), 1296.
86. H.R. Rep. No. 94–1476, at 53 (1976). See also Cook, "Moving to a New Beat," 1288.
87. H.R. Rep. No. 94–1476, at 53–54 (1976).
88. *Maralasco v. Fantasy, Inc.*, 953 F.2d 469, 473 (9th Cir. 1991).
89. US Copyright Office, *Compendium II*.
90. *Horgan v. MacMillan*, 789 F.2d 157, 161 (2d Cir. 1986).
91. US Copyright Office, *Compendium II*, § 4500.01.
92. Ibid., § 450.06.
93. Ibid.
94. Margaret Hunter describes colorism as "the system that privileges the lighter-skinned over darker-skinned people within a community of color." Margaret Hunter, "If You're Light, You're Alright': Light Skin Color as Social Capital for Women of Color," *Gender and Society* 16 (2002): 176. See also Margaret Hunter, *Race, Gender and the Politics of Skin Tone* (New York: Taylor and Francis, 2005), 70.

2 Comparing Aesthetics of Whiteness and Nonwhiteness in Relation to American Dance

*I am indebted to Patricia Hilliard-Nunn, for her generous support and intellectual contributions to the development of this chapter.

1. See Nancy Fraser, "Rethinking the Public Sphere: A Contribution to the Critique of Actually Existing Democracy," *Social Text*, no. 25/26 (1990): 57.
2. Joseph William Singer, *Property Law: Rules, Policies and Practices*, 2nd ed. (New York: Aspen Law & Business, 1997), xli.
3. Jacques Derrida, *Writing and Difference*, trans. Alan Bass (Chicago: University of Chicago Press, 1978).
4. Michel Foucault, *Discipline and Punish: The Birth of the Prison*, 2nd ed. (New York: Vintage, 1995).
5. Simone De Beauvoir, *The Second Sex*, trans. Constance Borde and Sheila Malovany Chevallier (New York: Vintage, 2011).
6. Luce Irigaray, *Marine Lover of Friedrich Nietzsche*, trans. Gillian C. Gill (New York: Columbia University Press, 1991).
7. Derrida notes: "In a classical philosophical opposition we are not dealing with the peaceful coexistence of a vis-à-vis, but rather with a violent hierarchy. One of the two terms governs the other (axiologically, logically, etc.), or has the upper hand." Jacques Derrida, "Interview with Julia Kristeva," in *Positions*, trans. Alan Bass (Chicago: University of Chicago Press, 1981), 42.
8. Dyer, *White*.
9. Gerald Jonas, *Dancing: The Pleasure, Power and Art of Movement* (New York: Harry N. Abrams, 1998), 23.
10. Ibid., 22.
11. Selma Jean Cohen, "Next Week Swan Lake: Reflections on Dance and Dances," in *What is Dance?*, eds. Roger Copeland and Marshall Cohen (New York: Oxford University Press, 1983), 341.
12. Jonas, *Dancing*, 158.
13. Ibid.
14. Ibid.
15. Ibid.
16. Cohen, "Next Week Swan Lake," 341.
17. Havelock Ellis, *Dance of Life* (Boston: Houghton Mifflin, 1923).
18. Jonas, *Dancing*, 131.
19. Cohen, "Next Week Swan Lake," 341.
20. Ibid., 342.
21. Ibid., 342–43.
22. Ibid., 343–44.
23. Ibid., 344.
24. Jonas, *Dancing*, 130.
25. Taper, *Balanchine: A Biography*, 293.

26. Jonas, *Dancing*, 130.
27. Nancy Reynolds and Malcolm McCormick, *No Fixed Points: Dance in the Twentieth Century* (New Haven and London: Yale University Press, 2003), 300.
28. Ibid., 130–31.
29. Ibid., 227.
30. Robert Gottlieb, *George Balanchine: The Ballet Maker* (New York: Harper Collins Publishers, 2004), 80.
31. Reynolds and McCormick, *No Fixed Points*, 300.
32. Taper, *Balanchine: A Biography,* 136.
33. Cynthia Jean Cohen Bull, "Sense, Meaning and Perception in Three Dance Cultures," in *Meaning in Motion*, ed. Jane C. Desmond (Durham, NC: Duke University Press, 1997), 272.
34. Jonas, *Dancing*, 227.
35. Ibid.
36. Cohen Bull, "Sense, Meaning and Perception," 272.
37. Ibid., 275.
38. Jonas, *Dancing*, 226.
39. Laura Mulvey, "Visual Pleasure and Narrative Cinema," in *The Sexual Subject: A Screen Reader in Sexuality* (London and New York: Routledge, 1992), 22–34.
40. Jonas, *Dancing*, 227.
41. I am indebted to Patricia Hilliard-Nunn for advising me to choose, in this context, "Black Aesthetic," which she traces to thinkers like Alain Locke, Larry Neal, Amiri Baraka and others. If I were to track the approach this book uses, it is more akin to Alain Locke's philosophical approach, which is rooted in pragmatism. While the strong social activist elements characteristic of Larry Neal's and Amiri Baraka's viewpoints could flow from this analysis, my principal focus is, like Locke's, on establishing a schema for understanding how value systems work, but as embodied in the collective imagination of dance, during a crucial time period in American dance, as the template for what passes as "copyrightable" and deserving of full protection, forms. This is not to say that I draw deeply from Locke's philosophy, but from his fundamental stance—that these racial distinctions are cultural and value-laden, and one has to begin, first, with understanding the logic of these systems, in order to reveal their foundations, prior to taking the deconstructive turn. See generally Leonard Harris, ed., *The Philosophy of Alain Locke: Harlem Renaissance and Beyond* (Philadelphia: Temple University Press, 1989); Alain Locke, "Art or Propaganda?," *Harlem* 1, no. 1 (1928): 12–13, http://nationalhumanitiescenter.org/pds/maai3/protest/text10/lockeartorpropaganda.pdf; Larry Neal, "The Black Arts Movement," *Drama Review*, Summer 1968, http://nationalhumanitiescenter.org/pds/maai3/community/text8/blackartsmovement.pdf; Larry Neal, *Visions of a Liberated Future: Black Arts Movement Writings*, ed. Michael Schwartz (New York: Thunder's Mouth Press, 1989); Amiri Baraka, *The Leroi Jones/Amiri Baraka*

Reader, 2nd ed., ed. William J. Harris (New York: Basic Books, 1999); Amiri Baraka, *Somebody Blew Up America and Other Poems* (New York: House of Nehesi Publishers, 2003).

42. Brenda Dixon Gottschild, *The Black Dancing Body: A Geography from Coon to Cool* (New York: Palgrave Macmillan, 2003), 10.
43. Cynthia Jean Cohen Bull (a.k.a. Cynthia Novack) was a choreographer, dancer and scholar who pioneered the study of dance as a cultural practice through her book, *Sharing the Dance: Contact Improvisation and American Culture* (Madison, WI: University of Wisconsin Press, 1990).
44. Felix Begho, influenced by the work of Kariamu Welsh Asante, establishes a very detailed taxonomy of Nigerian dances, both traditional and contemporary. Like Cohen Bull, he acknowledges that "entertainment dances" constitute an "overwhelming preponderance" of the dances. Felix Begho, "Traditional African Dance in Context," in *African Dance: An Artistic, Historical and Philosophical Inquiry*, ed. Kariamu Welsh Asante (Trenton, NJ: African World Press, 1996), 174. Begho's focus, though, is not on the kinesthetic or choreographic elements of these Nigerian dances, but what social functions they are associated with, whether sacred, ceremonial, entertainment or recreational, for example. Ibid.
45. See Susan Manning, "Black Voices, White Bodies: The Performance of Race and Gender in How Long Brethren," *American Quarterly* 50 (March 1998): 24–46.
46. Constance Valis Hill, "Collaborating with Balanchine on *Cabin in the Sky*: Interviews with Katherine Dunham," in *Kaiso! Writings by and about Katherine Dunham*, eds. Vévé A. Clark and Sara E. Johnson (Madison, WI: University of Wisconsin Press, 2005), 246–47.
47. Cohen Bull, *Sharing the Dance*, 278–79.
48. Ibid., 278. Cohen Bull does not identify a specific ethnic Ghanaian group from which she builds these observations. But then again, neither does Begho, in his taxonomy of Nigerian dances. Begho, "Traditional African Dance in Context," 163–82. Ultimately, the kind of sketch Cohen Bull sets up is general enough that it could be said to transcend ethnic and even national boundaries. I thank Patricia Hilliard-Nunn for this insight.
49. Cohen Bull, *Sharing the Dance*, 279.
50. Ibid.
51. Brenda Dixon Gottschild, "Crossroads, Continuities, and Contradictions: The Afro-Euro-Caribbean Triangle," in *Caribbean Dance from Abakuá to Zouk: How Movement Shapes Identity*, ed. Susanna Sloat (Gainesville, FL: University Press of Florida, 2002), 5.
52. Cohen Bull, *Sharing the Dance*, 279.
53. Ibid.
54. Cohen Bull acknowledges that leadership and coordination are elements of movement in her analysis of traditional Ghanaian dance, but these elements of synchronicity, in her view, do not necessarily require the same kind of exact military precision that a ballet corps does.
55. Cohen Bull, *Sharing the Dance*, 281.

56. For Cohen Bull, what is groundbreaking about her vision of traditional Ghanaian dance is that it sets up a *different* type of community, opposed to the ballet corps, one potentially more "democratic" and less hierarchical. This is not intended to imply that African dance, in general, is devoid of a long history or a method of professionalizing those who specialize in dance. Robert W. Nicholls affirms this aspect of Cohen Bull's characterization of "African dance" when he writes: "The role of audience and performer is often interchangeable, and, depending on the occasion, the ranks of the spectators might be broken by an individual eager to demonstrate his or her own dancing skills. Due to their mult-dimensional character, the integration of different art forms, and the lack of rigid distinctions between performers and audience, traditional dance performances might be described as 'whole theater.'" Robert W. Nicholls, "African Dance: Transition and Continuity," in *African Dance: An Artistic, Historical and Philosophical Inquiry*, ed. Kariamu Welsh Asante (Trenton, NJ: African World Press, 1996), 44.
57. Cohen Bull, *Sharing the Dance*, 281.
58. Ibid.
59. Cohen Bull does not think there are no rules concerning gender, or age, or specialization in traditional Ghanaian dance; she does think, in comparison with classical ballet, that there are more aesthetic possibilities that can be allowed (e.g., in some contexts, in traditional Ghanaian dance, older dancers are actually better dancers than younger dancers, which would normally be inconceivable in Balanchine's world, unless, of course, one is Balanchine himself, who danced the part of Don Quixote with the then nineteen year old Suzanne Farrell as Dulcinea, his muse, in 1965, when Balanchine was 61. The performance has been generally regarded with embarrassment by critics; to quote Reynolds and McCormick: "The ballet [*Don Quixote*] as a whole, burdened by drab music and featuring an old man as the protagonist, never really came alive, but for Balanchine it was a unique and seemingly very personal experiment. . . ." Reynolds and McCormick, *No Fixed Points*, 522.
60. Cohen Bull, *Sharing the Dance*, 281.
61. Gottschild, "Crossroads, Continuities, and Contradictions," 4.
62. Ibid., 7.
63. Robert Farris Thompson, *African Art in Motion* (Los Angeles: University of California Press, 1979), 7.
64. Gottschild, "Crossroads, Continuities, and Contradictions," 7.
65. The kind of "circles" Cohen Bull talks about, in relation to traditional Ghanaian dance, are not circular *theatres*, but are more akin to contemporary contact improvisation circles on the ground, in which participants and dancers literally form circles on the same floor, and take turns spectating and performing. Cynthia Jean Cohen Bull, "Looking at Movement as Culture: Contact Improvisation to Disco," in *Moving History/Dancing Cultures: A Dance History Reader*, eds. Ann Dils and Ann Cooper Albright (Middletown, CT: Wesleyan University Press, 2001), 406. Furthermore, the type of central vantage point—geared towards the gaze or spectatorship of a powerful patron—Cohen Bull speaks of is one deeply rooted in European

traditions, iconized, for example, in not only the architecture of European theatre but also in their conventions of painting. See, for example, Mary D. Garrard, "Leonardo da Vinci and Creative Female Nature," in *Feminism and Tradition in Aesthetics*, eds. Peggy Zeglin Brand and Carolyn Korsmeyer (University Park, PA: Pennsylvania State University Press, 1995), 326–53.

66. Gottschild, "Crossroads, Continuities, and Contradictions," 9.
67. Ibid., 5.
68. See generally, Yvonne Daniel, *Rumba: Dance and Social Change in Contemporary Cuba* (Bloomington, IN: Indiana University Press, 1995).
69. See generally, Sheila S. Walker, *Ceremonial Spirit Possession in Africa and Afro-America: Forms, Meanings, and Functional Significance for Individual Social Group* (Leiden, Netherlands: Brill, 1972).
70. Geneva Gay and Willie L. Baber, *Expressively Black: The Cultural Basis of Ethnic Identity* (New York: Praeger, 1987), 11.
71. Gottschild, *The Black Dancing Body*, 15.
72. Ibid., 4.
73. Brenda Dixon Gottschild, *Joan Myers Brown and the Audacious Hope of the Black Ballerina* (New York: Palgrave Macmillan, 2012), xxvii.
74. Vanessa Thomas Smith, quoted in Gottschild, *Joan Myers Brown*, 127.
75. Gottschild, *Joan Myers Brown*, 127.
76. Ananya Chatterjea, afterward to *Joan Myers Brown and the Audacious Hope of the Black Ballerina*, by Brenda Dixon Gottschild (New York: Palgrave Macmillan, 2012), 260.
77. Joan Myers Brown, quoted in Gottschild, *Joan Myers Brown*, 119.
78. Deborah Manning St. Charles, quoted in Gottschild, *Joan Myers Brown*, 119.
79. Gottschild, *Joan Myers Brown*, 120.
80. Gottschild, *The Black Dancing Body*, 76.
81. See Derrida, "Interview with Julia Kristeva," 42–43.
82. See, for example, Thomas DeFrantz's essay, comparing the Urban Bushwomen's choreographic treatment of "booty control" with Phildanco's version. Thomas F. DeFrantz, "Booty Control," in *Dancing Many Drums: Excavations in African American Dance*, ed. Thomas F. DeFrantz (Madison, WI: University of Wisconsin Press, 2002), 24–25.

3 Loíe Fuller, "Goddess of Light" and Josephine Baker, "Black Venus": Non-narrative Choreography as Mere "Spectacle"

*Selections reprinted with permission from Caroline Joan S. Picart, "A Tango between Copyright and Critical Race Theory: Whiteness as Status Property in Balanchine's Ballets, Fuller's Serpentine Dance and Graham's Modern Dances." *Cardozo Journal of Law and Gender* 18, no. 3 (Spring 2012): 685–725.

1. Suzanne Gordon, *Off Balance: The Real World of Ballet* (New York: Pantheon, 1983), 97. For remarks regarding the hyper-whitened, skeletally thin ballerina, see Paula T. Kelso, "Behind the Curtain: The Body, Control, and Ballet," *Edwardsville Journal of Sociology* 3, no. 2 (2003), http://www.siue.edu/sociology/EJS/v32kelso.htm.
2. Loïe Fuller, *Fifteen Years of a Dancer's Life* (Boston: Small, Maynard & Co., 1913), 28.
3. Ibid., 31.
4. Gerald Jonas, *Dancing: The Pleasure, Power and Art of Movement* (New York: Harry N. Abrams, 1998), 192.
5. Ibid.
6. Jody Sperling, "Loïe Fuller's Serpentine Dance: A Discussion of its Origins in Skirt Dancing and a Creative Reconstruction," in *Proceedings Society of Dance History Scholars: Twenty Second Annual Conference*, comp. Juliette Willis (Birmingham, AL: Society of Dance History Scholars, 1999), 53.
7. *New York Times*, "Dancing and Copyright," June 19, 1892.
8. See *Fuller v. Bemis*, 50 F. 926 (C.C.S.D.N.Y. 1892).
9. Ibid. at 929.
10. Ibid.
11. *Glazer v. Hoffman*, 16 So. 2d 53, 55 (Fla. 1943).
12. Ibid.
13. Ann Cooper Albright, *Traces of Light: Absence and Presence in the Work of Loïe Fuller* (Middletown, CT: Wesleyan University Press, 2007), 17.
14. J. E. Crawford Flitch, *Modern Dancing and Dancers* (London: Grant Richards, Ltd., 1912), 72.
15. Ibid.
16. Albright, *Traces of Light*, 18.
17. Stéphanie Mallarmé, *Oeuvres Complètes,* ed, Georges Jean-Aubrey and Henri Mondor (Cambridge, MA: Schoenhof's Foreign Books, 1945), 304.
18. Rhonda K. Garelick, *Electric Salome: Loïe Fuller's Performance of Modernism* (Princeton, NJ: Princeton University Press, 2009), 3.
19. Ibid.
20. Fuller, *Fifteen Years of a Dancer's Life*, 141–42.
21. Ibid., 6.
22. Ibid., 4.
23. See *New York Times*, "Miss Fuller's New Dance," January 24, 1896, http://query.nytimes.com/mem/archive-free/pdf?res=9907E0D6153EE333A25757C2A9679C94679ED7CF.
24. Albright, *Traces of Light*, 126.
25. *New York Times,* "Miss Fuller's New Dance."
26. Jean Lorraine, *Poussiéres de Paris* (Paris: P. Ollendorf, 1902), 143; English translation from Margaret Haile Harris, *Loïe Fuller: Magician of Light* (Richmond: Virginia Museum of Fine Arts, 1979), 20.
27. See, for example, Lynn Garafola, "The Travesty Dancer in Nineteenth-Century Ballet," in *Legacies of Twentieth-Century Dance* (Middletown, CT: Wesleyan University Press, 2005), 137–47.

28. Lorraine, *Poussiéres de Paris*, 144, translated in Harris, *Loïe Fuller: Magician of Light*, 20.
29. Albright, *Traces of Light*, 135.
30. Ibid., 139.
31. Ibid., 138.
32. Albright, *Traces of Light*, 139.
33. Ibid., 185.
34. Ibid., 38.
35. *New York Times*, "'La Loïe' Talks of Her Art," March 1, 1896, http://query.nytimes.com/mem/archive-free/pdf?res=F40B17FF3C5C17738DDDA80894DB405B8685F0D3.
36. Garelick, *Electric Salome*, 17.
37. I am indebted to Anita Anantharam, for her generous support and facilitation of the development of this book chapter, in relation to her seminar on Advanced Feminisms.
38. Copyright Revision Act of 1976, H.R. Rep. No. 94–1476, at 53 (1976). The Copyright Revision Act of 1976 recognized choreography as a significant art form that merits copyright protection. Copyright Revision Act of 1976, Pub. L. No. 94–553, 90 Stat. 2541 (1976).
39. See, for example, Wendy Martin, "'Remembering the Jungle': Josephine Baker and the Modernist Parody," in *Prehistories of the Future: The Primitivist Project and the Culture of Modernism*, ed. Elazar Barkan and Ronald Bush (Palo Alto, CA: Stanford University Press, 1996), 310–25; Nancy Nenno, "Femininity, the Primitive, and Modern Urban Space: Josephine Baker in Berlin," in *Women in the Metropolis: Gender and Modernity in Weimar Culture*, ed. Katharina von Ankum (Berkeley, CA: University of California Press, 1997), 145–61; Elizabeth Coffman, "Uncanny Performances in Colonial Narratives: Josephine Baker in Princess Tam Tam," *Paradoxa: Studies in World Literary Genres* 3, no. 3–4 (1997): 379–94.
40. Josephine Baker is reported to have exclaimed: "I would get children from every race, every creed, every religion. They would be every color of the rainbow. Then it hit me all at once. They would be the Rainbow Children of Josephine Baker." Stephen Papich, *Remembering Josephine* (Indianapolis, IN: Bobbs-Merrill, 1976), 135.
41. Jean-Claude Baker and Chris Chase, *Josephine: The Hungry Heart* (New York: Cooper Square Press, 2001), 261–63.
42. See generally, Mary L. Dudziak, "Josephine Baker, Racial Protest and the Cold War," in *Global Critical Race Feminism: An International Reader*, ed. Adrien Katherine Wing (New York: New York University Press, 2000), 179–91.
43. Unlike George Balanchine, for example, for whom his public choreography and his private love life were inseparable, Baker's dancing remained theatrically insulated from her love affairs. As Lester Strong observes: "In the U.S., [Baker's] lovers and husbands seem to have been exclusively black; in Europe, her lovers were white as well as black, and her husbands were exclusively white. More was known publicly about her male lovers than her female lovers

partly because heterosexual behavior was socially acceptable, while queer behavior was not, but also because, as a sex symbol, she had much to gain professionally by the rumors-and sometimes the public acknowledgment-of her liaisons with men. As for female lovers, if Josephine had seen any career advantage to announcing to the world, no doubt she would have done so. But because she could see no upside to it, she kept quiet about her affairs with women." Lester Strong, "Josephine Baker's Hungry Heart," *Gay and Lesbian Review Worldwide*, September/October 2006, http://www.glreview.com/issues/13.5/13.5-strong.php.

44. Phyllis Rose, *Jazz Cleopatra: Josephine Baker in Her Time* (New York: Doubleday, 1989), 230–31.
45. Baker and Chase, *Josephine: The Hungry Heart*, xvii.
46. Ibid., 3.
47. Ibid.
48. Bennetta Jules-Rosette, *Josephine Baker in Art and Life: The Icon and the Image* (Champaign, IL: University of Illinois Press, 2007), 47.
49. Rose, *Jazz Cleopatra*, 21.
50. Baker and Chase, *Josephine: The Hungry Heart*, 5.
51. Rose, *Jazz Cleopatra*, 21.
52. Baker and Chase, *Josephine: The Hungry Heart*, 5–6.
53. Quoted in Josephine Baker and Jo Bouillon, *Josephine*, trans. Mariana Fitzpatrick (New York: Harper & Row, 1977), 51–52.
54. Michele Faith Wallace, "The Good Lynching and *The Birth of a Nation*: Discourses and Aesthetics of Jim Crow," *Cinema Journal* 43, no. 1 (Fall 2003): 85–104.
55. For an example of how Baker, like Fuller, electrified many of Paris' artists and intellectuals, see Paul Colins's Art Deco lithographs in Paul Colin, *Josephine Baker and La Revue Négre: Paul Colin's Lithographs of Le Tumult Noir in Paris, 1927* (New York: Henry N. Abrams, 1998).
56. T. Denean Sharpley-Whiting, *Black Venus: Sexualized Savages, Primal Fears, and Primitive Narratives in French* (Durham, NC: Duke University Press, 1999), 251.
57. Terri Francis, "The Audacious Josephine Baker: Stardom, Cinema, Paris" in *Black Europe and the African Diaspora*, ed. Darlene Clark Hine, Trica Danielle Keaton, and Stephen Small (Champaign, IL: University of Illinois Press, 2009), 251.
58. Brenda Dixon Gottschild, *The Black Dancing Body: A Geography from Coon to Cool* (New York: Palgrave Macmillan, 2003), 157.
59. Ann Stoler noted that archives, which in this case, included cultural memories of Baartman's dissected genital "apron" as the trace that constituted Baartman's identity as a "Black Venus," embodied "codes of recognition and systems of expectation at the very heart of what we still need to learn about colonial polities." Ann Laura Stoler, "Colonial Archives and Arts of Governance," *Archival Science* 2 (2002):109.
60. Baker and Bouillon, *Josephine*, 53.
61. Rose, *Jazz Cleopatra*, 21.

62. Jules-Rosette, *Josephine Baker*, 178–79.
63. Rose, *Jazz Cleopatra*, 47.
64. Judith Butler, "Performative Acts and Gender Constitution: An Essay in Phenomenology and Feminist Theory," *Theatre Journal* 40, no. 4 (1988): 525.
65. Jules-Rosette, *Josephine Baker*, 49.
66. Foulkes similarly locates Baker's rise to stardom as part of the flowering of the Harlem Renaissance in the 1920's: "In Paris, Josephine Baker thrilled audiences at the Théâtre de Champs-Elysées in 1925 and the Folies Bergerés in 1926; in New York, Bill "Bojangles" Robinson dominated the tap scene in Broadway shows and then in movies of the 1930's, and Florence Mills made a splash with her dancing and singing ability in the 1924 all-black revue *Dixie to Broadway*, which differed from previous shows that usually centered around male comedians.... "Julia L. Foulkes, *Modern Bodies: Dance and American Modernism from Martha Graham to Alvin Ailey* (Chapel Hill, NC: University of North Carolina Press, 2002), 23.
67. Rose, *Jazz Cleopatra*, 47.
68. Quoted in Baker and Bouillon, *Josephine*, 55.
69. Baker and Chase, *Josephine: The Hungry Heart*, 227.
70. Phyllis Rose notes that as Baker's career rose, so did the number of instances in which she was dogged by claims of breach of contract. See Rose, *Jazz Cleopatra*, 82.
71. Jules-Rosette, *Josephine Baker*, 145.
72. Baker and Bouillon, *Josephine*, 5.
73. Baker and Chase, *Josephine: The Hungry Heart*, 116.
74. Ibid., 153.
75. Edward Said makes parallel observations concerning the complicity of those privileged by empire's structures (e.g., the colonial intelligentsia, or intellectual elite) with the colonialist's grand myth of a moral duty to subjugate and civilize "inferior" and "savage" cultures. "There was a commitment to [colonialists] over and above profit, a commitment in constant circulation and recirculation, which, on the one hand, allowed decent men and women to accept the notion that distant territories and their native peoples *should* be subjugated and, on the other hand, replenished metropolitan energies so that these decent people could think of the *imperium* as a protracted, almost metaphysical obligation to rule subordinate, inferior or less advanced people. We must not forget that there was very little domestic resistance to these empires." Edward Said, *Culture and Imperialism* (New York: Vintage, 1993), 10.
76. Jules-Rosette, *Josephine Baker*, 74. For a detailed analysis of the Black Cinderella and Pygmalion narratives in Baker's films, see ibid., 72–123.
77. Samir Dayal, "Blackness as Symptom: Josephine Baker and European Identity," in *Blackening Europe: The African American Presence*, ed. Heike Raphael-Hernandez (London and New York: Routledge, 2004), 41.
78. For an extended account of how Baker repeatedly abandoned choreography and chose improvisation on the spot, thus often driving the orchestra (and

sometimes the lighting crew) to follow her lead, see Papich, *Remembering Josephine*, 61.

79. Nancy Reynolds and Malcolm McCormick, *No Fixed Points: Dance in the Twentieth Century* (New Haven and London: Yale University Press, 2003), 690.
80. See Anthea Kraut, "White Womanhood, Property Rights and the Campaign for Choreographic Copyright: Loïe Fuller's *Serpentine Dance*," *Dance Research Journal* 43, no. 1 (Summer 2011): 3.
81. See Albright, *Traces of Light*, 185.
82. See *Fuller v. Bemis*, 50 F. 926 (S.D.N.Y. 1892).
83. Rose, *Jazz Cleopatra*, 100–01.
84. *Fuller v. Bemis*, 50 F. 926, 929 (C.C.S.D.N.Y. 1892).
85. *Martinetti v. Maguire*, 16 F. Cas. 920 (C.C.Cal. 1867); *Barnes v. Miner*, 122 F. 480 (C.C.S.D.N.Y. 1903); *Dane v. M. & H. Co.*, 136 U.S.P.Q. 426 (N.Y. 1963).
86. US Const. art. I, § 8, cl. 8.
87. Richard L. Schur, *Parodies of Ownership: Hip-Hop Aesthetics and Intellectual Property Law* (Ann Arbor, MI: University of Michigan Press, 2009), 164, 107.
88. Anthea Kraut, "'Stealing Steps' and Signature Moves: Embodied Theories of Dance as Intellectual Property," *Theatre Journal* 62, no. 2 (May 2010): 178. See Lawrence Levine, *Highbrow/Lowbrow: The Emergence of Cultural Hierarchy in America* (Cambridge, MA: Harvard University Press, 1988) regarding the racial genealogy of the terms "highbrow" and "lowbrow," which in turn sprang from the nineteenth century (racially problematic) pseudo-science of phrenology.
89. Thomas Streeter, "Broadcast Copyright and the Bureaucratization of Property," in *The Construction of Authorship: Textual Appropriation in Law and Literature*, ed. Martha Woodmansee and Peter Jaszi (Durham, NC: Duke University Press, 1994), 306.
90. Marlon B. Ross, "The New Negro Displayed: Self-Ownership, Proprietary Sites/Sights, and the Bonds/Bounds of Race," in *Claiming the Stones, Naming the Bones: Cultural Property and the Negotiation of National and Ethnic Identity*, ed. Elazar Barkan and Ronald Bush (Los Angeles: Getty Research Institute, 2002), 259.
91. Martha Woodmansee, "The Genius and the Copyright: Economic and Legal Conditions of the Emergence of the 'Author'," *Eighteenth Century Studies* 17, no. 4 (Summer 1984): 434, 447.
92. James Boyle, *Shahmans, Software and Spleens: Law and the Construction of the Information Society* (Cambridge, MA: Harvard University Press, 1996), xiv.
93. Martha M. Traylor, "Choreography, Pantomime and the Copyright Revision Act of 1976," *New England Law Review* 16 (1980): 234, 237.
94. Kraut, "'Stealing Steps'," 178.
95. Dayal, "Blackness as Symptom," 50.

4 George Balanchine, "Genius of American Dance": Whiteness, Choreography, Copyrightability in American Dance

*Selections reprinted with permission from Caroline Joan S. Picart, "A Tango between Copyright and Critical Race Theory: Whiteness as Status Property in Balanchine's Ballets, Fuller's Serpentine Dance and Graham's Modern Dances," *Cardozo Journal of Law and Gender* 18, no. 3 (Spring 2012): 685–725.

1. George Balanchine Foundation, "Biography: George Balanchine 1904–1983," accessed November 29, 2012, http://www.balanchine.org/balanchine/01/bio .html.
2. Bernard Taper, *Balanchine: A Biography with a New Epilogue* (Berkeley, CA: University of California Press, 1984), 152.
3. Ibid., 147.
4. Ibid., 150. Prior to working with Kerstein, Balanchine already had an impressive resume as a choreographer and ballet master; he had worked with Serge Diaghilev and his renowned Ballets Russes, the Royal Danish Ballet in Copenhagen, and the Ballets Russes de Monte Carlo, among others. George Balanchine Foundation, "Biography: George Balanchine 1904–1983."
5. Taper, *Balanchine: A Biography,* 154.
6. George Balanchine Foundation, "Biography: George Balanchine 1904–1983," 1–2.
7. Ibid.
8. Robert Gottlieb, *George Balanchine: The Ballet Maker* (New York: Harper Collins Publishers, 2004), 2.
9. Ibid., 3.
10. Taper, *Balanchine: A Biography,* 6.
11. Ibid.
12. Ibid., 13.
13. Ibid., 213.
14. Ibid., 215.
15. Ibid., 212.
16. Ibid., 213.
17. Ibid., 215–16.
18. For an overall look at Balanchine's oeuvre by a dance critic, see generally, Nancy Goldner, *Balanchine Variations* (Gainesville, FL: University Press of Florida 2008).
19. Gottlieb, *George Balanchine*, 91.
20. Ibid., 92.
21. Ibid., 93.
22. Ibid., 94–95.
23. Ibid., 103.
24. Ibid., 104.
25. Taper, *Balanchine: A Biography,* 185.

26. Ibid., 324.
27. Gottlieb, *George Balanchine*, 130–31.
28. Ibid., 130.
29. Suzanne Farrell and Toni Bentley, *Holding on to the Air: An Autobiography* (Gainesville, FL: University Press of Florida, 2002), 80.
30. Gottlieb, *George Balanchine*, 131.
31. Ibid.
32. Ibid.
33. Ibid., 131.
34. Farrell and Bentley, *Holding on to the Air*, 90.
35. Ibid., 259.
36. Ibid., 110.
37. Taper, *Balanchine: A Biography*, 399.
38. Ibid.
39. Ibid., 400.
40. Ibid.
41. Ibid.
42. Ibid.
43. Ibid., 324.
44. Ibid., 341–42.
45. Ibid., 401.
46. Ibid., 400.
47. Ibid.
48. Ibid.
49. Ibid., 401.
50. Ibid.
51. Ibid.
52. Ibid.
53. Ibid.
54. Ibid.
55. Ibid., 402.
56. Ibid., 402–03.
57. Ibid., 403.
58. Ibid.
59. Ibid.
60. Ibid.
61. Ibid., 404.
62. Ibid.
63. Ibid.
64. Ibid.
65. Ibid., 404–05.
66. Ibid., 405.
67. Ibid., 406.
68. Ibid.
69. Ibid.
70. Ibid., 407.

71. Ibid.
72. *Horgan v. MacMillan, Inc.*, 621 F. Supp. 1169 (S.D.N.Y. 1985) [hereinafter, *Horgan I*]; Horgan v. MacMillan, Inc., 789 F.2d 157 (2d. Cir. 1986) [hereinafter *Horgan II*].
73. *Horgan I*, 621 F. Supp. at 1169.
74. Ibid. at 1170 n.2.
75. Ibid. at 1170.
76. Ibid.
77. *Horgan II*, 789 F.2d at 164.
78. Ibid. at 163.
79. Ibid. at 164.
80. Ibid. at 162.
81. For a detailed review of the facts of both cases, see Patrician Solan Gennerich, "One Moment in Time: The Second Circuit Ponders Choreographic Photography as a Copyright Infringement: Horgan v. MacMillan, Inc.," *Brooklyn Law Review* 53 (Spring 1987): 383–89.
82. *Horgan I*, 621 F. Supp. at 1170.
83. Ibid.
84. Ibid.
85. Ibid. at 1170 n.1.
86. Ibid. at 1170.
87. Ibid.
88. Ibid. at 1169.
89. Ibid.
90. Ibid.
91. *Horgan II*, 789 F.2d at 159.
92. Ibid. at 158.
93. Taper, *Balanchine: A Biography,* 8.
94. *Horgan II*, 789 F.2d at 158.
95. Ibid.
96. Ibid.
97. Ibid.
98. Ibid.
99. Ibid.
100. Ibid.
101. Ibid. at 159.
102. Ibid.
103. Ibid.
104. Ibid.
105. Ibid.
106. Ibid. at 161.
107. Ibid.
108. Ibid.
109. Ibid.
110. Ibid. at 162.
111. Ibid.

112. Ibid.
113. Ibid., citing *Peter Pan Fabrics, Inc. v. Martin Weiner Corp.*, 274 F.2d 487, 489 (2d Cir. 1960).
114. *Horgan II*, 789 F.2d at 162.
115. Ibid.
116. Ibid.
117. Ibid.
118. Ibid., citing *Roy Export Co. Establishment v. Columbia Broadcasting System, Inc.*, 503 F. Supp. 1137, 1145 (S.D.N.Y. 1980), *aff'd*, 672 F.2d 1095 (2d Cir. 1982).
119. Ibid. at 162–63, citing *Elsmere Music, Inc. v. National Broadcasting Co.*, 482 F. Supp. 741, 744 (S.D.N.Y. 1980), *aff'd*, 623 F.2d 252 (2d Cir. 1980).
120. Ibid. at 163.
121. Ibid.
122. Ibid.
123. Ibid.
124. Ibid. at 163 n.8.
125. Ibid. at 163.
126. Ibid.
127. Taper, *Balanchine: A Biography*, 409.
128. Ibid., 410.
129. Ibid.
130. Ibid.
131. Bruno Latour, *Science in Action: How to Follow Scientists and Engineers through Society* (Cambridge, MA: Harvard University Press, 1987), 4, 13.
132. Thomas Kuhn, *The Structure of Scientific Revolutions* (Chicago: University of Chicago Press, 1970), viii.

5 Martha Graham, "Picasso of American Dance," and Katherine Dunham, "Matriarch of Black Dance": Exoticism and Nonwhiteness in American Dance

* Selections reprinted with permission from Caroline Joan S. Picart, "A Tango between Copyright and Critical Race Theory: Whiteness as Status Property in Balanchine's Ballets, Fuller's Serpentine Dance and Graham's Modern Dances," *Cardozo Journal of Law and Gender* 18, no. 3 (Spring 2012): 685–725.

1. Diane Solway, "When the Choreographer Is out of the Picture," *New York Times*, January 7, 2007, http://www.nytimes.com/2007/01/07/arts/dance/07solw.html?ref=ronprotas.
2. See PBS: American Masters, "Martha Graham: About the Dancer," September 16, 2005, http://www.pbs.org/wnet/americanmasters/episodes/martha-graham/about-the-dancer/497/.

3. Ibid.
4. Ibid.
5. Bernard Taper, *Balanchine: A Biography with a New Epilogue*, (Berkeley, CA: University of California Press, 1984), 15.
6. Don McDonagh, *Martha Graham*, 2nd ed. (New York: Warner Books, 1978), 53.
7. Ibid., 75.
8. Ibid., 225.
9. Ibid., 67.
10. Ibid., 8.
11. Russell Freedman, *Martha Graham: A Dancer's Life* (New York: Clarion Books, 1998), 15.
12. Ibid., 56.
13. Ibid., 58.
14. Ibid., 56–57.
15. Ibid., 27.
16. Ibid., 27–28.
17. Ibid., 30.
18. McDonagh, *Martha Graham*, 26.
19. Ibid., 26.
20. Ibid., 26, 28.
21. Agnes De Mille, *Martha: The Life and Work of Martha Graham* (New York: Random House, 1991), 67.
22. Freedman, *Martha Graham*, 38.
23. See, for example, Martha Graham, *Blood Memory: An Autobiography* (New York: Doubleday, 1991), 93 (where Graham admitted that the other female entertainers called her "Princess" because she was "more than a little arrogant" and she kept insisting that what she did was "art," not show business); Julia L. Foulkes, *Modern Bodies: Dance and American Modernism from Martha Graham to Alvin Ailey* (Chapel Hill, NC: University of North Carolina Press, 2002), 41 (where a caricature of Martha Graham, as opposed to Sally Rand, a popular entertainer, underlines the differences that separated the realm of "serious art" versus "simply entertainment" that Graham fiercely advocated).
24. Freedman, *Martha Graham*, 41.
25. Ibid., 42.
26. McDonagh, *Martha Graham*, 37.
27. Graham repeatedly resisted attributing any direct influences on her art. For example, because many critics noted that 'Primitive Mysteries" (1931) visually resembled the work of Mexican muralists, which were then the rave in the art world, Graham allowed herself to admit, "with her characteristic flair"... that she had been "influenced by the painter José Clemente Orozco but that she had not used him as a model to be copied or even approximated." Ibid., 85.
28. Ibid., 37.
29. Ibid., 26.
30. Ibid.

31. Deborah Jowitt, "Monumental Martha," in *What is Dance?*, ed. Roger Copeland and Marshall Cohen (New York: Oxford University Press, 1983), 456–58.
32. Freedman, *Martha Graham*, 120.
33. Ibid., 135.
34. Ibid.
35. Ibid., 141.
36. Ibid., 120.
37. Ibid., 137.
38. De Mille, *Martha*, 382.
39. Ibid., 382–83.
40. Freedman, *Martha Graham*, 137.
41. Ibid., 140–41.
42. *Martha Graham Sch. & Dance Found., Inc. v. Martha Graham Ctr. of Contemporary Dance, Inc.*, 380 F.3d 624, 628 (2d Cir. 2004) [hereinafter *Graham III*].
43. *Martha Graham Sch. & Dance Found., Inc. v. Martha Graham Ctr. of Contemporary Dance, Inc.*, 224 F. Supp. 2d 567, 572 (S.D.N.Y. 2002) [hereinafter *Graham II*].
44. *Graham III*, 380 F.3d at 629.
45. Ibid.
46. Ibid.
47. *Graham II*, 224 F.Supp. 2d at 572.
48. *Graham III*, 380 F.3d at 637.
49. Ibid. at 629.
50. Ibid. at 637.
51. Ibid. at 638.
52. Ibid.
53. See Ibid.
54. *Graham II*, 224 F. Supp. 2d at 573.
55. Ibid.
56. *Graham III*, 380 F.3d at 639.
57. Ibid. at 630.
58. Ibid.
59. Ibid.
60. Ibid.
61. Ibid. See also Jennifer Dunning, "Martha Graham's Legacy: How the Dances Will Now Be Danced," *New York Times*, September 8, 1999, http://partners.nytimes.com/library/dance/090899dance-graham.html; Jennifer Dunning, "Martha Graham Board Seeks to Remove Director," *New York Times*, March 25, 2000, http://www.nytimes.com/2000/03/25/arts/martha-graham-board-seeks-to-remove-director.html?src=pm.
62. *Graham III*, 380 F.3d at 630. See also Jennifer Dunning, "Performances Are Suspended In Dance Group Graham Started," *New York Times*, May 26, 2000, http://www.nytimes.com/2000/05/26/nyregion/performances-are-suspended-in-dance-group-graham-started.html.

63. See *Graham III*, 380 F.3d at 630.
64. Ibid.
65. Ibid.
66. *Graham III*, 380 F.3d at 631. See also Doreen Carvajal, "Bitter Standoff Imperils a Cherished Dance Legacy," *New York Times*, July 6, 2000, http://www.nytimes.com/2000/07/06/arts/bitter-standoff-imperils-a-cherished-dance-legacy.html; Jennifer Dunning, "Challenging Graham Board, Director Reveals A Rival Plan," *New York Times*, November 1, 2000, http://www.nytimes.com/2000/11/01/arts/challenging-graham-board-director-reveals-a-rival-plan.html.
67. See *Graham II*, 224 F. Supp. 2d at 607–09. See generally Joseph Carman, "DANCE; Who Owns A Dance? It Depends on the Maker," *New York Times*, December 23, 2001, http://query.nytimes.com/gst/fullpage.html?res=9D0DEFDC153EF930A15751C1A9679C8B63.
68. *Graham II*, 224 F. Supp. 2d at 521.
69. See *Graham II*, 224 F. Supp. 2d at 570. See also Jennifer Dunning, "In Ruling, Dance Center May Use Graham Name," *New York Times*, August 8, 2001, http://www.nytimes.com/2001/08/08/nyregion/in-ruling-dance-center-may-use-the-graham-name.html.
70. *Graham II*, 224 F. Supp. 2d at 570.
71. *Graham III*, 380 F.3d at 632.
72. Ibid. at 637–42. See also Jennifer Dunning, "Metro Briefing: New York: Manhattan: Martha Graham Center Wins Dance Rights," *New York Times*, August 19, 2004, http://query.nytimes.com/gst/fullpage.html?res=9E0CE3D91E3FF93AA2575BC0A9629C8B63; Felicia R. Lee, "Graham Legacy, on the Stage Again," *New York Times*, September 29, 2004, http://www.nytimes.com/2004/09/29/arts/dance/29grah.html?_r=1&ref=ronprotas; John Rockwell, "Arts, Briefly; Martha Graham Center Wins Court Ruling," *New York Times*, July 14, 2006, http://query.nytimes.com/gst/fullpage.html?res=9D05EED71E30F937A25754C0A9609C8B63&ref=ronprotas.
73. *See* 17 U.S.C. §101 (2000) (defining work for hire as "(1) a work prepared by an employee within the scope of his or her employment; or (2) a work specially ordered or commissioned for use as a contribution to a collective work" in enumerated instances.)
74. *Graham III*, 380 F.3d at 647.
75. Ibid.
76. *Graham III*, 380 F.3d at 639–40.
77. See Ibid. at 637–39.
78. See Ibid. at 638.
79. Ibid. at 640.
80. For detailed examinations of the history of the work for hire doctrine leading up to *Reid*, see Katherine B. Marik, "*Community for Creative Non-Violence v. Reid*: New Certainty for the Copyright Work for Hire Doctrine," *Pepperdine Law Review* 18, no. 3 (1991): 591–608; Christine Leahy Weinberg, "*Community For Creative Non-Violence v. Reid*: A Specious Solution to the

'Works Made for Hire' Problem," *Boston College Law Review* 32, no. 3:3 (1991): 666.

81. The Reid factors to be considered include the skill required, the source of the instrumentalities and tools used in creating the work, where the work was created, the duration of the relationship between the parties, whether the hiring party has the right to assign additional projects to the hired party, the method of payment, the extent of the hired party's discretion over when and how long to work, the hired party's role in hiring and paying assistants, whether the hiring party is in business and whether the work is part of the regular business of the hiring party, the provision of employee benefits, and the tax treatment of the hired party. *Cmty. for Creative Non-Violence v. Reid*, 490 U.S. 730, 751–52 (1989).
82. See *Aymes v. Bonelli*, 980 F.2d 857, 861 (2d Cir. 1992) (holding that the Second Circuit pays special attention to "(1) the hiring party's right to control the manner and means of creation; (2) the skill required; (3) provision of employee benefits; (4) the tax treatment of the hired party; and (5) whether the hiring party has the right to assign additional projects to the hired party.")
83. *Graham III*, 380 F.3d at 642.
84. Ibid.
85. *Graham III*, 380 F.3d at 642; see generally, *Graham II*, 224 F. Supp.2d at 569.
86. *Graham I*, 153 F. Supp.2d at 514.
87. *Horgan II*, 789 F.2d at 158.
88. Encyclopedia of World Biography, "Katherine Dunham," accessed November 30, 2012, http://www.notablebiographies.com/newsmakers2/2007-Co-Lh/Dunham-Katherine.html.
89. Ibid.
90. Dunham is claimed to have said, in relation to the financial stability of her dance company, "Katherine Dunham: Dancer," Missouri Historical Society, accessed November 30, 2012, http://www.mohistory.org/KatherineDunham/dancer.htm.
91. Ibid.
92. Ibid.
93. Ibid.
94. Ibid.
95. For examples of the rivalry between Dunham and Baker, especially in Paris, see Joyce Aschenbrenner, *Katherine Dunham: Dancing a Life* (Chicago, IL: University of Chicago Press, 2002), 143 (where Baker offers to introduce Dunham to Paris, and Dunham refuses, and Baker attempts to curry favor with Dunham's company members); Stephen Papich, *Remembering Josephine* (Indianapolis, IN: Bobbs-Merrill, 1976), 3 (where Baker refers to Dunham as "that colored woman from America"); Jean-Claude Baker and Chris Chase, *Josephine: The Hungry Heart* (New York: Cooper Square Press, 2001), 285 (where Baker and Dunham try to outdo each other in terms of jewelry, with Dunham wearing emeralds and Baker wearing diamonds).

96. Foulkes, *Modern Bodies*, 72.
97. Sally Sommer, "Free to Dance Biographies: Katherine Dunham," PBS: Great Performances, accessed December 3, 2012, http://www.pbs.org/wnet/freetodance/biographies/dunham.html.
98. Ibid.
99. Ann Barzel, Mark Turbyfill, and Ruth Page, "The Lost Ten Years: The Untold Story of the Dunham-Turbyfill Alliance," in *Kaiso! Writings by and about Katherine Dunham*, ed. Vévé A. Clark and Sara E. Johnson (Madison, WI: University of Wisconsin Press, 2005), 179.
100. Katherine Dunham, quoted by Harriet Jackson in "American Dancer, Negro," *Dance Magazine*, September 1966, 40. See also Katherine Dunham's autobiography, *A Touch of Innocence: Memoirs of Childhood* (Chicago: University of Chicago Press, 1994).
101. Aschenbrenner, *Katherine Dunham:Dancing a Life*, 7.
102. Ibid.
103. Ibid.
104. Ibid.
105. Ibid., 9.
106. Barzel, Turbyfill, and Page, "The Lost Ten Years," 181.
107. Library of Congress, "Katherine Dunham Timeline," Selections from the Katherine Dunham Collection at the Library of Congress, accessed December 3, 2012, http://lcweb2.loc.gov/diglib/ihas/html/dunham/dunham-timeline.html.
108. Ibid.
109. Barzel, Turbyfill, and Page, "The Lost Ten Years," 179.
110. Ibid., 187.
111. Sommer, "Free to Dance," 1.
112. Barzel, Turbyfill, and Page, "The Lost Ten Years," 187.
113. Ibid., note 1.
114. Ibid.
115. Aschenbrenner, *Katherine Dunham:Dancing a Life*, 27.
116. Ibid.
117. Frederick L. Orme, "The Negro in Dance, as Katherine Dunham Sees Him," in *Kaiso! Writings by and about Katherine Dunham*, ed. Vévé A. Clark and Sara E. Johnson (Madison, WI: University of Wisconsin Press, 2005), 192.
118. Ibid.
119. Kennedy Center, "Katherine Dunham," accessed December 3, 2012, http://www.kennedy-center.org/explorer/artists/?entity_id=3721.
120. Foulkes, *Modern Bodies*, 72–73.
121. Aschenbrenner, *Katherine Dunham:Dancing a Life*, 29.
122. Ibid., 32.
123. Franz Boas, *Race, Language and Culture* (New York: Macmillan, 1940), cited in Aschenbrenner, *Katherine Dunham:Dancing a Life*, 32–33.
124. Encyclopedia of World Biography, "Katherine Dunham."

125. Nancy Reynolds and Malcolm McCormick, *No Fixed Points: Dance in the Twentieth Century* (New Haven and London: Yale University Press, 2003), 341.
126. Sommer, "Free to Dance," 1.
127. An earlier edition of Dunham's thesis appears to be have been published by the University of California at Los Angeles Press in 1983, as revisions of "Las Danzas di Haití" in *Acta Anthropologica* 2, no. 4 (Mexico, 1947), and Katherine Dunham, *Les Dances de Haiti* (Paris: Fasquel Press, 1957); Dorothea Fischer-Hornung, "'Jungle in the Spotlight?': Primitivism and Esteem: Katherine Dunham's 1954 German Tour," in *Blackening Europe: The African American Presence*, ed. Heike Raphael-Hernandez (London and New York: Routledge, 2004), 67, note 37.
128. Fischer-Hornung, "Katherine Dunham's 1954 German Tour," 67, note 37.
129. Foulkes, *Modern Bodies*, 73.
130. Ibid.
131. Fischer-Hornung, "Katherine Dunham's 1954 German Tour," 60. For a detailed examination of American critics' struggles to reconcile Dunham's status as an intellectual and a dancer who did not flinch from the sexualized elements at the center of her choreography, see Ramsay Burt, "Katherine Dunham's *Rite de Passage*: Censorship and Sexuality," in *EmBODYing Liberation: The Black Body in American Dance*, ed. Dorothea Fischer-Hornung and Alison D. Goeller (Hamburg and London: LIT Verlag, Münster, 2001).
132. Fischer-Hornung, "Katherine Dunham's 1954 German Tour," 60.
133. Ibid. at 61.
134. Ibid. Fischer-Hornung explains the confusion over Dunham's alleged "Ph.D." is because she was awarded a Ph.B.—a Bachelor of Philosophy from the University of Chicago in 1936, and her alleged "professorship" at Yale is traceable to the dust jacket of *Katherine Dunham's Journey to Accompong*, where Dunham is described as having delivered a lecture and demonstration to the Anthropology Club at Yale University. Ibid., 70, note 50.
135. Vévé A. Clark, "Designing Dunham: John Pratt's Method in Costume and Décor: An Interview with John Pratt," in *Kaiso! Writings by and about Katherine Dunham*, ed. Vévé A. Clark and Sara E. Johnson (Madison, WI: University of Wisconsin Press, 2005), 208.
136. Fischer-Hornung, "Katherine Dunham's 1954 German Tour," 64–65.
137. Reynolds and McCormick, *No Fixed Points*, 341.
138. See generally, Melville Herkovits, *Myth of the Negro Past* (New York: Harper & Bros., 1941).
139. Joyce Aschenbrenner, "Katherine Dunham: Reflections on the Social and Political Contexts of Afro-American Dance," *Dance Research Journal Annual XI* (Congress on Research in Dance, 1980), 45 quoting from Katherine Dunham, "The Future of the Negro Dance," *Dance Herald* (1938): 5.
140. Katherine Dunham, *Island Possessed* (New York: Doubleday, 1969; Chicago: University of Chicago Press, 1994), 91.

141. Aschenbrenner, *Katherine Dunham: Dancing a Life*, 73.
142. Dunham, *Island Possessed*, 130–31.
143. Ibid.
144. Aschenbrenner, *Katherine Dunham: Dancing a Life*, 82–83.
145. Ibid., 83.
146. Ibid., 84.
147. Ibid.
148. Sommer, "Free to Dance," 2.
149. Ibid.
150. Constance Valis Hill, "Collaborating with Balanchine on *Cabin in the Sky*: Interviews with Katherine Dunham," in *Kaiso! Writings by and about Katherine Dunham*, ed. Vévé A. Clark and Sara E. Johnson, 235–47 (Madison, WI: University of Wisconsin Press, 2005), 235.
151. Aschenbrenner, *Katherine Dunham: Dancing a Life*, 124.
152. Taper, *Balanchine: A Biography*, 195.
153. Ibid.
154. For the invisibility of black choreographers in relation to white theater goers, see generally, Danielle Robinson, "'Oh, You Black Bottom!' Appropriation, Authenticity, and Opportunity in the Jazz Dance Teaching of 1920s New York," *Dance Research Journal* 38, no. 1/2 (2006): 19–42.
155. Aschenbrenner, *Katherine Dunham: Dancing a Life*, 125–25. See also Marshall Stearns and Jean Stearns, *Jazz Dance: The Story of American Vernacular Dance* (London: Macmillan, 1968), 309.
156. Valis Hill, "Collaborating with Balanchine," 235.
157. Reynolds and McCormick, *No Fixed Points*, 341.
158. Valis Hill, "Collaborating with Balanchine," 238.
159. Ibid., 239.
160. Ibid., 246.
161. Aschenbrenner, *Katherine Dunham: Dancing a Life*, 125.
162. Sol Hurok and Ruth Goode, *Impresario: A Memoir* (New York: Random House, 1946), 286. See also Aschenbrenner's interview with Tommy Gomez in Aschenbrenner, *Katherine Dunham: Dancing a Life*, 261, note 81.
163. Valis Hill, "Collaborating with Balanchine," 242.
164. Ibid., 242.
165. Ibid., 243–44.
166. Ibid., 244.
167. Ibid., 238.
168. Ibid.
169. Aschenbrenner, *Katherine Dunham: Dancing a Life*, 125.
170. Ibid., 125–26.
171. Elizabeth Chin, "Katherine Dunham's Dance as Public Anthropology," *American Anthropologist* 112, no. 4 (December 2010): 641.
172. Library of Congress. "Katherine Dunham Timeline," 8.
173. Ibid.
174. For a detailed description of the content of *Southland* as well as its historical reception, see Constance Valis Hill, "'Katherine Dunham's Southland'

Protest in the Face of Repression," in *Dancing Many Drums: Excavations in African American Dance*, ed. Thomas F. DeFrance (Madison, WI: University of Wisconsin Press, 2002), 289–316.

175. Reynolds and McCormick, *No Fixed Points*, 342.
176. Ibid., 344.
177. Foulkes, *Modern Bodies*, 73.
178. Ibid., 74. See also *Dance Observer* 10, no. 8 (October 1943): 88.
179. Foulkes, *Modern Bodies*, 74.
180. Halifu Osumare, "Dancing the Black Atlantic: Katherine Dunham's Research-to-Performance Method," in "Migration of Movement: Dance Across Americas," special issue, *AmeriQuest* 7, no 2 (2010): http://ejournals.library.vanderbilt.edu/index.php/ameriquests/article/view/165.
181. For example, Graham was the first dancer to win the Guggenheim Fellowship in 1930, and spent the grant exploring Aztec and Mayan archeological sites; "Primitive Mysteries," staged in 1931, had no clear connection to this trip or her experiences, and Graham disavowed any literal influence on her work. See Freedman, *Martha Graham*, 68–70; McDonagh, *Martha Graham*, 85.
182. Reynolds and McCormick, *No Fixed Points*, 146.
183. Ibid.
184. Ibid., 147.
185. Ibid., 148.
186. Jowitt, "Monumental Martha," 456–57.
187. Foulkes, *Modern Bodies*, 48.
188. Graham quoted in Merle Armitage, *Martha Graham: The Early Years* (New York: Da Capo Press, 1937), 97.
189. Reynolds and McCormick, *No Fixed Points*, 341.
190. Katherine Dunham, "Need for Study of Dances of Primitive Peoples," in *Kaiso! Writings by and about Katherine Dunham*, ed. Vévé A. Clark and Sara E. Johnson (Madison, WI: University of Wisconsin Press, 2005), 520.
191. Albirda Rose, "Dunham Technique: Barre Work and Center Progressions," in *Kaiso! Writings by and about Katherine Dunham*, ed. Vévé A. Clark and Sara E. Johnson (Madison, WI: University of Wisconsin Press, 2005), 488–89.
192. Ibid., 489.
193. Ibid., 493.
194. Ibid., 494.
195. Ibid.
196. Ibid.
197. Aschenbrenner, *Katherine Dunham: Dancing a Life*, 205.
198. Ibid.
199. Ibid., 207.
200. Library of Congress. "Katherine Dunham Timeline," 10.
201. Vévé A. Clark, "Performing the Memory of Difference in Afro-Caribbean Dance: Katherine Dunham's Choreography, 1938–1987," in *Kaiso! Writings*

by and about Katherine Dunham, ed. Vévé A. Clark and Sara E. Johnson (Madison, WI: University of Wisconsin Press, 2005), 324.

202. Aschenbrenner, *Katherine Dunham: Dancing a Life*, 230.
203. Ibid.
204. Ibid.
205. Ibid.
206. Library of Congress. "Katherine Dunham Timeline," 14.

6 Moving into New Directions: Cunningham and Ailey

1. Gerald Jonas, *Dancing: The Pleasure, Power and Art of Movement* (New York: Harry N. Abrams, 1998), 228.
2. Joseph H. Mazo, *Prime Movers: The Makers of Modern Dance in America* (New York: William Morrow and Company, 1977), 226.
3. Merce Cunningham, "You Have to Love Dancing to Stick to It," *The Vision of Modern Dance: In the Words of Its Creators*, 2nd edn., ed. Jean Morrison Brown, Naomi Mindlin and Charles H. Woodford (Hightstown, NJ: Princeton Book Company, 1998), 91.
4. Merce Cunningham, "Choreography and the Dance," in *Merce Cunningham*, ed. Germano Celant (Milan, Italy: Charta, 1999), 42.
5. Merce Cunningham in conversation with Jacqueline Lesschaeve, "The Dancer and the Dance," in *Reading Dance: A Gathering of Memoirs, Reportage, Criticism, Profiles, Interviews, and Some Uncategorizable* Extras, ed. and intro., Robert Gottlieb (New York: Pantheon Books, 2008), p. 462. See also Cunningham, "Choreography and the Dance," 49.
6. Encyclopedia Britannica, "Merce Cunningham," accessed December 19, 2012, http://www.britannica.com/EBchecked/topic/146610/Merce-Cunningham.
7. Mazo, *Prime Movers*, 215.
8. Ibid.
9. Encyclopedia Britannica. "Merce Cunningham."
10. Mazo, *Prime Movers*, 215.
11. Ibid.
12. Encyclopedia Britannica. "Merce Cunningham."
13. Ibid.; Lesschaeve, "The Dancer and the Dance," 465–66.
14. Ibid., 466.
15. Ibid.
16. Nancy Reynolds and Malcolm McCormick, *No Fixed Points: Dance in the Twentieth Century* (New Haven and London: Yale University Press, 2003), 355.
17. Lesschaeve, "The Dancer and the Dance," 466.
18. Carolyn Brown, Douglas Dunn, Viola Farber, Steve Paxton, Marianne Preger-Simon, Valda Setterfield, Gus Solomons Jr., and David Vaughan, "Cunningham and His Dancers," in *Merce Cunningham*, ed. Germano Celant (Milan, Italy: Charta, 1999), 236.
19. Joseph Mazo, "Martha Remembered," *Dance Magazine*, July 1991, 44.

20. Ibid., 52.
21. Deborah Jowitt, *Time and the Dancing Image* (New York: William Morrow and Company, 1988), 228–29.
22. Reynolds and McCormick, *No Fixed Points*, 355.
23. Ibid.
24. Mazo, *Prime Movers*, 216.
25. Ibid.
26. Ibid.
27. Simone Forti quoted in Roger Copeland, "Merce Cunningham and the Politics of Perception," in *Merce Cunningham*, ed. Germano Celant (Milan, Italy: Charta, 1999), 161.
28. Reynolds and McCormick, *No Fixed Points*, 355.
29. Ibid.
30. Ibid.
31. Ibid.
32. Ibid., 355–56.
33. Germano Celant, "Merce Cunningham and John Cage," in *Merce Cunningham*, ed. Germano Celant (Milan, Italy: Charta, 1999), 81.
34. Reynolds and McCormick, *No Fixed Points*, 356.
35. James Klosty, "Introduction," in *Merce Cunningham*, ed. James Klosty (New York: E.P. Dutton and Company, 1985), 11.
36. Reynolds and McCormick, *No Fixed Points*, 356.
37. Ibid.
38. Mazo, *Prime Movers*, 219.
39. Ibid.
40. Ibid.
41. Reynolds and McCormick, *No Fixed Points*, 360.
42. Ibid.
43. Ibid.
44. Merce Cunningham, "Two Questions and Five Dances" in "Time to Walk in Space," *Dance Perspectives* 34 (Summer 1968): 51.
45. Carolyn Brown, untitled essay in *Merce Cunningham*, ed. James Klosty (New York: E.P. Dutton and Company, 1985), 24.
46. Cunningham, "Choreography and the Dance," 47–48.
47. Gordon Mumma, "From Where the Circus Went," in *Merce Cunningham*, ed. James Klosty (New York: E.P. Dutton and Company, 1985), 66.
48. Ibid.
49. Mazo, *Prime Movers*, 219.
50. Carolyn Brown, untitled essay in *Merce Cunningham*, 22.
51. Brown et al., "Cunningham and His Dancers (1999)" 228.
52. Ibid., 229.
53. Ibid.
54. Ibid., 230.
55. Karen Eliot, *Dancing Lives: Five Female Dancers from the Ballet d'Action to Merce Cunningham* (Urbana and Chicago: University of Chicago Press, 2007), 121.

56. Brown et al., "Cunningham and His Dancers (1999)," 236.
57. Ibid., 237.
58. Klosty, "Introduction," 12.
59. "Contact improvisation," a term coined by modern dancer Steve Paxton (one of Cunningham's former dancers), describe it as an "art-sport"—a dance form whose interaction with the audience resembles the way Cohen Bull describes the relationship traditional Ghanian professional dancers have with their audiences: as providing both a communal movement experience as well as serving as an exemplar for the audience. Rather than relying on sight, '[t]he dancers in contact improvisation focus on the physical sensations of touching, leaning, supporting, counterbalancing, and falling with other people, thus carrying on a physical dialogue." Cynthia J. Novack, *Sharing the Dance: Contact Improvisation and American Culture* (Madison, WI: University of Wisconsin Press, 1990), 8, 10.
60. Mazo, *Prime Movers*, 203.
61. Brown et al., "Cunningham and His Dancers (1999)," 229.
62. Ibid., 230–31.
63. Copeland, "Merce Cunningham and the Politics of Perception," 154.
64. Klosty, "Introduction," 12.
65. Noél Carroll and Sally Banes, "Cunningham and Duchamp," in *Merce Cunningham*, ed. Germano Celant (Milan, Italy: Charta, 1999), 179.
66. Reynolds and McCormick, *No Fixed Points*, 366.
67. Mazo, *Prime Movers*, 228.
68. Ibid.
69. Reynolds and McCormick, *No Fixed Points*, 369.
70. Ibid.
71. Ibid.
72. Cunningham quoted in David Vaughn, "Merce Cunningham: Five More Years," in *Merce Cunningham*, ed. Germano Celant (Milan, Italy: Charta, 1999), 296.
73. Vaughn, "Merce Cunningham: Five More Years," 297.
74. Ibid., 305.
75. Ibid.
76. Ibid.
77. Terry Teachout, "Pale Horse, Pale Rider," in *Reading Dance: A Gathering of Memoirs, Reportage, Criticism, Profiles, Interviews, and Some Uncategorizable Extras*, ed. Robert Gottlieb (New York: Pantheon Books, 2008), 479–87.
78. David Vaughn, "Merce Cunningham," in *Merce Cunningham*, ed. Germano Celant (Milan, Italy: Charta, 1999), 99.
79. Cunningham declared: "The relationship between dance and music is one of co-existence, that is being related simply because they exist at the same time." Merce Cunningham, *Changes: Notes on Choreography* (New York: Something Else Press, 1968) quoted in Germano Celant, "Merce Cunningham and John Cage," 82.
80. Ramsay Burt, *The Male Dancer: Bodies, Spectacle, Sexualities*, 2nd edn. (New York: Routledge, 2007), 122.

81. Jonas, *Dancing*, 230.
82. Carolyn Brown, untitled essay in *Merce Cunningham*, 26.
83. Eliot, *Dancing Lives*, p. 138.
84. Earle Brown, untitled essay in *Merce Cunningham*, ed. James Klosty (New York: E.P. Dutton and Company, 1985), 76.
85. Ibid.
86. Ibid.
87. Teachout, "Pale Horse, Pale Rider," 485.
88. Jill Johnston, "Jigs, Japes and Joyce," *Art in America* (January 1987): 103–05.
89. Susan Leigh Foster, "Closets Full of Dances: Modern Dance's Performance of Masculinity and Sexuality," in *Dancing Desires*, ed. Jane Desmond (Madison, WI: University of Wisconsin Press, 2001), 154–69.
90. Yutian Wong's argument is that Cunningham and Cage appropriated aspects of Chinese and Japanese cultural beliefs (e.g., the Book of Changes, tenets of Zen Buddhism), without acknowledging their privilege as white, Western, male artists. Yutian Wong, "Towards a New Asian American Dance Theory: Locating the Dancing Asian American Body," *Discourses in Dance* 1, no. 1 (2002): 69–90.
91. Alistair Macauley, "The Merce Experience," *Dancing Times*, September 1987, 1051.
92. Brown, untitled essay in *Merce Cunningham*, 25.
93. Carolyn Brown, Douglas Dunn, Viola Farber, Steve Paxton, Valda Setterfield, Gus Solomons, Jr., and David Vaughn, "Cunningham and His Dancers," in *Merce Cunningham: Dancing in Space and Time* (New York: Da Capo Press, 1992), 111.
94. Jonathan D. Katz, "Identification," in *Difference/Indifference*, ed. Moira Roth (Amsterdam: Gordon and Breach, 1998), 49–70.
95. Burt, *The Male Dancer*, 123.
96. Moira Roth, "The Aesthetic of Indifference," *Artforum* (November 1977): 45–53.
97. Ibid.
98. Burt, *The Male Dancer*, 125.
99. Marcia Siegel, *Shapes of Change* (Berkeley and Los Angeles: University of California Press, 1985), 325.
100. Burt, *The Male Dancer*, 127.
101. Eliot, *Dancing Lives*, 128.
102. Ibid., 129.
103. Brown, untitled essay in *Merce Cunningham*, 31.
104. Reynolds and McCormick, *No Fixed Points*, 368.
105. Lawrence Halprin, "About Anna Halprin," accessed December 24, 2012, http://www.annahalprin.org/about_bio.html.
106. Cunningham, "Choreography and the Dance," 46.
107. Merce Cunningham Trust, "Honors and Awards," accessed December 24, 2012, http://www.mercecunningham.org/merce-cunningham/.
108. Ibid.

109. Ibid.
110. Merce Cunningham Trust, "Staff/Trustees," accessed December 24, 2012, http://www.mercecunningham.org/trust/.
111. Ibid.
112. Merce Cunningham Trust, "New York Public Library for the Performing Arts," accessed December 24, 2012, http://www.mercecunningham.org/archives/.
113. Daniel J. Wakin, "Merce Cunningham Sets Plan for his Dance Legacy," *New York Times*, June 9, 2009, http://www.nytimes.com/2009/06/10/arts/dance/10merc.html?ref=mercecunningham&_r=0.
114. Ibid.
115. Sutton Stracke, "A Final Goodbye," *Suttons Law* (blog), March 18, 2012, http://suttons-law.blogspot.com/2012/03/final-goodbye.html.
116. Robert Pogrebin, "Dance is Never Far from his Mind," *New York Times*, December 7, 2012, http://www.nytimes.com/2012/12/09/nyregion/for-robert-battle-alvin-ailey-director-dance-is-never-far-from-mind.html?_r=0.
117. See generally, Jennifer Dunning, *Alvin Ailey: A Life in Dance* (New York: Da Capo Press, 1996), 1–5.
118. Ibid., 19.
119. Ibid.
120. Ibid., 18.
121. Joseph H. Mazo, *The Alvin Ailey American Dance Theater* (New York: William Morrow and Company, 1978), 111.
122. Ibid.
123. "Alvin Ailey: Biography," Biography, accessed December 26, 2012, http://www.biography.com/people/alvin-ailey-9177959.
124. Dunning, *Alvin Ailey: A Life in Dance*, 34.
125. Alvin Ailey and A. Peter Bailey, *Revelations: The Autobiography of Alvin Ailey* (New York: Carol Publishing Group, 1995) 42–43.
126. Dunning, *Alvin Ailey: A Life in Dance*, 19.
127. Ailey and Bailey, *Revelations*, 44.
128. Ibid.
129. Encyclopedia of World Biography, "Alvin Ailey Biography,", accessed December 27, 2012, http://www.notablebiographies.com/A-An/Ailey-Alvin.html.
130. Ailey and Bailey, *Revelations*, 44.
131. Robert Tracy, "Early Days: Revelations," in *Ailey Spirit: The Journey of an American Dance Company* (New York: Stewart, Tabori and Chang, 2004), 16.
132. Ailey described his first impression of de Lavallade as a "beautiful, honey-colored creature in a pink leotard, pink skirt, and pink shoes;" he said that from the first moment he set eyes on her, he was in a "state of pure awe." Ailey and Bailey, *Revelations*, 43.
133. Dunning, *Alvin Ailey: A Life in Dance*, 42.
134. Ibid.
135. Ibid.

136. Ibid., 42–43.
137. Ibid., 43.
138. Tracy, "Early Days: Revelations," 16.
139. Ibid., 17.
140. Ibid., 16.
141. Ibid.
142. Dunning, *Alvin Ailey: A Life of Dance*, 48.
143. Ailey and Bailey, *Revelations*, 51.
144. Ibid.
145. Tracy, "Early Days: Revelations," 16.
146. Ibid. For an extended discussion of *Morning Mourning*, see Dunning, *Alvin Ailey: A Life in Dance*, 75.
147. For detailed synopses of these reviews, both positive and negative, see Dunning, *Alvin Ailey: A Life in Dance, 75–77.*
148. Ibid., 76.
149. Tracy, "Early Days: Revelations," 16.
150. Dunning, *Alvin Ailey: A Life in Dance*, 77–78.
151. Ibid., 78.
152. Tracy, "Early Days: Revelations," 17.
153. Ailey and Bailey, *Revelations*, 119.
154. Ibid.
155. Tracy, "Early Days: Revelations," 17.
156. Ibid. See also Dunning, *Alvin Ailey: A Life in Dance*, 85.
157. Dunning, *Alvin Ailey: A Life in Dance*, 88.
158. Ibid.
159. Ibid., 89.
160. Ibid., 89–90.
161. Ibid., 90.
162. Ibid.
163. Tracy, "Early Days: Revelations," 17.
164. Ibid.
165. Dunning, *Alvin Ailey: A Life in Dance*, 94.
166. Tracy, "Early Days: Revelations," 17.
167. Ibid.
168. Ibid.
169. Dunning, *Alvin Ailey: A Life in Dance*, 98.
170. Ailey and Bailey, *Revelations*, 82.
171. Mazo, *The Alvin Ailey American Dance Theater*, 11.
172. Ibid.
173. Ibid., 39.
174. Ibid., 11–12.
175. Ibid.
176. Ibid., 39.
177. Ibid.
178. Ailey and Bailey, *Revelations*, 92.
179. Ibid.

180. Dunning, *Alvin Ailey: A Life in Dance*, 125.
181. Mazo, *The Alvin Ailey American Dance Theater*, 14.
182. Szilard quoted in Dunning, *Alvin Ailey: A Life in Dance*, 128.
183. Mazo, *The Alvin Ailey American Dance Theater*, 14.
184. Ibid.
185. Ibid., 14–15.
186. Ibid.
187. Naima Prevots, *Dance for Export: Cultural Diplomacy and the Cold War* (Hanover, NH: Wesleyan University Press, 1998), 53–54.
188. Ibid., 56.
189. Ibid., 93–101.
190. "Alvin Ailey," *Wikipedia*, last modified April 23, 2013, http://en.wikipedia .org/wiki/Alvin_Ailey.
191. Ibid.
192. PBS, "Free to Dance Biographies: Alvin Ailey,", accessed December 28, 2012 http://www.pbs.org/wnet/freetodance/biographies/ailey.html.
193. Mazo, *Prime Movers*, 256.
194. Mazo, *The Alvin Ailey American Dance Theater*, 15.
195. Ailey and Bailey, *Revelations*, 70.
196. Ibid.
197. Ibid.
198. Mazo, *The Alvin Ailey American Dance Theater*, 15.
199. Ibid.
200. Alvin Ailey, "It's About Dance," in *The Vision of Modern Dance: In the Words of Its Creators*, 2nd edn., ed. Jean Morrison Brown, Naomi Mindlin and Charles H. Woodford (Hightstown, NJ: Princeton Book Company, 1998), 132.
201. Ibid.
202. Reynolds and McCormick, *No Fixed Points*, 348.
203. Ailey and Bailey, *Revelations*, 129.
204. Ibid.
205. Mazo, *The Alvin Ailey American Dance Theater*, 107.
206. Ibid.
207. Encyclopedia of World Biography, "Alvin Ailey Biography."
208. Ailey, "It's About Dance," 133.
209. Ibid.
210. "Alvin Ailey," *Wikipedia*, last modified April 23, 2013, http://en.wikipedia .org/wiki/Alvin_Ailey.
211. Ailey, "It's About Dance," 133.
212. Ibid.
213. Burt, *The Male Dancer*, 117.
214. For Burt, "Ailey gradually synthesized white European- and African-derived dance and music traditions." Ibid.
215. Marcia Siegel, *At the Vanishing Point: A Critic Looks at Dance* (New York: Saturday Review Press, 1972), 161.
216. Ibid.

217. Ailey quoted in Mazo, *The Alvin Ailey American Dance Theater*, 8.
218. "Alvin Ailey," *Wikipedia*, last modified April 23, 2013, http://en.wikipedia.org/wiki/Alvin_Ailey. See also "Alvin Ailey: Biography," *Biography.com*, accessed December 26, 2012, http://www.biography.com/people/alvin-ailey-9177959.
219. Ailey and Bailey, *Revelations*, 134–38.
220. Dunning, *Alvin Ailey: A Life in Dance*, 330–42.
221. American Ballet Theatre Foundation, "Alvin Ailey: Biography," accessed December 28, 2012, http://www.abt.org/education/archive/choreographers/ailey_a.html.
222. Encyclopedia of World Biography, "Alvin Ailey Biography."
223. "Alvin Ailey," *Texas Online*, accessed December 28, 2012, http://www.texas-on-line.com/graphic/alvinailey.htm.
224. Ibid.
225. PBS, "Free to Dance Biographies: Alvin Ailey."
226. Ibid.
227. Ibid.
228. Ailey and Bailey, *Revelations*, 131.
229. Ibid.
230. Ibid.
231. Ibid.

7 Conclusions: Quo Vadis?

* "Conclusions: Quo Vadis?" adapted with permission from Caroline Joan S Picart, "A Tango between Copyright and Critical Race Theory: Whiteness as Status Property in Balanchine's Ballets, Fuller's Serpentine Dance and Graham's Modern Dances," *Cardozo Journal of Law and Gender* 18, no. 3 (Spring 2012): 685–725.

"Quo Vadis: A Postscript" adapted with permission from Caroline Joan S. Picart and Marlowe Fox. "Beyond Unbridled Optimism and Fear: Indigenous Peoples, Intellectual Property, Human Rights and the Globalization of Traditional Knowledge and Expressions of Folklore (Part I)" *International Community Law Review* 15, no. 3 (2013): 319–339.

1. Cynthia Novack (a.k.a. Cynthia Jean Cohen Bull) pioneered the ethnographic analysis of dance through her book, *Sharing the Dance: Contact Improvisation and American Culture* (Madison, WI: University of Wisconsin Press, 1990).
2. Loïe Fuller, *Fifteen Years of a Dancer's Life* (Boston: Small, Maynard & Co., 1913), 27–28.
3. Ibid., 61, 20–21.
4. *Fuller v. Bemis*, 50 F. 926, 929 (C.C.S.D.N.Y. 1892).
5. Bernard Taper, *Balanchine: A Biography with a New Epilogue* (Berkeley, CA: University of California Press, 1984), 152.

6. Krystina Lopez de Quintana posits that copyright law often proves ineffective in protecting lesser-known choreographers (unlike Balanchine) who don't have the financial backing or time that large companies have. Krystina Lopez de Quintana, "The Balancing Act: How Copyright and Customary Practices Protect Large Dance Companies over Pioneering Choreographers," *Villanova Sports and Entertainment Law Journal* 11 (2004): 152.
7. Taper, *Balanchine: A Biography,* 13.
8. Barbara Horgan, Balanchine's personal assistant, managed many pragmatic tasks, freeing Balanchine to pursue his choreographic passion. Ibid., 329.
9. J. E. Crawford Flitch characterized the skirt dance as a "compromise between the overly academic ballet of the time and the more outrageous step-kick dancing, such as the can-can...". J. E. Flitch, Crawford, *Modern Dancing and Dancers* (London: Grant Richards, Ltd., 1912), 72.
10. For descriptions of Balanchine's authoritativeness, see Taper, *Balanchine: A Biography,* 23.
11. For examples of how much control Graham had over her dancers, see Don McDonagh, *Martha Graham.* 2nd ed. (New York: Warner Books, 1978), 224–25.
12. Graham's first students, when she had broken away from the Denishawn Company, were secretaries, salesclerks, waitresses, and artists' models by day. Russell Freedman, *Martha Graham: A Dancer's Life* (New York: Clarion Books, 1998), 50.
13. Encyclopedia of World Biography, "Katherine Dunham," accessed November 30, 2012. http://www.notablebiographies.com/newsmakers2/2007-Co-Lh/Dunham-Katherine.html."
14. Martha Graham, *Blood Memory: An Autobiography* (New York: Doubleday, 1991),110.
15. See, for example, Martha as the central figure, dressed completely in white, surrounded by 12 women in blue in *Primitive Mysteries*. Freedman, *Martha Graham*, 68–69.
16. For the depth of adoration Graham had for St. Denis, see McDonagh, *Martha Graham*, 126.
17. As Ted Shawn observed, Graham was "not 'the Northern European, peaches-and-cream blonde,' and her high cheekbones made her exotic." Ibid., 26.
18. For a description of St. Denis' performance that convinced Graham that her "fate was sealed. [She] couldn't wait to learn to dance as the goddess [St. Denis] did," see Freedman, *Martha Graham*, 21–22.
19. *Martha Graham Sch. & Dance Found., Inc. v. Martha Graham* Ctr. of Contemporary Dance, Inc., 380 F.3d 624, 628 (2d Cir. 2004).
20. For example, for an account of the failure of Balanchine's collaboration with the Metropolitan Opera in March, 1938, see Taper, *Balanchine: A Biography,* 175.
21. See *Fuller v. Bemis*, 50 F. 926, 929 (C.C.S.D.N.Y. 1892).
22. See Agnes De Mille, *Martha: The Life and Work of Martha Graham* (New York: Random House, 1991), vii–viii, note 194.
23. See *Graham II*, 380 F.3d at 639–40.

24. For an example of an ecstatic review of Fuller's surreal performances, see Jody Sperling, "Loïe Fuller's Serpentine Dance: A Discussion of its Origins in Skirt Dancing and a Creative Reconstruction," in *Proceedings: Society of Dance History Scholars: Twenty Second Annual Conference*, compiled by Juliette Willis (Birmingham, AL: Society of Dance History Scholars, 1999), 53.
25. Freedman, *Martha Graham*, 112.
26. Taper, *Balanchine: A Biography*, 409.
27. Ibid., 410.
28. Ibid.
29. Ibid.
30. For an example of how Baker, like Fuller, electrified many of Paris' artists and intellectuals, see Paul Colins' Art Deco lithographs in Paul Colin, *Josephine Baker and La Revue Négre: Paul Colin's Lithographs of Le Tumult Noir in Paris, 1927* (New York: Henry N. Abrams, 1998).
31. Bennetta Jules-Rosette, *Josephine Baker in Art and Life: The Icon and the Image* (Champaign, IL: University of Illinois Press, 2007), 49.
32. For an extended account of how Baker repeatedly abandoned choreography and chose improvisation on the spot, thus often driving the orchestra (and sometimes the lighting crew) to follow her lead, see Stephen Papich, *Remembering Josephine* (Indianapolis, IN: Bobbs-Merrill, 1976), 61.
33. See Anthea Kraut, "White Womanhood, Property Rights and the Campaign for Choreographic Copyright: Loïe Fuller's *Serpentine Dance*," *Dance Research Journal* 43, no. 1 (Summer 2011): 3.
34. See Ann Cooper Albright, *Traces of Light: Absence and Presence in the Work of Loïe Fuller* (Middletown, CT: Wesleyan University Press, 2007), 185.
35. See *Fuller v. Bemis*, 50 F. 926 (C.C.S.D.N.Y. 1892).
36. *Fuller v. Bemis*, 50 F. 926, 929 (C.C.S.D.N.Y. 1892).
37. *Martinetti v. Maguire*, 16 F. Cas. 920 (C.C.Cal. 1867); Barnes v. Miner, 122 F. 480 (C.C.S.D.N.Y. 1903); Dane v. M. & H. Co., 136 U.S.P.Q. 426 (N.Y. 1963).
38. US Const. art. I, § 8, cl. 8.
39. Julia L. Foulkes, *Modern Bodies: Dance and American Modernism from Martha Graham to Alvin Ailey* (Chapel Hill, NC: University of North Carolina Press, 2002), 72.
40. Sally Sommer, "Free to Dance Biographies: Katherine Dunham," PBS: Great Performances, accessed December 3, 2012, http://www.pbs.org/wnet/freetodance/biographies/dunham.html."
41. Ann Barzel, Mark Turbyfill, and Ruth Page, "The Lost Ten Years: The Untold Story of the Dunham-Turbyfill Alliance," in *Kaiso! Writings by and about Katherine Dunham*, ed. Vévé A. Clark and Sara E. Johnson, 177–88 (Madison, WI: University of Wisconsin Press, 2005), 179.
42. Katherine Dunham, quoted by Harriet Jackson in "American Dancer, Negro," *Dance Magazine* (September 1966): 40. This same information is stated in Dunham's autobiography, *A Touch of Innocence: Memoirs of Childhood* (Chicago: University of Chicago Press, 1994).

43. Constance Valis Hill, "Collaborating with Balanchine on *Cabin in the Sky*: Interviews with Katherine Dunham," in *Kaiso! Writings by and about Katherine Dunham*, ed. Vévé A. Clark and Sara E. Johnson (Madison, WI: University of Wisconsin Press, 2005), 235.
44. Joyce Aschenbrenner, *Katherine Dunham: Dancing a Life* (Chicago, IL: University of Chicago Press, 2002), 125.
45. Robert Tracy, "Early Days: Revelations," in *Ailey Spirit: The Journey of an American Dance Company* (New York: Stewart, Tabori and Chang, 2004), 17.
46. Merce Cunningham, "Space, Time and Dance," in *Merce Cunningham: Dancing in Space and Time* (New York: Da Capo Press, 1992), 38–39.
47. Gerald Jonas, *Dancing: The Pleasure, Power and Art of Movement* (New York: Harry N. Abrams, 1998), 228.
48. Karen Eliot, *Dancing Lives: Five Female Dancers from the Ballet d'Action to Merce Cunningham* (Urbana and Chicago: University of Chicago Press, 2007), 121.
49. Marcia Siegel, *Shapes of Change* (Berkeley and Los Angeles: University of California Press, 1985), 328.
50. Jill Johnston, "Jigs, Japes and Joyce," *Art in America* (January 1987): 105.
51. James Klosty, "Introduction," in *Merce Cunningham*, ed. James Klosty, 11–18 (New York: E.P. Dutton and Company, 1985), 12.
52. Merce Cunningham, "Choreography and the Dance," in *Merce Cunningham*, ed. Germano Celant, 42–49 (Milan, Italy: Charta, 1999), 46.
53. Daniel J.Wakin, "Merce Cunningham Sets Plan for his Dance Legacy," *New York Times*, June 9, 2009, http://www.nytimes.com/2009/06/10/arts/dance/10merc.html?ref=mercecunningham&_r=0
54. Jacqueline Lesschaeve, "The Dancer and the Dance," in *Reading Dance: A Gathering of Memoirs, Reportage, Criticism, Profiles, Interviews, and Some Uncategorizable Extras*, ed. Robert Gottlieb, 462–74 (New York: Pantheon Books, 2008), 472.
55. Nancy Reynolds and Malcolm McCormick, *No Fixed Points: Dance in the Twentieth Century* (New Haven and London: Yale University Press, 2003), 366.
56. Sutton Stracke, "A Final Goodbye," *Suttons Law* (blog), March 18, 2012, http://suttons-law.blogspot.com/2012/03/final-goodbye.html"
57. See generally, Stephanie Jordan, "Freedom from Music: Cunningham, Cage and Collaborations," in *Merce Cunningham*, ed. Germano Celant (Milan, Italy: Charta, 1999), 61–67.
58. Alvin Ailey and A. Peter Bailey, *Revelations: The Autobiography of Alvin Ailey* (New York: Carol Publishing Group, 1995), 49.
59. Jennifer Dunning, *Alvin Ailey: A Life in Dance* (New York: Da Capo Press, 1996), 75.
60. PBS, "Free to Dance Biographies: Alvin Ailey," accessed December 28, 2012. http://www.pbs.org/wnet/freetodance/biographies/ailey.html
61. Joseph H. Mazo, *Prime Movers: The Makers of Modern Dance in America* (New York: William Morrow and Company, 1977), 254.

62. Marcia Siegel, *Days on Earth: The Dance of Doris Humphrey* (New Haven, CT: Yale University Press, 1987), 307.
63. See generally, Richard Dyer, *White: Essays on Race and Culture* (London and New York: Routledge, 1997).
64. Mazo, *Prime Movers*, 254.
65. Ibid., 256.
66. Foulkes, *Modern Bodies*, 173.
67. For an analysis of the scope of protection given to choreography under the 1976 Act, and its uncertainties, see Kathleen Anne Fisher, "The Copyright in Choreographic Works: A Technical Analysis of the Copyright Act of 1976," *Copyright Law Symposium* 31(1984): 1450–1490;. Martha M. Traylor, "Choreography, Pantomime and the Copyright Revision Act of 1976," *New England Law Review* 16 (1980): 227–255.
68. *Horgan v. MacMillan, Inc.*, 789F.2d 157, 161 (2d. Cir. 1986).
69. See, e.g., H.R. Rep. No. 94–1476, at 53 (1976).
70. For a related analysis, see Robert Freedman, "Is Choreography Copyrightable?: A Study of the American and English Legal Interpretations of 'Drama'," *Duquesne Law Review* 2 (1963–1964): 78.
71. For an analysis of what "creativity" entails, in relation to copyright protection, see Fisher, "The Copyright in Choreographic Works," 149–51.
72. See generally Fred Astaire, *Steps in Time* (New York: Harper & Bros., 1959).
73. Caroline Joan S. Picart, *From Ballroom to DanceSport: Aesthetics, Athletics and Body Culture* (Albany, NY: State University of New York Press, 2006), 93–94. See generally, Marta Savigliano, *Tango and the Political Economy of Passion* (Boulder, CO: Westview, 1995); Juliet E. McMains, "Brownface: Representations of Latin-ness in DanceSport," *Dance Research Journal* 33, no. 2 (Winter 2001): 59.
74. Caroline Joan (Kay) Picart, "Beyond *Dancing with the Stars*: Sexual Sports Rhetoric in Competitive Ballroom Dance," in *Sexual Sports Rhetoric: Global and Universal Contexts*, ed. Linda K. Fuller (New York: Peter Lang, 2010), 57, 61.
75. Robert Farris Thompson, *Tango: The Art History of Love* (New York: Vintage, 2005), 8.
76. For a rough analogue in film, see generally Ella Shohat and Robert Stam, *Unthinking Eurocentrism: Multiculturalism and the Media* (London and New York: Routledge, 1994). For a general review of literature in relation to global dance and postcolonial ethnography, see Susan A. Reed, "The Politics and Poetics of Dance," *Annual Review of Anthropology* 27 (1998): 503–32.
77. Kariamu Welsh-Asante, "The Aesthetic Conceptualization of Nzuri," in *The African Aesthetic: Keeper of the Traditions*, ed. Kariamu Welsh-Asante (Westport, CT: Greenwood Press, 1993), 1.
78. Nyama McCarthy-Brown, "Dancing in the Margins: Experiences of African American Ballerinas," *Journal of African American Studies* 15 (2011): 385–408.

Bibliography

Ailey, Alvin. "It's About Dance." In *The Vision of Modern Dance: In the Words of Its Creators*, 2nd ed., edited by Jean Morrison Brown, Naomi Mindlin and Charles H. Woodford, 131–36. Hightstown, NJ: Princeton Book Company, 1998.

Ailey, Alvin and A. Peter Bailey. *Revelations: The Autobiography of Alvin Ailey*. New York: Carol Publishing Group, 1995.

Albright, Ann Cooper. *Traces of Light: Absence and Presence in the Work of Loïe Fuller*. Middletown, CT: Wesleyan University Press, 2007.

American Ballet Theatre Foundation. "Alvin Ailey: Biography." Accessed December 28, 2012. http://www.abt.org/education/archive/choreographers/ailey_a.html.

Arcomano, Nicholas. "Choreography and Copyright, Part One." *Dance Magazine*, April 1980, 58–59.

Armitage, Merle. *Martha Graham: The Early Years*. New York: Da Capo Press, 1937.

Aschenbrenner, Joyce. "Katherine Dunham: Reflections on the Social and Political Contexts of Afro-American Dance." *Dance Research Journal Annual XI* (Congress on Research in Dance, 1980).

Aschenbrenner, Joyce. *Katherine Dunham: Dancing a Life*. Chicago, IL: University of Chicago Press, 2002.

Astaire, Fred. *Steps in Time*. New York: Harper & Bros., 1959.

Baker, Jean-Claude and Chris Chase. *Josephine: The Hungry Heart*. New York: Cooper Square Press, 2001.

Baker, Josephine and Jo Bouillon. *Josephine*, translated by Mariana Fitzpatrick. New York: Harper & Row, 1977.

Baraka, Amiri. *The Leroi Jones/Amiri Baraka Reader*. 2nd ed. Edited by William J. Harris. New York: Basic Books, 1999.

Baraka, Amiri. *Somebody Blew Up America and Other Poems*. New York: House of Nehesi Publishers, 2003.

Barzel, Ann, Mark Turbyfill and Ruth Page. "The Lost Ten Years: The Untold Story of the Dunham-Turbyfill Alliance." In *Kaiso! Writings by and about Katherine Dunham*, edited by Vévé A. Clark and Sara E. Johnson, 177–88. Madison, WI: University of Wisconsin Press, 2005.

Begho, Felix. "Traditional African Dance in Context." In *African Dance: An Artistic, Historical and Philosophical Inquiry*, edited by Kariamu Welsh Asante, 163–82. Trenton, NJ: African World Press, 1996.

Benesh, Rudolf and Joan Benesh. *An Introduction to Benesh Movement Notation*. London: A & C Black, 1956.

Biagi, Shirley and Marilyn Kern-Foxworth, *Facing Difference: Race, Gender and Mass Media*. Thousand Oaks: Pine Forge Press, 1997.

Boas, Franz. *Race, Language and Culture*. New York: Macmillan, 1940.

Boyle, James. *Shahmans, Software and Spleens: Law and the Construction of the Information Society*. Cambridge, MA: Harvard University Press, 1996.

Brown, Carolyn. Untitled essay in *Merce Cunningham*, edited by James Klosty, 19–32. New York: E.P. Dutton and Company, 1985.

Brown, Carolyn, Douglas Dunn, Viola Farber, Steve Paxton, Marianne Preger-Simon, Valda Setterfield, Gus Solomons and David Vaughan. "Cunningham and His Dancers." In *Merce Cunningham*, edited by Germano Celant, 225–41. Milan, Italy: Charta, 1999.

Brown, Carolyn, Douglas Dunn, Viola Farber, Steve Paxton, Valda Setterfield, Gus Solomons, Jr. and David Vaughn. "Cunningham and His Dancers." In *Merce Cunningham: Dancing in Space and Time*, 101–23. New York: Da Capo Press, 1992.

Burt, Ramsay. "Katherine Dunham's *Rite de Passage*: Censorship and Sexuality." In *EmBODYing Liberation: The Black Body in American Dance*, edited by Dorothea Fischer-Hornung and Alison D. Goeller, 79–90. Hamburg and London: LIT Verlag, Münster, 2001.

Burt, Ramsay. *The Male Dancer: Bodies, Spectacle, Sexualities*. 2nd ed. New York: Routledge, 2007.

Butler, Judith. "Performative Acts and Gender Constitution: An Essay in Phenomenology and Feminist Theory." *Theatre Journal* 40, no. 4 (1988): 519–31.

Carman, Joseph. "DANCE; Who Owns A Dance? It Depends on the Maker." *New York Times*. December 23, 2001. http://query.nytimes.com/gst/fullpage.html?res=9D0DEFDC153EF930A15751C1A9679C8B63.

Carroll, Noél and Sally Banes. "Cunningham and Duchamp," In *Merce Cunningham*, edited by Germano Celant, 179–85. Milan, Italy: Charta, 1999.

Carvajal, Doreen. "Bitter Standoff Imperils a Cherished Dance Legacy." *New York Times*. July 6, 2000. http://www.nytimes.com/2000/07/06/arts/bitter-standoff-imperils-a-cherished-dance-legacy.html.

Celant, Germano. "Merce Cunningham and John Cage." In *Merce Cunningham*, edited by Germano Celant, 80–89. Milan, Italy: Charta, 1999.

Chatterjea, Ananya. Afterward to *Joan Myers Brown and the Audacious Hope of the Black Ballerina*, by Brenda Dixon Gottschild, 255–62. New York: Palgrave Macmillan, 2012.

Chin, Elizabeth. "Katherine Dunham's Dance as Public Anthropology." *American Anthropologist* 112, no. 4 (December 2010): 640–42.

Clark, Vévé A. "Designing Dunham: John Pratt's Method in Costume and Décor: An Interview with John Pratt." In *Kaiso! Writings by and about Katherine Dunham*, edited by Vévé A. Clark and Sara E. Johnson, 208–10. Madison, WI: University of Wisconsin Press, 2005.

Clark, Vévé A. "Performing the Memory of Difference in Afro-Caribbean Dance: Katherine Dunham's Choreography, 1938–1987." In *Kaiso! Writings by and about Katherine Dunham*, edited by Vévé A. Clark and Sara E. Johnson, 320–40. Madison, WI: University of Wisconsin Press, 2005.

Coffman, Elizabeth. "Uncanny Performances in Colonial Narratives: Josephine Baker in Princess Tam Tam." *Paradoxa: Studies in World Literary Genres* 3, no. 3–4 (1997): 379–94.

Cohen, Selma Jean. "Next Week Swan Lake: Reflections on Dance and Dances." In *What is Dance?*, edited by Roger Copeland and Marshall Cohen, 339–54. New York: Oxford University Press, 1983.

Cohen Bull, Cynthia Jean. "Looking at Movement as Culture: Contact Improvisation to Disco." In *Moving History/Dancing Cultures: A Dance History Reader*, edited by Ann Dils and Ann Cooper Albright, 404–13. Middletown, CT: Wesleyan University Press, 2001.

Cohen Bull, Cynthia Jean. *Sharing the Dance: Contact Improvisation and American Culture*. Madison, WI: University of Wisconsin Press, 1990.

Cohen Bull, Cynthia Jean. "Sense, Meaning and Perception in Three Dance Cultures." In *Meaning in Motion*, edited by Jane C. Desmond, 69–88. Durham, NC: Duke University Press, 1997.

Colin, Paul. *Josephine Baker and La Revue Négre: Paul Colin's Lithographs of Le Tumult Noir in Paris, 1927*. New York: Henry N. Abrams, 1998.

Cook, Melanie. "Moving to a New Beat: Copyright Protection for Choreographic Works." *UCLA Law Review* 24 (1976–1977): 1287–312.

Copeland, Roger. "Merce Cunningham and the Politics of Perception." In *Merce Cunningham*, edited by Germano Celant, 154–63. Milan, Italy: Charta, 1999.

Crenshaw, Kimberle, Neil Gotanda, Gary Peller, and Kendall Thomas, eds. *Critical Race Theory: The Key Writings that Formed the Movement*. New York: The New Press, 1995.

Crenshaw, Kimberle. "Mapping the Margins: Intersectionality, Identity Politics, and Violence Against Women of Color." In *Critical Race Theory: The Key Writings that Formed the Movement*, edited by Kimberle Crenshaw, Neil Gotanda, Gary Peller, and Kendall Thomas, 357–82. New York: The New Press, 1995.

Cunningham, Merce. *Changes: Notes on Choreography*. New York: Something Else Press, 1968.

Cunningham, Merce. "Two Questions and Five Dances." In Selma Jeanne Cohen. "Time to Walk in Space," *Dance Perspectives* 34 (Summer 1968).

Cunningham, Merce. "Space, Time and Dance." In *Merce Cunningham: Dancing in Space and Time*, 37–39. New York: Da Capo Press, 1992.

Cunningham, Merce. "You Have to Love Dancing to Stick to It." In *The Vision of Modern Dance: In the Words of Its Creators*, 2nd ed., edited by Jean Morrison Brown, Naomi Mindlin and Charles H. Woodford, 89–92. Hightstown, NJ: Princeton Book Company, 1998.

Cunningham, Merce. "Choreography and the Dance." In *Merce Cunningham*, edited by Germano Celant, 42–49. Milan, Italy: Charta, 1999.

Current, Richard and Marcia Ewing Current, *Loïe Fuller: Goddess of Light*. Lebanon, NH: Northeastern University Press, 1997.

Daniel, Yvonne. *Rumba: Dance and Social Change in Contemporary Cuba*. Bloomington, IN: Indiana University Press, 1995.

Dayal, Samir. "Blackness as Symptom: Josephine Baker and European Identity." In *Blackening Europe: The African American Presence*, edited by Heike Raphael-Hernandez, 35–52. London and New York: Routledge, 2004.

De Beauvoir, Simone. *The Second Sex*. Translated by Constance Borde and Sheila Malovany Chevallier. New York: Vintage, 2011.

De Mille, Agnes. *Martha: The Life and Work of Martha Graham*. New York: Random House, 1991.

DeFrantz, Thomas F. "Booty Control." In *Dancing Many Drums: Excavations in African American Dance*, edited by Thomas F. DeFrantz, 24–25. Madison, WI: University of Wisconsin Press, 2002.

Delgado, Richard and Jean Stefancic, eds. *Critical Race Theory: The Cutting Edge*, 2nd ed. Philadelphia, PA: Temple University Press, 2000.

Derrida, Jacques. "Interview with Julia Kristeva." In *Positions*, translated by Alan Bass, 15–36. Chicago: University of Chicago Press, 1981.

Derrida, Jacques. *Writing and Difference*. Translated by Alan Bass. Chicago: University of Chicago Press, 1978.

Dudziak, Mary L. "Josephine Baker, Racial Protest and the Cold War." In *Global Critical Race Feminism: An International Reader*, edited by Adrien Katherine Wing, 179–91. New York: New York University Press, 2000.

Dunham, Katherine. "The Future of the Negro Dance." *Dance Herald* (1938): 5.

Dunham, Katherine. *Katherine Dunham's Journey to Accompong*. New York: Henry Holt, 1946.

Dunham, Katherine. "Las Danzas di Haití" in *Acta Anthropologica* 2, no. 4 (Mexico, 1947).

Dunham, Katherine. *Les Dances de Haiti*. Paris: Fasquel Press, 1957.

Dunham, Katherine. *Island Possessed*. Chicago: University of Chicago Press, 1994. First published 1969 by Doubleday.

Dunham, Katherine. *Dances of Haiti*. Los Angeles: University of California Press, 1983.

Dunham, Katherine. *A Touch of Innocence: Memoirs of Childhood*. Chicago: University of Chicago Press, 1994.

Dunham, Katherine. "Need for Study of Dances of Primitive Peoples." In *Kaiso! Writings by and about Katherine Dunham*, edited by Vévé A. Clark and Sara E. Johnson, 520–21. Madison, WI: University of Wisconsin Press, 2005.

Dunning, Jennifer. "Martha Graham's Legacy: How the Dances Will Now Be Danced." *New York Times*. September 8, 1999. http://partners.nytimes.com/library/dance/090899dance-graham.html.

Dunning, Jennifer. *Alvin Ailey: A Life in Dance*. New York: Da Capo Press, 1996.

Dunning, Jennifer. "Martha Graham Board Seeks to Remove Director." *New York Times*. March 25, 2000. http://www.nytimes.com/2000/03/25/arts/martha-graham-board-seeks-to-remove-director.html?src=pm.

Dunning, Jennifer. "Performances Are Suspended In Dance Group Graham Started." *New York Times.* May 26, 2000. http://www.nytimes.com/2000/05/26/nyregion/performances-are-suspended-in-dance-group-graham-started.html.

Dunning, Jennifer. "Challenging Graham Board, Director Reveals A Rival Plan." *New York Times,* November 1, 2000. http://www.nytimes.com/2000/11/01/arts/challenging-graham-board-director-reveals-a-rival-plan.html.

Dunning, Jennifer. "In Ruling, Dance Center May Use Graham Name." *New York Times.* August 8, 2001. http://www.nytimes.com/2001/08/08/nyregion/in-ruling-dance-center-may-use-the-graham-name.html.

Dunning, Jennifer. "Metro Briefing: New York: Manhattan: Martha Graham Center Wins Dance Rights." *New York Times.* August 19, 2004. http://query.nytimes.com/gst/fullpage.html?res=9E0CE3D91E3FF93AA2575BC0A9629C8B63.

Dyer, Richard. *White: Essays on Race and Culture.* London and New York: Routledge, 1997.

Eliot, Karen. *Dancing Lives: Five Female Dancers from the Ballet d'Action to Merce Cunningham.* Urbana and Chicago: University of Chicago Press, 2007.

Ellis, Havelock. *Dance of Life.* Boston: Houghton Mifflin, 1923.

Encyclopedia Britannica. "Merce Cunningham." December 19, 2012. http://www.britannica.com/EBchecked/topic/146610/Merce-Cunningham.

Encyclopedia of World Biography. "Alvin Ailey Biography." Accessed December 27, 2012. http://www.notablebiographies.com/A-An/Ailey-Alvin.html.

Encyclopedia of World Biography. "Katherine Dunham." Accessed November 30, 2012. http://www.notablebiographies.com/newsmakers2/2007-Co-Lh/Dunham-Katherine.html.

Farrell, Suzanne and Toni Bentley. *Holding on to the Air: An Autobiography.* Gainesville, FL: University Press of Florida, 2002.

Fischer-Hornung, Dorothea. "'Jungle in the Spotlight?': Primitivism and Esteem: Katherine Dunham's 1954 German Tour." In *Blackening Europe: The African American Presence,* edited by Heike Raphael-Hernandez, 53–72. London and New York: Routledge, 2004.

Fisher, Kathleen Anne. "The Copyright in Choreographic Works: A Technical Analysis of the Copyright Act of 1976." *Copyright Law Symposium* 31 (1984): 1450–90.

Flitch, J.E. Crawford. *Modern Dancing and Dancers.* London: Grant Richards, Ltd., 1912.

Foster, Susan Leigh. "Closets Full of Dances: Modern Dance's Performance of Masculinity and Sexuality." In *Dancing Desires,* edited by Jane Desmond, 147–208. Madison, WI: University of Wisconsin Press, 2001.

Foucault, Michel. *Discipline and Punish: The Birth of the Prison.* 2nd ed. New York: Vintage, 1995.

Foulkes, Julia L. *Modern Bodies: Dance and American Modernism from Martha Graham to Alvin Ailey.* Chapel Hill, NC: University of North Carolina Press, 2002.

Francis, Terri. "The Audacious Josephine Baker: Stardom, Cinema, Paris." In *Black Europe and the African Diaspora,* edited by Darlene Clark Hine, Trica

Danielle Keaton, and Stephen Small, 238–59. Champaign, IL: University of Illinois Press, 2009.

Fraser, Nancy. "Rethinking the Public Sphere: A Contribution to the Critique of Actually Existing Democracy." *Social Text*, no. 25/26 (1990): 56–80.

Freedman, Robert. "Is Choreography Copyrightable?: A Study of the American and English Legal Interpretations of 'Drama'." *Duquesne Law Review* 2 (1963–1964): 77–95.

Freedman, Russell. *Martha Graham: A Dancer's Life*. New York: Clarion Books, 1998.

Fuller v. Bemis, 50 F. 926 (C.C.S.D.N.Y. 1892)

Fuller, Loïe. *Fifteen Years of a Dancer's Life*. Boston: Small, Maynard & Co., 1913.

Garafola, Lynn. "The Travesty Dancer in Nineteenth-Century Ballet." In *Legacies of Twentieth-Century Dance*, 137–47. Middletown, CT: Wesleyan University Press, 2005.

Garelick, Rhonda K. *Electric Salome: Loïe Fuller's Performance of Modernism*. Princeton, NJ: Princeton University Press, 2009.

Garrard, Mary D. "Leonardo da Vinci and Creative Female Nature." In *Feminism and Tradition in Aesthetics*, edited by Peggy Zeglin Brand and Carolyn Korsmeyer, 326–53. University Park, PA: Pennsylvania State University Press, 1995.

Gay, Geneva and Willie L. Baber. *Expressively Black: The Cultural Basis of Ethnic Identity*. New York: Praeger, 1987.

Gennerich, Patrician Solan. "One Moment in Time: The Second Circuit Ponders Choreographic Photography as a Copyright Infringement: Horgan v. MacMillan, Inc." *Brooklyn Law Review* 53 (Spring 1987): 379–407.

George Balanchine Foundation. "Biography: George Balanchine 1904–1983." Accessed November 29, 2012. http://www.balanchine.org/balanchine/01/bio.html.

Goldner, Nancy. *Balanchine Variations*. Gainesville, FL: University Press of Florida 2008.

Gordon, Suzanne. *Off Balance: The Real World of Ballet*. New York: Pantheon, 1983.

Gottlieb, Robert., *George Balanchine: The Ballet Maker*. New York: HarperCollins Publishers, 2004.

Gottschild, Brenda Dixon. "Crossroads, Continuities, and Contradictions: The Afro-Euro-Caribbean Triangle." In *Caribbean Dance from Abakuá to Zouk: How Movement Shapes Identity*, edited by Susanna Sloat, 3–10. Gainesville, FL: University Press of Florida, 2002.

Gottschild, Brenda Dixon. *The Black Dancing Body: A Geography from Coon to Cool*. New York: Palgrave Macmillan, 2003.

Gottschild, Brenda Dixon. *Joan Myers Brown and the Audacious Hope of the Black Ballerina*. New York: Palgrave Macmillan, 2012.

Graham, Martha. *Blood Memory: An Autobiography*. New York: Doubleday, 1991.

Greene, Kevin J. "Papa's Got a Brand New Bag: James Brown, Innovation, and Copyright Law." In *African American Culture and Legal Discourse*, edited by Lovalerie King and Richard Schur, 177–90. New York: Palgrave Macmillan, 2009.

Greene, Stuart and Dawn Abt-Perkins, eds. *Making Race Visible: Literacy Research for Cultural Understanding*. New York: Teacher's College Press, 2003.

Halprin, Lawrence. "About Anna Halprin." Accessed December 24, 2012. http://www.annahalprin.org/about_bio.html.

Haraway, Donna J. "A Cyborg Manifesto: Science, Technology, and Socialist-Feminism in the Late Twentieth Century." In *Simians, Cyborgs and Women: The Reinvention of Nature*, 149–82. New York: Routledge, 1991.

Harris, Cheryl. "Whiteness as Property." *Harvard Law Review* 106 (1993): 1707–91.

Harris, Leonard, ed. of *The Philosophy of Alain Locke: Harlem Renaissance and Beyond*. Philadelphia: Temple University Press, 1989.

Harris, Margaret Haile. *Loïe Fuller: Magician of Light*. Richmond: Virginia Museum of Fine Arts, 1979.

Herkovits, Melville. *Myth of the Negro Past*. New York: Harper & Bros., 1941.

Horgan v. MacMillan, 789 F.2d 157, 161 (2d Cir. 1986)

Hunter, Margaret. "If You're Light, You're Alright': Light Skin Color as Social Capital for Women of Color." *Gender and Society* 16 (2002): 176–93.

Hunter, Margaret. *Race, Gender and the Politics of Skin Tone*. New York: Taylor and Francis, 2005.

Hurok, Sol and Ruth Goode. *Impresario: A Memoir*. New York: Random House, 1946.

Irigaray, Luce. *Marine Lover of Friedrich Nietzsche*. Translated by Gillian C. Gill. New York: Columbia University Press, 1991.

Jackson, Harriet. "American Dancer, Negro." *Dance Magazine*, September 1966, 35–42.

Jonas, Gerald. *Dancing: The Pleasure, Power and Art of Movement*. New York: Harry N. Abrams, 1998.

Johnston, Jill. "Jigs, Japes and Joyce." *Art in America* (January 1987): 103–5.

Jordan, Stephanie. "Freedom from Music: Cunningham, Cage and Collaborations." In *Merce Cunningham*, edited by Germano Celant, 61–67. Milan, Italy: Charta, 1999.

Jowitt, Deborah. "Monumental Martha." In *What is Dance?*, edited by Roger Copeland and Marshall Cohen, 456–58. New York: Oxford University Press, 1983.

Jowitt, Deborah. *Time and the Dancing Image*. New York: William Morrow and Company, 1988.

Jules-Rosette, Bennetta. *Josephine Baker in Art and Life: The Icon and the Image*. Champaign, IL: University of Illinois Press, 2007.

Katz, Jonathan D. "Identification." In *Difference/Indifference*, edited by Moira Roth, 49–70. Amsterdam: Gordon and Breach, 1998.

Kelso, Paula T. "Behind the Curtain: The Body, Control, and Ballet." *Edwardsville Journal of Sociology* 3, no. 2 (2003): http://www.siue.edu/sociology/EJS/v32kelso.htm.

Kennedy Center. "Katherine Dunham." Accessed December 3, 2012. http://www.kennedy-center.org/explorer/artists/?entity_id=3721.

Klosty, James. "Introduction." In *Merce Cunningham*, edited by James Klosty, 11–18. New York: E.P. Dutton and Company, 1985.

Kraut, Anthea. *Choreographing the Folk: The Dance Stagings of Zora Neale Hurston (Indigenous Americas)*. Minneapolis, MN: University of Minnesota Press, 2008.

Kraut, Anthea. "'Stealing Steps' and Signature Moves: Embodied Theories of Dance as Intellectual Property." *Theatre Journal* 62, no. 2 (May 2010): 173–89.

Kraut, Anthea. "White Womanhood, Property Rights and the Campaign for Choreographic Copyright: Loïe Fuller's *Serpentine Dance*." *Dance Research Journal* 43, no. 1 (Summer 2011): 2–26.

Kuhn, Thomas. *The Structure of Scientific Revolutions*. Chicago: University of Chicago Press, 1970.

Lakes, Joi Michelle. "A Pas De Deux for Choreography and Copyright." *New York University Law Review* 80 (2005): 1829–61.

Latour, Bruno. *Science in Action: How to Follow Scientists and Engineers through Society*. Cambridge, MA: Harvard University Press, 1987.

Lee, Felicia R. "Graham Legacy, on the Stage Again." *New York Times*. September 29, 2004. http://www.nytimes.com/2004/09/29/arts/dance/29grah.html?_r=1&ref=ronprotas.

Lesschaeve, Jacqueline. "The Dancer and the Dance." In *Reading Dance: A Gathering of Memoirs, Reportage, Criticism, Profiles, Interviews, and Some Uncategorizable Extras*, edited by Robert Gottlieb, 462–74. New York: Pantheon Books, 2008

Levine, Lawrence. *Highbrow/Lowbrow: The Emergence of Cultural Hierarchy in America*. Cambridge, MA: Harvard University Press, 1988.

Library of Congress. "Katherine Dunham Timeline." Selections from the Katherine Dunham Collection at the Library of Congress. Accessed December 3, 2012. http://lcweb2.loc.gov/diglib/ihas/html/dunham/dunham-timeline.html.

Locke, Alain. "Art or Propaganda?" *Harlem* 1, no. 1 (1928): 12–13. http://nationalhumanitiescenter.org/pds/maai3/protest/text10/lockeartorpropaganda.pdf.

Lopez de Quintana, Krystina. "The Balancing Act: How Copyright and Customary Practices Protect Large Dance Companies over Pioneering Choreographers." *Villanova Sports and Entertainment Law Journal* 11 (2004): 139–72.

Lorraine, Jean. *Poussiéres de Paris*. Paris: P. Ollendorf, 1902.

Lyle, Cynthia. *Dancers on Dancing*. New York: Drake, 1977.

Macauley, Alistair. "The Merce Experience." *Dancing Times*, September 1987, 1050–52.

Manning, Susan. "Black Voices, White Bodies: The Performance of Race and Gender in How Long Brethren." *American Quarterly* 50 (March 1998): 24–46.

Mallarmé, Stéphanie. *Oeuvres Complètes*. Edited by Georges Jean-Aubrey and Henri Mondor. Cambridge, MA: Schoenhof's Foreign Books, 1945.

Marik, Katherine B. "*Community for Creative Non-Violence v. Reid*: New Certainty for the Copyright Work for Hire Doctrine." *Pepperdine Law Review* 18, no. 3 (1991): 598–621.

Martin, Wendy. "'Remembering the Jungle': Josephine Baker and the Modernist Parody." In *Prehistories of the Future: The Primitivist Project and the Culture of*

Modernism, edited by Elazar Barkan and Ronald Bush, 310–25. Palo Alto, CA: Stanford University Press, 1996.

Massine, Leonide. *Massine on Choreography: Theory and Exercises in Composition.* London: Faber & Faber, 1971.

Mazo, Joseph H. *Prime Movers: The Makers of Modern Dance in America.* New York: William Morrow and Company, 1977.

Mazo, Joseph H. *The Alvin Ailey American Dance Theater.* New York: William Morrow and Company, 1978.

Mazo, Joseph. "Martha Remembered." *Dance Magazine*, July 1991, 34–45.

Merce Cunningham Trust. "Honors and Awards." Accessed December 24, 2012. http://www.mercecunningham.org/merce-cunningham/.

Merce Cunningham Trust. "Staff/Trustees." Accessed December 24, 2012. http://www.mercecunningham.org/trust/.

Merce Cunningham Trust. "New York Public Library for the Performing Arts." Accessed December 24, 2012. http://www.mercecunningham.org/archives/.

McCarthy-Brown, Nyama. "Dancing in the Margins: Experiences of African American Ballerinas." *Journal of African American Studies* 15 (2011): 385–408.

McDonough, Don. *Martha Graham: A Biography.* New York: Popular Library, 1973.

McDonagh, Don. *Martha Graham.* 2nd ed. New York: Warner Books, 1978.

McMains, Juliet E. "Brownface: Representations of Latin-ness in DanceSport." *Dance Research Journal* 33, no. 2 (Winter 2001): 54–71.

Missouri Historical Society. "Katherine Dunham: Dancer." Accessed November 30, 2012. http://www.mohistory.org/KatherineDunham/dancer.htm.

Mulvey, Laura. "Visual Pleasure and Narrative Cinema." In *The Sexual Subject: A Screen Reader in Sexuality*, 22–34. London and New York: Routledge, 1992.

Mumma, Gordon. "From Where the Circus Went." In *Merce Cunningham*, edited by James Klosty, 65–74. New York: E.P. Dutton and Company, 1985.

Mutua, Makau. *Kenya's Quest for Democracy: Taming Leviathan.* Boulder, CO: Lynne Rienner Publishers, 2008.

Mutua, Makau, ed., *Human Rights NGOs in East Africa: Political and Normative Tensions.* Philadelphia, PA: University of Pennsylvania Press, 2008.

Mutua, Makau. *Human Rights: A Political and Cultural Critique.* Philadelphia, PA: University of Pennsylvania Press, 2008.

Nagel, Joane. *Race, Ethnicity and Sexuality: Intimate Intersections, Forbidden Frontiers.* New York: Oxford University Press, 2003.

Neal, Larry. "The Black Arts Movement." *Drama Review*, Summer 1968. http://nationalhumanitiescenter.org/pds/maai3/community/text8/blackartsmovement.pdf.

Neal, Larry. *Visions of a Liberated Future: Black Arts Movement Writings.* Edited by Michael Schwartz. New York: Thunder's Mouth Press, 1989.

Nenno, Nancy. "Femininity, the Primitive, and Modern Urban Space: Josephine Baker in Berlin." In *Women in the Metropolis: Gender and Modernity in Weimar Culture*, edited by Katharina von Ankum, 145–61. Berkeley, CA: University of California Press, 1997.

New York Times. "Dancing and Copyright." June 19, 1892.

New York Times. "Miss Fuller's New Dance." January 24, 1896. http://query.nytimes.com/mem/archive-free/pdf?res=9907E0D6153EE333A25757C2A9679C94679ED7CF.

New York Times. "'La Loïe' Talks of Her Art." March 1, 1896. http://query.nytimes.com/mem/archive-free/pdf?res=F40B17FF3C5C17738DDDA80894DB405B8685F0D3.

Nicholls, Robert W. "African Dance: Transition and Continuity." In *African Dance: An Artistic, Historical and Philosophical Inquiry*, edited by Kariamu Welsh Asante, 41–62. Trenton, NJ: African World Press, 1996.

Nimmer, Melville B. "The Subject Matter of Copyright under the Act of 1976." *UCLA Law Review* 24 (1977): 978–1024.

Nimmer, Melville B. and David Nimmer. *Nimmer on Copyright*. New York: Matthew Bender, 1981.

Novack, Cynthia J. *Sharing the Dance: Contact Improvisation and American Culture*. Madison, WI: University of Wisconsin Press, 1990.

Nunn, Kenneth B. "Law as Eurocentric Enterprise." *Law and Inequality* 15 (1997): 323–70.

Ordway, Gary D. "Choreography and Copyright." *Bulletin of the Copyright Society U.S.A.* 13 (1965–1966): 225–40.

Orme, Frederick L. "The Negro in Dance, as Katherine Dunham Sees Him." In *Kaiso! Writings by and about Katherine Dunham*, edited by Vévé A. Clark and Sara E. Johnson, 191–94. Madison, WI: University of Wisconsin Press, 2005.

Osumare, Halifu. "Dancing the Black Atlantic: Katherine Dunham's Research-to-Performance Method." In "Migration of Movement: Dance Across Americas." Special issue, *AmeriQuest* 7, no 2 (2010). http://ejournals.library.vanderbilt.edu/index.php/ameriquests/article/view/165.

Papich, Stephen. *Remembering Josephine*. Indianapolis, IN: Bobbs-Merrill, 1976.

Patry, William. "Choreography and Alternatives to Copyright Law." *The Patry Copyright Blog*, August 18, 2005. http://williampatry.blogspot.com/2005/08/choreography-and-alternatives-to.html.

PBS. "Free to Dance Biographies: Alvin Ailey." Accessed December 28, 2012. http://www.pbs.org/wnet/freetodance/biographies/ailey.html.

PBS: American Masters. "Martha Graham: About the Dancer." September 16, 2005. http://www.pbs.org/wnet/americanmasters/episodes/martha-graham/about-the-dancer/497/.

Percival, John. *Experimental Dance*. London: Studio Vista, 1971.

Picart, Caroline Joan S. *Inside Notes from the Outside*. Lanham, MD: Lexington Press, 2004.

Picart, Caroline Joan S. *From Ballroom to DanceSport: Aesthetics, Athletics and Body Culture*. Albany, NY: State University of New York Press, 2006.

Picart, Caroline Joan (Kay). "Beyond *Dancing with the Stars*: Sexual Sports Rhetoric in Competitive Ballroom Dance." In *Sexual Sports Rhetoric: Global and Universal Contexts*, edited by Linda K. Fuller, 57–68. New York: Peter Lang, 2010.

Picart, Caroline Joan S. "A Tango between Copyright and Critical Race Theory: Whiteness as Status Property in Balanchine's Ballets, Fuller's Serpentine Dance and Graham's Modern Dances." *Cardozo Journal of Law and Gender* 18, no. 3 (Spring 2012): 685–725.

Picart, Caroline Joan S. and Marlowe Fox, "Beyond Unbridled Optimism and Fear: Indigenous Peoples, Intellectual Property, Human Rights and the Globalization of Traditional Knowledge and Expressions of Folklore (Part I), *International Community Law Review* 15 no. 3 (2013): 319–339.

Pogrebin, Robert. "Dance is Never Far from his Mind." *New York Times*, December 7, 2012. http://www.nytimes.com/2012/12/09/nyregion/for-robert-battle-alvin-ailey-director-dance-is-never-far-from-mind.html?_r=0.

Prevots, Naima. *Dance for Export: Cultural Diplomacy and the Cold War*. Hanover, NH: Wesleyan University Press, 1998.

Putnam, Margaret. "Notation Takes Steps to Preserve Dance." *Dallas Morning News*, December 6, 1998.

Reed, Susan A. "The Politics and Poetics of Dance." *Annual Review of Anthropology* 27 (1998): 503–32.

Reynolds, Nancy and Malcolm McCormick. *No Fixed Points: Dance in the Twentieth Century*. New Haven and London: Yale University Press, 2003.

Robinson, Danielle. "'Oh, You Black Bottom!' Appropriation, Authenticity, and Opportunity in the Jazz Dance Teaching of 1920s New York." *Dance Research Journal* 38, no. 1/2 (2006): 19–42.

Robinson, Reginald Leamon. "Race, Myth and Narrative in the Social Construction of the Black Self." *Howard Law Journal* 40 (1996): 1–144.

Rockwell, John. "Arts, Briefly; Martha Graham Center Wins Court Ruling." *New York Times*. July 14, 2006. http://query.nytimes.com/gst/fullpage.html?res=9D05EED71E30F937A25754C0A9609C8B63&ref=ronprotas.

Rose, Albirda. "Dunham Technique: Barre Work and Center Progressions." In *Kaiso! Writings by and about Katherine Dunham*, edited by Vévé A. Clark and Sara E. Johnson, 488–95. Madison, WI: University of Wisconsin Press, 2005.

Rose, Phyllis. *Jazz Cleopatra: Josephine Baker in Her Time*. New York: Doubleday, 1989.

Ross, Marlon B. "The New Negro Displayed: Self-Ownership, Proprietary Sites/Sights, and the Bonds/Bounds of Race." In *Claiming the Stones, Naming the Bones: Cultural Property and the Negotiation of National and Ethnic Identity*, edited by Elazar Barkan and Ronald Bush, 259–301. Los Angeles: Getty Research Institute, 2002.

Roth, Moira. "The Aesthetic of Indifference." *Artforum* (November 1977): 45–53.

Said, Edward W. *Orientalism*. New York: Random House, 1978.

Said, Edward. *Culture and Imperialism*. New York: Vintage, 1993.

Savigliano, Marta. *Tango and the Political Economy of Passion*. Boulder, CO: Westview, 1995.

Schur, Richard L. *Parodies of Ownership: Hip-Hop Aesthetics and Intellectual Property Law*. Ann Arbor, MI: University of Michigan Press, 2009.

Sharpley-Whiting, T. Denean. *Black Venus: Sexualized Savages, Primal Fears, and Primitive Narratives in French*. Durham, NC: Duke University Press, 1999.

Shohat, Ella and Robert Stam. *Unthinking Eurocentrism: Multiculturalism and the Media*. London and New York: Routledge, 1994.

Siegel, Marcia. *At the Vanishing Point: A Critic Looks at Dance*. New York: Saturday Review Press, 1972.

Siegel, Marcia. *Shapes of Change*. Berkeley and Los Angeles: University of California Press, 1985.

Siegel, Marcia. *Days on Earth: The Dance of Doris Humphrey*. New Haven, CT: Yale University Press, 1987.

Singer, Joseph William. *Property Law: Rules, Policies and Practices*. 2nd ed. New York: Aspen Law & Business, 1997.

Solway, Diane. "When the Choreographer Is out of the Picture." *New York Times*, January 7, 2007. http://www.nytimes.com/2007/01/07/arts/dance/07solw.html?ref=ronprotas.

Sommer, Sally. "Loïe Fuller." *The Drama Review* 19, no. 1 (1975): 53–67.

Sommer, Sally. "Free to Dance Biographies: Katherine Dunham." PBS: Great Performances. Accessed December 3, 2012. http://www.pbs.org/wnet/freetodance/biographies/dunham.html.

Sparshott, Francis. *A Measured Pace, toward a Philosophical Understanding of the Arts of Dance*. Toronto: University of Toronto Press, 1995.

Sperling, Jody. "Loïe Fuller's Serpentine Dance: A Discussion of its Origins in Skirt Dancing and a Creative Reconstruction." In *Proceedings: Society of Dance History Scholars: Twenty Second Annual Conference*, compiled by Juliette Willis, 53–56. Birmingham, AL: Society of Dance History Scholars, 1999.

Stearns Marshall and Jean Stearns. *Jazz Dance: The Story of American Vernacular Dance*. London: Macmillan, 1968.

Stoler, Ann Laura. "Colonial Archives and Arts of Governance." *Archival Science* 2 (2002): 87–109.

Stracke, Sutton. "A Final Goodbye." *Suttons Law* (blog), March 18, 2012. http://suttons-law.blogspot.com/2012/03/final-goodbye.html.

Streeter, Thomas. "Broadcast Copyright and the Bureaucratization of Property." In *The Construction of Authorship: Textual Appropriation in Law and Literature*, edited by Martha Woodmansee and Peter Jaszi, 303–26. Durham, NC: Duke University Press, 1994.

Strong, Lester. "Josephine Baker's Hungry Heart." *Gay and Lesbian Review Worldwide*, September/October 2006. http://www.glreview.com/issues/13.5/13.5-strong.php.

Switzer, Ellen. *The Nutcracker: A Story & a Ballet*. New York: Atheneum, 1985.

Taper, Bernard. *Balanchine: A Biography with a New Epilogue*. Berkeley, CA: University of California Press, 1984.

Teachout, Terry. "Pale Horse, Pale Rider." In *Reading Dance: A Gathering of Memoirs, Reportage, Criticism, Profiles, Interviews, and Some Uncategorizable Extras*, edited by Robert Gottlieb, 479–87. New York: Pantheon Books, 2008.

Thompson, Robert Farris. *African Art in Motion*. Los Angeles: University of California Press, 1979.

Thompson, Robert Farris. *Tango: The Art History of Love*. New York: Vintage, 2005.

Torrance, Lee Ann. "Copyright and Dance." *Explore!* (blog), March 15, 2010. http://leeanntorrans.com/copyright-and-dance (post discontinued).

Tracy, Robert. "Early Days: Revelations." In *Ailey Spirit: The Journey of an American Dance Company*, 15–37. New York: Stewart, Tabori and Chang, 2004.

Traylor, Martha M. "Choreography, Pantomime and the Copyright Revision Act of 1976." *New England Law Review* 16 (1980): 227–55.

"United States Copyright Law: Copyright Clause and First Copyright Law." History of Copyright: What are Copyrights? http://www.historyofcopyright.org/pb/wp_fe548a29/wp_fe548a29.html?0.9602877043269001.

US Copyright Office. *Copyright Law of the United States and Related Laws Contained in Title 17 of the United States Code*. Washington, DC: US Copyright Office, 1978. http://www.copyright.gov/title17/92chap1.html.

US Copyright Office. *Compendium II: Compendium of Copyright Office Practices*. Washington, DC: US Copyright Office, 1984.

Valis Hall, Constance. "'Katherine Dunham's Southland' Protest in the Face of Repression." In *Dancing Many Drums: Excavations in African American Dance*, edited by Thomas F. DeFrantz, 289–316. Madison, WI: University of Wisconsin Press, 2002.

Valis Hill, Constance. "Collaborating with Balanchine on *Cabin in the Sky*: Interviews with Katherine Dunham." In *Kaiso! Writings by and about Katherine Dunham*, edited by Vévé A. Clark and Sara E. Johnson, 235–47. Madison, WI: University of Wisconsin Press, 2005.

Van Camp, Julie. "Copyright of Choreographic Works." In *1994–95 Entertainment, Publishing and the Arts Handbook*, edited by Stephen F. Breimer, Robert Thorne, and John David Viera, 59–92. New York: Clark, Boardman and Callaghan, 1994. http://www.csulb.edu/~jvancamp/copyrigh.html.

Vaughn, David. "Merce Cunningham," In *Merce Cunningham*, edited by Germano Celant, 96–99. Milan, Italy: Charta, 1999.

Vaughn, David. "Merce Cunningham: Five More Years," In *Merce Cunningham*, edited by Germano Celant, 295–305. Milan, Italy: Charta, 1999.

Wakin, Daniel J. "Merce Cunningham Sets Plan for his Dance Legacy." *New York Times*, June 9, 2009. http://www.nytimes.com/2009/06/10/arts/dance/10merc.html?ref=mercecunningham&_r=0.

Walker, Sheila S. *Ceremonial Spirit Possession in Africa and Afro-America: Forms, Meanings, and Functional Significance for Individual Social Group*. Leiden, Netherlands: Brill, 1972.

Wallace, Michele Faith. "The Good Lynching and *The Birth of a Nation*: Discourses and Aesthetics of Jim Crow." *Cinema Journal* 43, no. 1 (Fall 2003): 85–104.

Wallis, Leslie Erin. "The Different Art: Choreography and Copyright." *UCLA Law Review* 33 (1986): 1442–71.

Weinberg, Christine Leahy. "*Community For Creative Non-Violence v. Reid*: A Specious Solution to the 'Works Made for Hire' Problem." *Boston College Law Review* 32, no. 3:3 (1991): 663–702.

Welsh-Asante, Kariamu. "The Aesthetic Conceptualization of Nzuri." In *The African Aesthetic: Keeper of the Traditions*, edited by Kariamu Welsh-Asante, 1–20. Westport, CT: Greenwood Press, 1993.

Wong, Yutian. "Towards a New Asian American Dance Theory: Locating the Dancing Asian American Body." *Discourses in Dance*, 1(1) (2002): 69–90.

Woodmansee, Martha. "The Genius and the Copyright: Economic and Legal Conditions of the Emergence of the 'Author'." *Eighteenth Century Studies* 17, no. 4 (Summer 1984): 425–48.

Yeoh, Francis. "The Value of Documenting Dance." *Ballet-Dance Magazine*, June 2007. http://www.ballet-dance.com/200706/articles/Yeoh200706.html.

Author's Biography

Caroline Joan ("Kay") S. Picart was born in the Philippines, and has been educated in the Philippines; Cambridge, England; and the UnitedStates. Kay was the Sir Run Run Shaw Scholar and Wolfson Prize Winner (given to the top student) in History and Philosophy of Science at Cambridge University. She went on to finish a PhD in Political Philosophy (with doctoral minors in Aesthetics & Criticism and Comparative Literature) from the Pennsylvania State University as well as a postdoctoral fellowship on Jurisprudence with the Cornell School of Criticism and Theory. Prior to law school, she was a tenured associate professor of English and Humanities, and has authored/contracted 16 books with university and scholarly presses, three of which were published or contracted, while she was a full-time law student; she also published 25 peer-reviewed articles in scholarly journals (six while in law school) and 24 book chapters published by university or scholarly presses (ten while in law school). She has published articles on the Violence Against Women Act; the Tokyo IMT, and issues regarding the international litigation of crimes of violence against women during war; and as well Intellectual Property and Critical Race Theory. In 2010, she was a Florida Bar Foundation Fellow, and worked on Public Interest Law, protecting the rights of prisoners and underprivileged persons under the supervision of the Florida Institutional Legal Services; in 2010–2011, she was an extern, and also completed her pro bono certification hours, with the Gainesville State Attorney's Office, Domestic Violence Unit. From 2011 to 2012, she concurrently served as editor-in-chief of the *Florida Journal of International Law*, and the communications executive and former articles editor and research editor for the *Journal of Technology Law and Policy*. From 2012 to 2013, Kay was awarded the Tybel Spivack Pre-Doctoral Fellowship in Women's Studies, and designed and taught a course on Humanities Perspectives on Gender and Sexuality, while finishing coursework for Program Certificates on Intellectual Property and International Law and an MA in Women's Studies. In May, 2013, Kay graduated, *cum laude*, with a *Juris Doctor* with Certificates in Intellectual Property and International Law, and an MA in Women's Studies from the University of Florida. In her spare time, as a US Open Champion in ballroom dance and a visual artist who has exhibited and sold work nationally and internationally, Kay is the owner-manager of a business consultancy in dance and original visual art, Kinesthetics, LLC. But amidst all her accomplishments, what she is most proud of is her marriage to her beloved husband, Jerry Rivera.

Index

Note: Locators followed by 'n' refer to notes.

abstraction, 8, 12, 47, 52, 87, 132
According to St. Francis (1953), 145
Acrobats of God (1969), 94
Adler, Stella, 146
African American, 6–7, 10–11, 39–42, 62–4, 102–3, 108, 167–8, 172, 177n42, 184n82, 188n77, 199n127, 201n174, 213n78
African dance, 33–4, 38–9, 97, 155, 167–8, 182n44, 182n48, 183n56
"Africanisms," in choreography, 103, 109
Africanist, 35–8, 44, 62, 97, 162, 167
Ailey, Alvin, 19–20, 40, 42–3, 88, 110, 117–19, 139–59, 169–74, 188n66, 194n23, 206–9nn116–231, 211n39, 212n45, 212nn58–60
Albright, Ann Cooper, 11, 52–3, 177n44, 183n65, 185n13, 185n16, 185n24, 186nn29–32, 189n81, 211n34
Alex, Joe, 56–7
Alvin Ailey American Dance Theater, 40, 139, 149–52, 206n121, 207nn171–7, 208n181, 208n183, 208n194, 208n198, 208n205, 209n217
Alvin Ailey Dance Company, 110, 117
"ambassador with hips," 97
American Ballet Theater, The, 156
"American choreographer," 19, 159, 171
American Dance, 12, 18, 21–4, 28, 31–2, 40, 52, 54
American in Paris (1951), 5
American modern ballet, 88
American modern dance, 3, 4, 13, 23, 28, 33, 47, 55, 84–5, 88, 96–8, 109, 111–15, 118, 123, 128, 134, 141, 143, 144, 147, 150–74, 175, 178n70, 184, 185n14, 185n18, 188n66, 190, 193, 194n23, 198n96, 198n120, 199n129, 201n177, 201n179, 201n187, 202nn2–3, 204n59, 205n89, 208n200, 209, 210n9, 211n39, 212, 212n61, 213n66
American National Theater and Academy (ANTA), 151
Angelou, Maya, 147
anthropology, 100, 101, 103, 199n134, 200n171, 213n76
  in dance, 100
arabesque, 155
art nouveau, 46, 49
artistic film, 5, 8, 13, 16–19, 23, 30–1, 62, 68, 70, 82, 116, 129–31, 134, 148, 155, 159, 161, 170, 174, 188n76, 213n76
Aschenbrenner, Joyce, 99, 101–8, 168, 197n95, 198n101, 198n115, 198n121–3, 199–200nn139–41, 200n144, 200n151, 200n155, 200nn161–2, 200n169, 201n197, 202nn202–5, 212n44

Astaire, Fred, 143, 172–3, 213n72
avant-garde, 19, 122, 129, 143, 159
avant-garde art, 19, 129, 159
avant-garde rebellion, 117

Baartman, Sara, 9, 57–8, 187n59
Baber, Willie L., 38, 184n70
Bailey, Peter, 140, 206n125, 206n127, 206n130, 206n132, 207n143, 207n153, 207n170, 207n178, 208n195, 208n203, 209n219, 209n228, 212n58
Baker, Jean-Claude, 56–7, 186n41, 197n95
Baker, Josephine, 3–10, 18–20, 34, 43, 45–65, 97, 99, 100, 102–3, 108, 111, 113, 121, 145, 147, 149, 151, 158, 163, 166–9, 177n40, 184, 186–7nn39–48, 187n50, 187nn52–3, 187n55, 187n57, 187n60, 188n62, 188n65, 188n66, 188nn68–73, 188n176–8, 197n95, 211nn30–2
Balanchine, George, 3–14, 18–20, 23–39, 43, 45, 54, 63, 67–85, 87–9, 91, 95–6, 105–8, 110–11, 117, 119–20, 125–6, 128–9, 132–3, 134, 136, 137–8, 141, 145–6, 150, 152, 154, 157–8, 161, 163–6, 168–73, 175, 176n13, 177n43, 178n64–8, 180n25, 181n30, 181n32, 182n46, 183n59, 184, 186n43, 190–3, 194n5, 200n150, 200n152, 200n156, 200n158, 200n163, 209, 209n5, 210n6, 210nn7–8, 210n10, 210n20, 211n26, 212n43
Balanchine: A Biography with a New Epilogue, 11, 176n13, 190n2, 194n5, 209n5
Balanchine Trust, 14, 67, 75–6
Balanchivadze, Georgi Melitonovitch, *see* George Balanchine
Baldwin, James, 144
ballerina, characteristics of, 8, 23, 25, 28–31, 37–8, 40–1, 43, 45, 70, 72–3, 89, 98–9, 108, 111–12, 136, 164, 184n73, 184n76, 185n1, 213n78
ballet, 4, 14, 16–19, 23–43, 45, 49, 54, 64–5, 67–79, 81–5, 88–90, 95–9, 107–8, 110–15, 118–21, 126–9, 134–5, 139–41, 143–9, 151–8, 161–2, 164–7, 169–70, 172–4, 175, 179n72, 181n30, 182n54, 183n56, 183n59, 184, 185n1, 185n27, 190, 190n4, 190nn8–9, 193, 203n55, 209n221, 209, 210n9, 212n48
ballet master, 28, 31, 35, 67, 79, 84, 88, 96, 107, 111, 164, 169, 190n4
Banes, Sally, 128, 204n65
Barrelhouse (1950), 108
Bates, Clara, 143
Battles, Robert, 139
Beach Birds for Camera (1992), 131, 133
Bellefonte, Harry, 147
Bemis, Minnie Renwood, 4, 11, 18, 48–9, 52, 163, 175n3, 178n56, 185n8, 189n82, 189n84, 209n4, 210n21, 211nn35–6
Benesh Notation, 16
black ballerina, 40–1, 99, 184n73, 184n76
"black ballet," 18–9, 40, 42
"Black Cinderella," 60, 62, 188n76
black dancers, 42, 99, 106, 112–13, 141, 144, 147, 153, 155–6
"Black Madonna," 62
"Black Venus," 9, 18, 43, 45, 55–9, 163, 166, 184, 187n56, 187n59
black vernacular, 109
Bloch, Gabrielle, 51
Blues Suite, 149–50, 156
Bongard, David, 145
Bouillon, Jo, 187n53, 187n60, 188n68, 188n72

Boyle, James, 65, 189n92
Brahms-Schoenberg Quartet (1966), 74
British Laurence Olivier Award (1985), 138
Broadway, 40, 90, 105–7, 145–8, 153, 168, 188n66
Brown I (1954), 7
Brown II (1955), 7
Brown, Carolyn, 119, 124–6, 132–4, 202n18, 203n45, 203n50, 205n82, 205n93
Brown, Trisha, 137
Bryars, Gavin, 130
burlesque, 45, 49, 70, 85, 112, 174
Butler, Judith, 9, 58, 177n38, 188n64

Cabin in the Sky (1940), 33, 105–11, 168–9, 182n46, 200n150, 212n43
Cage, John, 119–24, 135, 137, 170–1, 178, 203n33, 204n79, 205n90, 212n57
Capezio Award, The (1979), 157
Caras, Steven (photographer), 78, 80, 83
Carefree Tree, The (1955), 147
Caribbean Calypso Carnival (1956), 147
Caribbean Cultural Center, The, 114–16
Caribbean-African dance, 97, 168
Carroll, Noél, 128, 204n65
celebrity, 9, 12, 18, 47, 50–1, 53–4, 63, 84, 97, 102, 108, 115, 165, 167, 173
Charlip, Remy, 134
Chaya, Masazumi, 158
choreographic *oeuvre,* 126
Choreographing the Folk: The Dance Stagings of Zora Neale Hurston, 10, 177n41
choreography, 2–6, 8–11, 13–20, 23–4, 27–9, 31–2, 36, 43–5, 48, 52, 54–5, 63, 65, 67, 73–5, 77–85, 87–8, 90–1, 93–5, 97, 104–7, 113–14, 116–18, 121, 123–9, 131–3, 135, 137–8, 141, 143, 145–6, 147, 149, 152–4, 156, 158–9, 161, 163–74, 177nn52–3, 179n74, 179n78, 179nn80–1, 179n84, 184, 186n38, 186n43, 188n78, 189n93, 190, 199n131, 201n201, 202nn4–5, 203n46, 204n79, 205n106, 211n32, 212n52, 213n67, 213n70
  "animal" qualities of, 58, 60, 62, 121, 149
Choros (1973), 151
Civil Rights Movement, The, 151
Clark, Vévé A., 115, 182n46, 198n99, 198n117, 199n135, 200n150, 201nn190–1, 201n201, 211, 212
class (social), 2–3, 4, 6–11, 17, 20, 23–4, 26, 28, 37, 41, 43, 45, 49, 51, 53, 55, 61, 63, 85, 98, 101, 105, 112–3, 162–4, 167, 173
classicism, revolt against, 19, 120, 128, 158, 170
Cocteau, Jean, 97
Cohen, Selma Jean, 25–7, 180n11
Cohen Bull, Cynthia Jean, 20, 29, 32–6, 97, 127, 162, 167, 174, 181n33, 181n36, 182nn43–4, 182nn47–50, 182n52, 182–3nn54–60, 183n65, 204n59, 209n1
Cold War, The, 135, 186n42, 208n187
Coltrane, Alice, 155
commercial film, 70
"commercialism," of dance, 156–7
Compendium (1973), 16–17
Compendium II (1984), 16–17, 80–1, 179n82, 179n89, 179n91
conventions, in dance, 18–19, 24–7, 30, 39, 41, 89, 111, 113, 120–5, 127, 130, 133, 134–7, 142, 146, 152, 156, 159, 169–72
Copp, Aaron, 130

copyright, 2–6, 8, 10–20, 22–3, 32, 43–4, 45, 47–9, 52–5, 63–5, 67, 73, 75–85, 87–8, 93–5, 110, 117, 124, 129, 131–2, 137–8, 146, 154, 159, 161, 163–5, 167, 169–70, 172–4, 175, 177n42, 177–8nn51–5, 178nn69–71, 179n74, 179n78, 179n80, 179n82, 179n84, 179n85, 179n89, 179n91, 181n41, 184, 185n7, 186n38, 189n80, 189n89, 189n91, 189n93, 190, 192n81, 193, 196n80, 209, 210n6, 211n33, 213n67, 213nn70–1
  history of, 3–6, 8, 10–20, 22–3, 32, 43–4, 45, 47–9, 52–5, 63–5, 67, 73, 75–85, 87–8, 93–5, 110, 117, 124, 129, 131–2, 137–8, 146, 154, 159, 161, 163–5, 167, 169–70, 172–4, 175, 177n42, 177–8nn51–5, 178nn69–71, 179n74, 179n78, 179n80, 179n82, 179n84, 179n85, 179n89, 179n91, 181n41, 184, 185n7, 186n38, 189n80, 189n89, 189n91, 189n93, 190, 192n81, 193, 196n80, 209, 210n6, 211n33, 213n67, 213nn70–1
  infringement of, 4, 16, 17–8, 48–9, 52, 77, 79, 81–2, 84, 88, 117, 165, 173, 192n81
  protection, 3–4, 6, 8, 10–13, 15–16, 18–19, 45, 48, 54, 63, 65, 67, 73, 79–80, 83–5, 87–8, 117, 124, 132, 161, 163, 165, 167, 169–70, 172–4, 178n70, 179n85, 181n41, 186n38, 213n67, 213n71
Copyright Act of 1909, 13, 16
Copyright Act of 1976, 3, 13–17, 73, 85, 95, 164, 172, 177n54, 179n78, 179nn85–7, 186n38, 189n93, 213n67
"copyrightable," 3–4, 8, 12–13, 15, 17–18, 20, 22–3, 32, 44, 52–5, 64, 81, 83, 85, 88, 161, 163, 172–3, 181n41, 213n70
Cornish School of Fine and Applied Arts, 119
corps de ballet, 27, 29, 39
Costas, Ron (photographer), 78, 80, 83
costumes, 51, 56, 60–1, 63, 78–9, 81, 83, 91, 103, 105, 109, 115–16, 121, 132, 141–2, 144, 149, 162–4, 168, 199n135
costuming, 19, 43–4, 61–2, 81, 84, 159, 164, 171
Cowell, Henry, 122
Craft, Randal J., Jr., 76
Crenshaw, Kimberle, 4, 7–8, 11, 175n8, 176nn22–5, 177n45
criminal law, 2–3
critical race theory, 2–4, 6, 10, 11, 22, 175, 175n8, 177nn45–6, 184, 190, 193, 209
Cry (1951), 155
Cuban influence, in dance, 110, 114–15
cultural, 3–5, 9–12, 15, 21, 23–4, 31–3, 38, 42, 44, 53–5, 58–60, 65, 83–5, 90, 99, 103, 105, 110, 112–16, 143, 151–2, 158, 162–3, 165–6, 169, 174, 176n10, 176n35, 177n47, 181n41, 182n43, 184n70, 187n59, 189n88, 205n90, 208n187, 213n76
Cunningham, Merce, 19–20, 88, 117–59, 169–72, 174, 178n70, 202nn3–6, 202n9, 202n12, 202n18, 203n27, 203n33, 203n35, 203nn44–8, 203–4nn50–6, 204n59, 204nn61–3, 204n65, 204nn72–6, 204nn78–9, 205n82, 205n84, 205n90, 205nn92–3, 205n103, 205–6nn106–14, 212n46, 212n48, 212n51–3, 212n57
Cunningham Dance Foundation, 131, 138

dadaesque, 122
Damballa, 104, 110, 114
d'Amboise, Jacques, 72

Dance Heritage Foundation, 116
Dance Magazine, 120, 134, 150, 157–8, 177n52, 179n72, 198n100, 202n19, 211n42
Dance Magazine Award, The (1975), 157
Dance Observer, 121, 201n178
Dance Theatre of Harlem, 157
Dances of Haiti, The (1947), 101, 199n127
Danilova, Alexandra, 29, 74
Danse de Sauvage, (La) (1925), 56–7
danseur, 30–1, 37, 41, 43, 135–6, 148
Davidova, Lucia, 71
Davis, Ossie, 148
de Beauvoir, Simone, 23, 180n5
de Lavallade, Carmen, 142–3, 145, 206n132
De Mille, Agnes, 107–8, 155–6, 194n21, 195n38, 210n22
Denby, Edwin, 12, 25
Denishawn School of Dance, 90
Denishawn Style, The, 91
Der Spiegel, 102
Derrida, Jacques, 23, 44, 180n3, 180n7, 184n81
discrimination, 12, 101
Don Quixote (1965), 37, 72, 74, 183n59
Doris Duke Charitable Foundation, 116
Dudley, Jane, 89
Duncan, Isadora, 20, 65, 174
Dunham, Albert, Jr., 98, 102
Dunham, Albert Millard, 97
Dunham, Katherine, 3–6, 9–10, 12, 18–20, 32–4, 42–3, 65, 87, 89, 91, 93, 95–116, 121, 139, 141–3, 146, 148–9, 151–2, 154, 157–8, 162, 166–9, 171, 174, 182n46, 193, 197n88, 197n90, 197n95, 198n97, 198nn99–101, 197n107, 198n115, 198n117, 198n119, 198n121, 198nn123–4, 199nn127–8, 199n131–2, 199nn134–6, 199nn139–40, 200nn141–2, 200n144, 200nn150–1, 200n155, 200nn161–2, 200n169, 200nn171–2, 200n174, 201n180, 201nn190–1, 201n197, 201nn200–2, 202n206, 210n13, 211nn40–44
Dunham Technique, 114, 116, 201n191
"Dunham Walk," 114
Dyer, Richard, 5, 8, 23–4, 31, 159, 161, 171, 176n11, 176n34, 176n36, 177n49, 180n8, 213n63

Eastman School of Music, 91
"Ebony Goddess," 56
"Ebony Venus," *see* "Black Venus"
Edinburgh Festival (1968), 152
Ellington, Duke, 144, 156
employee/"employee", 76, 93–5, 164–5, 196n73, 197nn81–2
see also independent contractor/ "independent contractor"
Encyclopedia of World Biography (Dunham), 101, 197n88, 198n124, 210n13
Enter (1993), 130
ephebe/ephebism, 37
Epstein, Paul H., 75
Erdman, Jean, 120
eroticism, 63, 113, 167
Eshkar, Shelley, 130
ethereal, 8–9, 24–6, 28–30, 39, 41, 47, 51, 63, 69, 71, 90, 112, 141, 167
ethnographic research, 34, 108–10, 115, 168–9, 209n1
Eurocentric culture, 8, 31, 64, 175–6nn9–10, 176nn26–33
European culture, 31, 162
"the exotic," 56, 62, 91, 102, 164, 168
expense test, 95
see also work/s for hire

Farber, Viola, 126, 128, 133, 202n18, 205n93
Farrell, Suzanne, 31, 37, 71–4, 133, 183n59, 191n29, 191n34
Federal District Court of New York, 77

feminine, 23, 25, 30, 50–1, 70, 72–3, 80–1, 84, 88, 100, 133, 136, 163, 165
ethereality, 8, 24–6, 30, 63, 71, 90, 141, 167
ideal, 51
femininity, 22, 112, 136, 170, 172, 186n39
Ficker, Roberta Sue, 72
see also Farrell, Suzanne
Fifteen Years of a Dancer's Life (Fuller), 46, 185n2, 185n20, 209n2
film, 5, 8, 13, 16–19, 23, 30–1, 62, 68, 70, 82, 116, 129–31, 134, 148, 155, 159, 161, 170, 174, 188n76, 213n76
use in dance, 8, 13, 16–17, 19, 23, 30, 31, 62, 68, 70, 82, 116, 129–31, 134, 148, 155, 159, 161, 170, 174, 188n76, 213n76
Firebird, The (1949), 43, 74
Fischer-Hornung, Dorothea, 102, 199nn127–8, 199nn131–4, 199n136
Flanner, Janet, 57
Flowers (1971), 156
folklore, 20, 110, 169, 209
Fort, Syvilla, 146
Forti, Simone, 121, 137, 203n27
Foster, Susan, 134, 205n89
Foucault, Michel, 23, 180n4
Francis, Terri, 57–8, 179n94, 187n57
Fuller, Loïe, 3–6, 8–9, 11–15, 18–20, 23, 43, 45–57, 59, 61–3, 65, 69–70, 83–5, 87, 97, 117, 145–6, 154, 158, 163, 165–7, 169, 174–5, 175n3, 176n12, 177n44, 178n56, 178nn69–70, 184, 185n2, 185n6, 185n8, 185n13, 185n18, 185n20, 185n23, 185n25, 185n26, 186n28, 186n35, 187n55, 189n80, 189n82, 189n84, 190, 193, 209, 209n2, 209n4, 210n21, 211n24, 211n30, 211nn33–6, 213n74
Fuller v. Bemis (1892), 4, 11, 18, 48, 175n3, 178n56, 185n8, 189n82, 189n84, 209n4, 210n21, 211n35, 211n36

"Gaiety Girls," 49
Gaiety Theatre, 49
Garelick, Rhonda K., 50, 53, 185n18, 186n36
"Garment for Dancers," 53
gay (sexuality), *see homosexuality*
gender, 2–4, 6–11, 17–20, 23–4, 30, 37, 39, 55, 58–9, 83, 85, 108, 111, 113, 132–6, 159, 161, 163–4, 166, 169, 171–2, 174–5, 176n35, 177n38, 179n94, 182n45, 189n59, 184, 186n39, 188n64, 190, 193, 209
Gershwin, George, 71
Gesamtkuntswerk (Wagner), 123
Geva, Tamara, 70
Ghanaian Dance, 32–7, 97, 127, 162, 167, 174, 182n54, 183n56, 183n59, 183n65
Gillaume, Fanny June, 98
Glazer v. Hoffman (1943), 48, 185n11
Goldwyn, Samuel, 5, 70–1
Goldwyn Follies, The, 70
Good, Alan, 131, 134
Gotanda Neil, 11, 175n8, 177n45
Gottlieb, Robert, 28, 68, 181n30, 190n8, 190n19, 191n27, 191n30, 202n5, 204n77, 212n54
Gottschild, Brenda Dixon, 32, 37–43, 58, 183n42, 183n51, 183n61, 183n64, 184n66, 184n71, 184nn73–80, 187n58
Graham, George Greenfield, 89
Graham, Martha, 3–6, 9–10, 12, 18–20, 23, 28, 33, 43, 56, 87–99, 101–3, 105, 107–21, 125–9, 135–8, 141–7, 150, 153–4, 156, 158, 163–7, 169–71, 174–5, 175nn5–6, 184, 188n66, 190, 193, 193n2, 194n6, 194n11, 194n18, 194n21–4, 194nn26–7,

195n32, 195n40, 195nn42–4, 195nn47–8, 195n54, 195n56, 195nn61–2, 196n63, 196nn66–72, 196n74, 196n76, 197n83, 197nn85–6, 201n181, 201n188, 209, 210nn11–2, 210nn14–19, 210nn22–3, 211n25, 211n39
Greene, Kevin J., 3, 10–11, 177n42
Greenwich Village Follies, 90
Ground Overlay (1995), 130

Hall, Constance Valis, 106, 168
Halprin, Ann, 137, 205
Haraway, Donna J., 1, 175n1
Harris, Cheryl, 4, 6–8, 175n7, 176n14
Hartwig, Eva Brigitta, 71
Hawkins, Erick, 91, 97, 119–20, 167
Herkovits, Melville, 101, 103, 199n138
heteronormative masculinity, 19, 158, 170
heterosexuality, 8, 31, 171
  in American dance, 24, 42, 161
hierarchy, American dance, 31, 41–2, 44, 64, 108, 111, 113–14, 161, 180n7, 189n88
"high art," 19, 64, 113, 128, 137–8, 146, 158, 170
Hinkson, Mary, 147
Holland Festival (1967), 152
Holm, Hanya, 146
homosexuality, 42, 135, 156, 170, 172
Horgan, Barbara, 14, 73–80, 210n8
Horgan I (1985), *see Horgan v. MacMillan*
Horgan II (1986), *see Horgan v. Macmillan II*
Horgan v. MacMillan (1985), 17–18, 77–8, 83, 164, 175n4, 179n90, 192nn72–3, 192nn81–2, 213n68
Horgan v. Macmillan II (1986), 4, 78, 83, 85, 95, 164, 172, 192n72, 192n77, 192n91, 192n94, 193n114, 197n87
Horne, Lena, 148
Horst, Louis, 120–1
Horton Dance Company, 145
Horton, Lester, 119, 141, 143–6, 149, 153–4, 171
House of Flowers (1954), 145
Hughes, Elinor, 102
Humphrey, Doris, 146, 213n62
Hurok, Sol, 101, 107, 200n162
hybrid ballet, 19, 114, 156, 170
hyperfeminized, 28–9, 59, 83, 164, 166
hypermasculinized, 148
"hypersexualized primitive," 100
hyper-whitened, *see* hyper-whiteness
hyper-whiteness, 8, 23, 25, 28, 50–3, 70–3, 80–1, 84–5, 88, 91, 100, 164–5, 173, 185n1

identity, 2, 4, 6, 8–10, 41, 49, 59, 83, 90–1, 163–4, 166, 182n51, 184n70, 187n59, 188n77, 189n90
identity politics, 7, 175n8
Immanuel, Isak, 137
independent contractor/"independent contractor," 95
  see also employee/"employee"
Ingram, Rex, 105
Internal Revenue Service (IRS), 75
"innate" qualities, in choreography, 149–50
"instance" test/prong, 95
  see also work for hire
intangible property, 5, 22–3, 74–5
intellectual property, 2–4, 8, 11–2, 20, 22–3, 43, 54–5, 63–5, 74–5, 77, 79, 92, 94, 96, 115–16, 124, 137–8, 164, 170, 189nn87–8, 209
intellectualism, in dance, 121, 171
International Exchange Program, 152
intersectional, 4, 7–8, 17, 20, 175n8
Iova-Koga, Dana, 137
Iova-Koga, Shinichi Momo, 137
Irigaray, Luce, 23, 180n6
Island Possessed (Dunham), 101, 199n140, 200n42
Ito, Michio, 143

Jacob's Pillow, 145
Jacob's Pillow Dance Award (2009), 138

Jamaica (1957), 148
Jamison, Judith, 155, 158
Japan's Praemium Imperiale (2005), 138
Jerome Robbins Dance Division, 138
Joffrey Ballet, 157
Jonas, Gerald, 118, 132, 180n9, 180n12, 180n18, 180n24, 181n26, 181n34, 181n38, 181n40, 185n4, 202n1, 205n81, 212n47
Joplin, Janis, 156
Journey to Accampong (Dunham), 101
Jowitt, Deborah, 112, 118, 120, 195n31, 201n186, 203n21
Judge Lacombe, 48
Judge Wilfred Feinberg, 77
Judson Church Group, 136–7
Judsonites, 136
Jules-Rosette, Benetta, 58–9, 61, 177n40, 187n48, 188n62, 188n65, 188n71, 188n76, 211n31

Katherine Dunham Legacy Project, 116
Keiser, Paul, 130
Kelly, Gene, 143
The Kennedy Center Honors Prize (1988), 157
Kerr, Catherine, 133–4
Kerstein, Lincoln, 67, 74, 83, 119, 163, 190n4
kinesthetic, 19, 35, 37, 127, 146, 162, 169–70, 182n44
  movement, 39
  techniques, 110, 153, 169
Kinetic Molpai (1935), 151
Kingsley, Gershon, 145
Kirstein, Lincoln, 25, 67
Klee, Paul, 144
Klosty, James, 127–8, 203n35, 203n45, 203n47, 204n58, 204n64, 205n84, 212n51
Kraut, Anthea, 10, 64–5, 177n41, 189n80, 189n88, 189n94, 211n33
Ku Klux Klan, 140

L'Ag'ya (1938), 102, 108
La Baker, 56
La Guiablesse, 98
La Loïe, *see* Fuller, Loie
La Revue Nègre, 56, 187n55, 211n30
La Scala Ballet, 157
La Sirène des tropiques (1927), 62
La tragédie de Salomé (1907), 52
Labanotation, 16, 130, 179n81
Latin ballroom, 109, 173
Latour, Bruno, 11, 85, 177n48, 193n131
Lawson, Christine, 148
Le Clercq, Tanaquil, 29, 70–1, 73–4, 76
"Le Jazz Hot": From Haiti to Harlem (1940), 103
Lee, Dohee, 137
Legacy Plan, The, 138
legal property, 54
legal protection, 85, 167, 172–3
"legitimate grounds," 23
Library of Congress, 46, 55, 68, 88, 96, 116, 139, 198n107, 200n172, 201n200, 202n206
Lieberson, Goddard, 71
Liebeslieder Walzer (1960), 74
LifeForms (computer software), 130
Lind, Letty, 49
linearity, in American dance, 31, 161
Long, Richard, 116
Lorca, Garcia, 144
Lorraine, Jean, 51, 185n26, 186n28
Louis XIV, 25

MacArthur Fellowship (1985), 138
Mahi, 114
"mainstream," 128
male gaze, 31, 58
maleness, 12, 149
Malinowski, Bronislaw, 101
Maralasco v. Fantasy, Inc (1991), 179n88
Martha Graham Center for Contemporary Dance, 92
Martha Graham School and Dance Foundation, 92–3

Martha Graham School for Contemporary Dance, 91
Martha Graham School v. Martha Graham Center II (2004), 4, 164
Martha Graham School v. Martha Graham Center III (2006), 4
The Martha Graham Trademark, 94
Martha Graham Trust, 93
Martin, John, 99–100, 147, 149
Martinetti v. Maguire (1867), 13, 178n57, 189n85, 211n37
masculine power, 30
masculinity, in dance, 19–20, 41, 135–6, 142–3, 149, 156, 158–9, 170–2, 205n89
Maslow, Sophie, 147
Mason, Audrey, 148
"Matriarch of Black Dance", 87, 97, 193
Mazo, Joseph, 124, 141, 153, 202n2, 202n7, 202n10, 202n19, 203n24, 203n38, 203n49, 204n60, 204n67, 206n121, 207n171, 208n181, 208n183, 208nn193–4, 208n198, 208n205, 209n217, 212n61, 213n64
McCarthy witch hunts, 135
McCormick, Malcolm, 109, 129, 181n27, 181n31, 183n59, 189n79, 199n125, 199n137, 200n157, 201n175, 201n182, 201n189, 202n16, 203n22, 203n28, 202n34, 203n36, 203n41, 204n66, 204n69, 205n104, 208n202, 212n55
McCullers, Carson, 144
McKayle, Donald, 147, 151
"Mechanism for the Production of Light Effects," 53
Meditation, 72, 74
Merce Cunningham Dance Company, 138
Merce Cunningham Trust, 138, 205n107, 206n110, 206n112
Milhaud, Darius, 145
mise en scene, 43, 71, 141, 149
Mitchell, Arthur, 20, 42–3
modern dance, 3, 13, 28, 33, 46, 84–5, 88, 96–8, 109, 114–15, 118, 128, 134, 141, 144, 147, 150–4, 157–8, 161–2, 165, 167, 169, 171–2, 175, 184, 190, 193, 202nn2–3, 204n59, 205n89, 208n200, 209, 212n60
"modicum of originality", in copyright law, 110, 169
Monk, Meredith, 137
Montalban, Ricardo, 148
Mooche, The (1975), 156
Moore, Charles, 150
moral, 21–2, 24–5, 32, 44, 70, 83, 105, 163, 188n75
movement, 16–7, 19, 24, 26–30, 35, 37–9, 41–2, 48, 51, 57, 59, 64–5, 80–1, 83, 89, 90–1, 97, 99–100, 105–6, 108–15, 118, 120–1, 123, 125–30, 133, 135–7, 142, 148–51, 153, 155, 157, 162–3, 167, 175n8, 177n45, 178n70, 179n81, 180n9, 181n41, 182n51, 182n54, 183n65, 185n4, 201n180, 202n1, 204n59, 212n47
  African styles of, 35–6, 104
  Caribbean styles of, 97, 100, 168
multiracial, 117, 139, 144–5, 148, 154–5
muse, 31, 69, 70–1, 183n59
Myers Brown, Joan, 40, 42, 184n73–9

National Association for the Advancement of Colored People, 157
National Medal of Arts (1990), 138
neoclassical, 27
neoclassical mambo, 146
New York City Ballet, 67, 71, 75–9, 83, 96, 120
Nicks, Walter, 147
Nietzsche, philosophy of, 1, 122
Nietzschean, 32
1909 Copyright Act, *see* Copyright Act of 1909
1976 Copyright Act, *see* Copyright Act of 1976

Ninety Degrees in the Shade (1965), 156
non-corporeality, in American dance, 8, 25, 31, 54, 161
"non-white," 9–10, 12, 19–20, 23–4, 32, 39–40, 42–4, 52, 65, 100, 121, 128, 139, 147, 158, 164, 170, 173
  aesthetic of, 5, 17, 21–2, 24, 31–2, 34, 38–9, 42, 54, 56, 65, 97, 127, 162–3, 166–7, 174
"non-whiteness," 8, 12, 17–25, 27, 29, 31–3, 35, 37, 39, 41–3, 52, 55, 63, 87, 139, 161, 167, 170, 173, 180, 193
nudity, 10, 57, 59, 61, 166
Nunn, Kenneth, 4–5, 8, 29, 38, 59, 175n9, 176n10, 176n26
Nutcracker, The (1892), 77
Nutcracker: A Story & A Ballet, The (1895), 77
Nyro, Laura, 155

objectification, 8
O'Donnell, May, 151
Officier of the Legion d'Honneur in France (2004), 138
"one-drop" rule, 31, 162
orientalist, 50, 52, 53, 69
orientalized other, 173
"original dance" steps, 172
Osumare, Halifu, 110, 201
"the other," 57
ownership, of choreographic works, 63, 67, 87, 93–6, 107, 115–16, 139, 154, 157, 158, 159, 164, 167, 169, 172, 189n87
  coownership, 76

Page, Ruth, 98–9, 198n99, 211n41
Pan-Africanist, 97
Paris Opera Ballet, 157
Parker, Charlie, 156
pas de deux, 30, 31, 74, 134, 170
Patry, William, 16, 179n80
Paxton, Steve, 125, 126, 202n18, 204n59, 205n93
Peller, Gary, 11, 175n8, 177n45
pelvic motion, in dance, 99, 109, 114, 149
  girdle, 34, 108
Perces, Marjorie, 153
performances, 5, 9–10, 11–12, 14, 34, 35, 38, 47, 51, 52, 56, 58, 59, 63, 195n62, 195n97, 211n4, 211n40
  physical, 90
  violent, 90
performative strategies, 10, 59, 166
Petipa, Marius, 28
Phildanco, 40–3, 184n82
Phillips, Jared, 130
Phoebe Snow (1959), 150
photographs, as evidence of copyright, 77–83, 97, 116
Picart, Caroline Joan S., 175, 175n1, 175n2, 184, 190, 193, 209, 213n73, 213n74
"Picasso of American Dance," 12, 18, 70, 78, 80, 87, 165, 193
Points in Space (1987), 134
Pratt, John, 103, 108–9, 168, 199n135
Premice, Josephine, 148
"prepared piano," 122
Prevots, Naima, 151, 208n197
Primitive Mysteries (1931), 33, 112, 115, 194n7, 201n181, 210n15
Primus, Pearl, 109–10, 169
Princesse TamTam (1935), 62
privilege, 2, 5, 6–7, 8–9, 12, 18, 21, 23–4, 28, 43, 44, 49, 52, 53, 55, 64, 108, 120, 127, 148, 154, 162, 164, 168, 171–2, 173, 179n94, 188n75, 205n90
props, in dance, 143
Proskauer, Rose, Goetz & Mendelsohn, 75
Protas, Ron, 92–4
public domain, 8, 11, 23, 64, 67, 77, 78, 79, 81, 94, 173, 178n54

race, 4, 6, 7, 9, 10, 11, 17, 19, 20, 22, 24, 41, 54, 55, 56, 59, 85, 101, 102, 103, 109, 117, 139, 141, 145, 149,

150, 155, 156, 159, 166, 169, 171, 172, 174, 175nn8–9, 117n11, 117n35, 177nn45–7, 179n94, 182n45, 186n40, 186n42, 189n90, 190, 193, 198n123, 209, 213n63
racial hierarchy, 41
racism, 7, 39, 98, 101, 108, 140, 144, 145
Radcliffe-Brown, A. R., 101
Rainbow 'Round My Shoulder (1973), 151
"Rainbow Tribe," 56
Rainer, Yvonne, 137
Ramsay, Burt, 134, 199n131, 204n80
rationality, in American dance, 8, 31, 161
raw material, 64, 65, 81, 120
Redfield, Robert, 101
Regnier, Paul, 57
Reid factors, 95, 197n81
see also work/s for hire
Revelations (1960), 140, 141, 150, 155, 156, 206n125, 206n127, 206n130, 206n131, 206n132, 207n138, 207n143, 207n145, 207n149, 207n152, 207n153, 207n155, 207n163, 207n166, 207n170, 207n178, 208n195, 208n203, 209n219, 209n228, 212n45, 212n58
Reynolds, Pearl, 148
"Right On, Be Free" (1970), 155
Rites of Passage (1943), 102
River, The (1970), 156
Rockettes, 39, 49
Rose, Albirda, 114, 201n191
Rose, Phyllis, 52, 58–9, 63, 187n44, 188n70
Rosenwald Travel Fellowship, 101
Ross, Bertram, 88, 119–20
Ross, Herbert, 145
Roth, Moira, 135, 205n94, 205n96
Royal Society of Anthropology, 103

Salomé, 51, 185n18, 186n36
Samuel H. Scripps American Dance Festival Award (1987), 157
Sapir, Edward, 101
Schaffer, Pierre, 124
Scheherazade (1888), 143
Schiffer, F. S., 97
Schoenberg, Arthur, 122
School of American Ballet, 75, 119
Schorer, Suki, 31
Schur, Richard, 64, 177n42, 189n87
Second Circuit, 18, 94–5, 164, 192n81, 197n82
Senegalese National Ballet, 115
Senghor, Leopold, 115
sensuality, in dance, 72, 149
Septet (1964), 135
Serenade (1934), 74
"serpentine" dance, 11, 13, 38, 45–53, 63, 167, 175, 184, 185n6, 189n80, 190, 193, 209, 211n24, 211n33
Setterfield, Valda, 128, 202n18, 205n93
seven chakras, 115
sexism, 7, 53
"sexlessness," 33, 113
sexuality, 2, 3, 9, 19, 20, 62, 89, 100, 102, 104–5, 110, 112, 134, 142, 146, 159, 169, 171, 172, 174, 176n35, 181n39, 199n131
in dance, 57, 90, 97, 115, 120, 156, 167, 204n80, 205n89
Shango (1945), 110
Shawn, Ted, 20, 90, 92, 102, 145, 151, 156, 171, 174
Shook, Karel, 146
Siegel, Marcia, 135, 157, 205n99, 208n215, 212n49, 213n62
Signals (1970), 129
Sing Man Sing (1956), 147
Singer, Joseph, 23, 180n2
skirt dance, 12, 47, 49, 53, 83, 84, 163, 165, 210n9
So You Think You Can Dance (2005–), 153
"social dance steps," 65, 81, 103, 168, 172
Sokolow, Anna, 147
Solo Suite in Space and Time (1953), 123, 133

"Something About John Coltrane," 155
Song of Hiawatha, The (1928), 143
Soto, G. Huffman, 137
Southern District of New York, 94
Southland (1951), 109, 200n174
"spectacle," 13–4, 24–5, 45, 48, 63, 70, 83, 85, 127, 163, 167, 184, 204n80
Speranzeva, Ludmilla, 98, 108
The Springarn Medal (1979), 157
staging, 26, 51, 78, 83, 84, 100, 105, 113, 115, 123–4, 131, 132, 146, 149, 151, 162, 163, 166, 168
  conventional, 159, 171
  theatrical, 19, 145, 159, 171
Standing at the Edge, We Dance (2001), 43
stardom, 4, 11, 18, 50, 53, 54, 55, 57, 60, 62, 63, 87, 89, 97, 108, 148, 156, 164, 166, 173, 174, 187n57, 188n66
status property, 4, 7, 9, 12, 17, 18, 19, 20, 44, 45, 51, 52, 53, 54, 73, 77, 80, 83, 83, 85, 87–8, 90, 96, 111, 113, 116, 163–4, 166, 169, 171, 173, 175, 184, 190, 193, 209
St. Denis, Ruth, 20, 65, 90, 91, 92, 102, 142, 164, 174, 210n16, 210n18
Steele, Jeannie, 130
stereotypes, 52, 147, 172
  of black dancers, 10, 42, 97, 99, 105, 108, 110, 112, 167, 173
Stokes, Adrian, 25
Stoler, Ann Laura, 9, 177n39, 187n59
Story (1963), 132
Stravinsky Violin Concerto (1931), 74
"street" dances, 59, 62, 65, 167
Suite for Five (1955), 123
Suspension (1972), 151
"Swan Lake" concept, 5, 71
Sysol, Theodore M., 73
Szilard, Paul, 150, 208n182

Tallchief, Maria, 43, 69–70, 71
tangible property, 5, 6, 7, 9, 63, 64, 162, 169
tap dance, 65, 119, 143, 188n66
Taper, Bernard, 11, 29, 68, 69, 74, 78, 105, 176n13, 177n43, 178n64, 180n25, 181n32, 190n2, 190n5, 190 n10, 190n125, 191n37, 192n93, 193n127, 194n5, 200n152, 209n5, 210n7, 210n10, 210n20, 211n26
Teachout, Terry, 130, 133, 204n77, 205n87
terra incognita, 113
Théâtre des Champs-Élysées, 56
"Theatrical Stage Mechanism," 53
Thomas, Kendall, 11, 175n8, 177n45
Thompson, Claude, 148
Thompson, Clive, 150
Thompson, Robert Farris, 173, 183n63, 213n75
Traces of Light: Absence and Presence in the Work of Loïe Fuller (Albright), 11, 177n44, 185n13, 185n16, 185n24, 186n29, 186n32, 186n81, 211n34
Trackers (1991), 130
trademark/s, 40, 63, 70, 84, 85, 94, 165, 166, 173
Trisler, Joyce, 157
The Triumph of St. Joan (1951), 91
Tropical Revue (1943), 101
Tropics (1940), 103
"token blacks," 146–7
Turbyfill, Mark, 98, 198n99, 198n106, 198n109, 198n112, 211n41
TV Re-run (1972), 129, 132

underlighting, 21, 53
"unisex" choreography, 132
US Constitution, 13

Variations V (1965), 129
vaudeville, 49, 60, 63, 98, 113, 119, 141, 167
Vaughn, David, 130, 131, 204nn72–3, 204n78, 205n93
Vega, Marta (Moreno), 114, 115
Verdy, Violette, 27, 72

video, use in dance, 16, 17, 19, 129, 131, 159, 170
Village Voice, 118
virtue, in American dance, 8, 24, 25, 30, 31, 135, 146, 152, 161
Voices of East Harlem, 155
von Aroldingen, Karin, 14, 73
Voudou religion, 101, 110
voudun, 104

Walker, Sheila, 38, 184n69
war dances, 37
Warner, Lloyd, 101
"Water Nymph," 71
Waters, Ethel, 105
Weidman, Charles, 109, 146
weightlessness, characteristics of danseurs, 25–7, 30, 35, 90
Welsh-Asante, Kariamu, 20, 174, 182n44, 183n56, 213n77
Wengerd, Tim, 119–20
"white," 22–4, 31, 39–43, 55, 91, 99, 128, 156, 161–2, 166
white aesthetic, 5, 17, 21–4, 31, 39–41, 52, 72, 146, 161, 163, 174
"white ballets," 25
whiteness, 4–55, 62–3, 67, 71, 77, 83, 85, 87–8, 90, 96, 111, 113, 116–17, 139, 159, 163–4, 166–7, 169, 171, 173–4, 175, 175n7, 176n14, 180, 184, 190, 193, 209
  aesthetic of (abstraction), 4–5, 8, 11–13, 17–44, 51–5, 67, 71, 83, 85, 87–8, 113, 161, 163, 166–7, 173–4, 175n2, 180
  as status property, 4–12, 15, 17–20, 22, 23, 32, 43–5, 52–4, 67, 77, 83, 85, 87–8, 90, 96, 111, 113, 116, 161, 163–73, 175, 175n7, 176n14, 180, 184, 190, 193, 209
Wigman, Mary, 113
Williams, Tennessee, 144–5
Wilson, Billy, 148
Wilson, Dooly, 105
Wong, Yutian, 134, 205n90
work/s for hire, 92–5, 164, 196n73, 196n80
  expense test/prong, 95
  instance test/prong, 95
  work for hire doctrine, 92, 95, 164, 196n73, 196n80, 222
  see also Reid factors
World Festival of Negro Arts in Dakar (1966), 152
World War II, 124, 129
Wright, Barbara, 148

Xochitl, 90

Yanvalou, 114
Yeoh, 15, 179n72

Zen Buddhism, 118, 122, 205n90
zepaules/"zepaules movement," 104
Zorina, Vera, 5, 70–1
ZouZou (1934), 62

Printed and bound by CPI Group (UK) Ltd, Croydon, CR0 4YY